Globalization and Labour Reforms

Globalization and Labour Reforms

The Politics of Interest Groups and Partisan Governments

ZAAD MAHMOOD

OXFORD
UNIVERSITY PRESS

OXFORD
UNIVERSITY PRESS

Oxford University Press is a department of the University of Oxford.
It furthers the University's objective of excellence in research, scholarship,
and education by publishing worldwide. Oxford is a registered trademark of
Oxford University Press in the UK and in certain other countries.

Published in India by
Oxford University Press
2/11 Ground Floor, Ansari Road, Daryaganj, New Delhi 110 002, India

First Edition published in 2017

ISBN-13: 978-0-19-947527-8
ISBN-10: 0-19-947527-X

Typeset in Dante MT Std 10.5/13
by Tranistics Data Technologies, New Delhi 110 044
Printed in India by Replika Press Pvt. Ltd

For Babuji and Maa

Dedicated to the love, compassion, support, and humanism of

my mother
Khadematul Ahmed

and

my late father
Barrister Mohiuddin Ahmed

Contents

Tables and Figures

Tables

Figures

Abbreviations

AIFB	All India Forward Bloc
AITC	All India Trinamool Congress
ASI	*Annual Survey of Industries*
BC	Backward Class
BJP	Bharatiya Janata Party
CII	Confederation of Indian Industries
Congress (O)	Congress (Organization)
CPI	Communist Party of India
CPI(M)	Communist Party of India, Marxist
CSO	Central Statistical Organization
ECI	Election Commission of India
ENPST	Effective Number of Parties according to Seat
EOU	Export-Oriented Unit
ESI	Employees' State Insurance
FICCI	Federation of Indian Chamber of Commerce and Industry
FDI	Foreign Direct Investment
GATT	General Agreement on Tariffs and Trade
GoI	Government of India
GCCI	Gujarat Chamber of Commerce and Industry
HOS	Heckscher–Ohlin–Samuelson
HDI	Human Development Index
ID	Industrial Disputes
IEM	Industrial Entrepreneur Memorandum
ILO	International Labour Organization
IMF	International Monetary Fund
INC	Indian National Congress

ISI	Import-substituting Industrialization
KHAM	Kshatriyas, Harijans, Adivasis, and Muslims
MLA	Member of State Legislative Assembly
MNC	Multinational Corporation
MP	Member of Parliament
NCP	Nationalist Congress Party
NDA	National Democratic Alliance
NSS	National Sample Survey
NSDP	National State Domestic Product
NSSO	National Sample Survey Organization
NTR	N.T. Rama Rao
NVA	Net Value Added
OECD	Organisation for Economic Co-operation and Development
OBC	Other Backward Classes
RBI	Reserve Bank of India
RSP	Revolutionary Socialist Party
SBR	State–Business Relation
SC	Scheduled Caste
SDP	State Domestic Product
ST	Scheduled Tribe
TDP	Telugu Desam Party
TRIMs	Agreement on Trade-Related Investment Measures
TU	Trade Union
UPA	United Progressive Alliance
WB	World Bank
WFPR	Workforce Participation Rate
WTO	World Trade Organization

Acknowledgements

This book is the outcome of my doctoral research undertaken at SOAS University of London, UK. The dissertation and the present work would not have been possible without the support of many kind and thoughtful people. I wish to convey my gratitude to some of them in my humble acknowledgement.

First and foremost, I would like to thank my research supervisor, Lawrence Sáez, for his careful supervision, guidance, and encouragement in both professional and personal matters. It was a thought-provoking, educative, and, above all, self-actualizing experience as his PhD student. I am also indebted to the Department of Politics and International Studies at SOAS, especially Tat Yan Kong for his incisive comments and Laleh Khalili for the constant reassurances and 'pastoral' care. The good advice and support of my research committee have been invaluable, for which I am extremely grateful. Kunal Sen of The University of Manchester, UK, and Subir Sinha of SOAS were the best examiners one could hope for and their suggestions have enriched this work.

My time at SOAS and in London was made enjoyable in large part due to the many friends who became a part of my life. I am thankful for the time spent with James Sunday, Andrea Valente, Konstantinos Tsimonis, Silvia Ferabolli, Mehr F. Hussain, Aditya Menon, Anwesha Ray, Leftaris Zampoulakis, Jaycob Baylon, Ritanjan Das, Zia Foley, Shamayita Chakraborty, and Shakyajit Bhattacharya. They have been a source of good advice and emotional strength during the troughs of my journey as a PhD student. A special thanks goes out to Niladri Chatterji for not only being the best housemate, but also my family away from home. Without him, this journey would have been long and lonely.

I would also like to thank my friends in Kolkata, India—colleagues from Seth Anandram Jaipuria College and Presidency University—for their encouragement and support. A few of them deserve special mention, particularly Advocate Priyankar Deb Sarkar who helped to codify labour amendments, and Zakaria Siddiqui and Subhanil Choudhury for taking the time to read and comment on my thesis. I must also acknowledge my teachers Rakhahari Chatterji and Satyabrata Chakraborty, both professors at University of Calcutta, for introducing me to political economy and encouraging me to pursue research. Anik Chatterjee, Pradip Basu, Abdus Samad Gayen, and the colleagues at Presidency University provided the impetus to convert the dissertation into a book.

Many arguments covered in the book were critically interrogated and refined through the intervention of journal referees, conferences, and informal discussions. Although too many to mention, Dibyesh Anand, Prerna Singh, Swagato Sarkar, Shibasish Chatterjee, Gautam Kumar Basu, Sunil Khilnani, Ashutosh Varshney, Tamaz Zubiashvili, Axel Gehring, and Suhas Palshikar deserve mention for their interest in my work. The discussions with Amiya Bagchi, Achin Chakraborty, and Supurna Banerjee of Institute of Development Studies, Kolkata, India; Dwaipayan Bhattacharya of Jawaharlal Nehru University, New Delhi, India; and Rajesh Bhattacharya of Indian Institute of Management Calcutta, India, helped shape many arguments of this book. I also thank the editorial boards and anonymous reviewers for their suggestions and comments which helped refine the arguments.

In the recent past, association with Pippa Norris, Ferran Martinez-i-coma, and Alessandro Nai of The University of Sydney, Australia, renewed the lessons of academic rigour which expedited the preparation of the manuscript. During my stint at Electoral Integrity Project, The University of Sydney, Jeffry Karp, Marta Regalia, Elizabeth Young, Max Gromping, and Miguel Angel Lara Otaola provided unwavering friendship for which I am indebted. I am also grateful to Abu Zaffer, Moni Zaffer, Arif, and Asif for their unflinching kindness and care.

The fieldwork for this research was greatly aided by Alakh Sharma of Indian Society of Labour Economics, New Delhi, India; M.M. Rahman of V.V. Giri Institute of Labour Research, Noida, India; Prasenjit Bose, Shovan Ray, Ritabrata Banerjee, as well as the national labour federations, business associations, and labour bureaucracy at the subnational states. My study drew upon their knowledge and experience and although too numerous to name, they are appreciated for their individual contributions. I must also acknowledge the insight gained from conversations with academics involved with labour politics, especially K.R. Shyam Sundar, Jesim Pais, Ghanshyam Shah, Narasimha Reddy, and Ramkrishna Chattopadhyay. The fieldwork across different parts of India would have been difficult without the hospitality and support of Maqbool Ahmed and Mansur Ahmed in New Delhi, Asif Ahmed in Hyderabad, K.F. Rahaman and his family in Mumbai, and Quamrunessa Murshed in London. They not only opened up their homes to me, but treated me as one of their own.

Research is an expensive proposition and this research would not have been possible without the funding agencies whose benevolence made my PhD study at SOAS possible. I sincerely thank the Felix Foundation and the anonymous benefactors who have helped many like me to pursue higher education at world-renowned institutes. I would also like to thank the University of London Central Research Fund for fieldwork support. I also acknowledge the academic and technical support of the SOAS University of London, UK, particularly the postgraduate research section. Marcus Cerny, the postgraduate research manager, Alicia Sales Fernandez, and Laura Jacobs provided a friendly and caring university office. Oxford University Press, especially the editorial team, deserves my gratitude for their professionalism and commitment in bringing out this book.

Finally, I would like to thank my family for all their love, support, and encouragement. My father, late Mohiuddin Ahmed, has been my inspiration and although he was there to see me off as I ventured into research, he is no longer here to see the completion of this journey. This work is dedicated to his memory. My mother, Khadematul Ahmed, who has raised me with sincerity and love and my brother, Saad Mahmood, have an immense contribution in what I am today. I must acknowledge the support, love, care, and encouragement of Rabeena Kamal, my wife. Her dedication and persistent confidence in me allowed me to pursue academics uninhibited by familial concerns. My father-in-law, Rabiul Kamal, and mother-in-law, Rumana Begum, also deserve mention for their support throughout, for which a mere expression of thanks does not suffice.

In the end, I would like to express my regret that I could not mention everyone individually. For any errors or inadequacies that may remain in this work, of course, the responsibility is entirely my own.

Introduction

Globalization and Policy Reform

'If the markets don't like your policies they will punish you.'
—Tony Blair
Chicago, April 1999

This terse sentence in the speech of the former British prime minister roughly sums up the conventional sentiments about the contemporary public policy. As is commonly understood, globalization—due to opening up of the economy, the creation of international networks, and multinationalization of production and distribution—limits the policy choices of nation states. It is observed that states increasingly adopt similar policies that expand the scope of markets, empower non-state actors, and encourage economic interdependence as policy autonomy is constrained under conditions of globalization (Strange 1996). In policy literature, such constraints on the policy autonomy of states have been framed in terms of democracy deficit, domination of neo-liberal capitalism, global interdependence, and policy convergence, among others (Aman 2004; Patnaik 2003). Consequently, the relevance of policymaking based on domestic socio-economic interests has increasingly come under question. Friedman (1999) famously used the metaphor of 'golden straitjacket' to signify increasing prosperity alongside limitations in state autonomy that characterize contemporary globalization.

Globalization and Public Policy

The idea of policy convergence has found immense currency with scholars and practitioners in the context of globalization. This, however, does not imply that the idea is considered inevitable or accepted uncritically by all. A survey of public policy literature reveals extensive debates about policy convergence, which can be broadly categorized into three contending positions.

According to one group of scholars, the influence of external economic and political factors on domestic policymaking has become decisive under conditions of globalization. Characterized as 'structural theorists', these scholars argue that policy convergence is dictated by external environment such as international economy, international regimes, and multilateral agreements that affect political units (Huber and Stephens 2001a; Omae 1995). Nation states have little control over the external environment and thus have to frame policies to accommodate global forces.

Contrary to the structural constraint argument, some scholars contend that states continue to have power over the market. To these scholars, policy convergence is a conscious political choice made by nation states (Downes, Gomez, and Gunderson 2004; Garrett 1998a). This idea of policy coordination holds that intensified economic competition, due to the mobility of capital and technological innovations, increases the cost of economic closure, leading to the adoption of similar policies by nation states. Thus, certain policies are adopted due to either emulation of best practices or competitive pressure to attract mobile capital (Mosley and Uno 2007).

Contending the materialist (structural and coordination) hypothesis[1] for convergence, the 'world society approach' locates the source of policy convergence in the realm of ideas. Focusing on the conscious adoption of neo-liberal policies by states, it argues that the impetus for policy consistency is from the spread of certain models and ideas through global, cultural, and associational processes. Such global ideational norms are usually facilitated through global scientific discourses,

---

[1] The structural hypothesis and policy coordination approaches argue that under conditions of globalization, policies of states converge due to the pressures of global market. The shift in policy is due to the changes in market forces which is an objective material reality.

international organizations, mimetic emulations, and the increased role of technocrats and academics who act as a pathway to elite consensus (Knill 2005).

The diverse theoretical approaches actually emanate from the observed differences in the extent of policy convergence across nation states. Empirical evidence of convergence towards neo-liberal policies has been somewhat mixed with instances of convergence along with the continuation of national heterogeneities.

Interestingly, some scholars such as Pierson (2001) and Kong (2006) have gone to the extent of contradicting the argument of convergence. They argue that substantial national heterogeneity persists even under conditions of globalization. The adoption or rejection of a particular set of policies is not merely conditioned by the growing internationalization of economic activities, but also by nation-specific political, institutional, and structural frameworks. The argument of non-convergence is reinforced by studies on the implementation of structural adjustment that highlights continued relevance of domestic political factors in policy reforms. Haggard and Webb (1993) have found that reforms guided by the World Bank (WB), International Monetary Fund (IMF), and other international economic institutions have not been coherently implemented and sustained in the majority of countries due to domestic considerations. Similarly, scholars subscribing to varieties of capitalism arguments attribute difference in economy—specifically, liberal market economies and coordinated market economies—to institutional and political dynamics (Hall and Soskice 2001). Welfare state literature also points to continued policy heterogeneity due to institutional impediments such as electoral system, legislature, and path dependence (Nelson, Meerman, and Rahman 2008; Pierson 2001).

Clearly, the status of public policy under conditions of globalization remains a contested terrain between perceived convergence and continued national heterogeneity. What is striking is that despite the contradictory positions of convergence and heterogeneity, there is an implicit agreement on the issue of marginalization of political agency under conditions of globalization. The literature on public policy primarily attributes policy diverge or convergence to either structural-economic or legal-institutional dynamics. The role of political agency is considered emaciated in the altered environment marked by the withdrawal of the nation state.

Role of Political Agency

This book intervenes in the existing debate about public policy under conditions of globalization by reflecting on the continued relevance of political variables in determining policy reforms. The need to reinstate politics in explaining public policies is necessary and important for mainly two reasons. First, political actors and practices exert considerable influence on policy transformation. Much of these processes, however, remain relatively understudied in macroanalyses of reforms. Second, emphasis on political factors signposts the intra-national dynamics of reform and domestic configurations of support that contribute to particular sets of reform. The underlying assumptions is that even if forces of globalization are attributed causal importance in explaining policy transformations, there exists a political logic behind such a process.

In order to resolve the issues outlined, this book examines the role of political dynamics in shaping reforms through a comparative study of labour market variation across India. Through the case studies,[2] this book shows that policy reforms are mediated and influenced by political factors—specifically, the partisan configuration of government and the nature of party competition.

The partisan configuration of government, that is, the socio-economic support base of the party in power, determines not only the orientation of government policies, but also the relative importance of particular interests in society. When the dominant support base of the party in government is relatively homogenous and has a presence of business groups, greater reform can be observed in the labour market. Such a government supports a constricted patronage network and has focused reform orientation. However, when the dominant support base is heterogeneous and wide, the government tends to reform slowly, formulating broader socio-economic policies and maintains a wider network of political patronage.

The case study of labour market variation in India suggests that regimes having relatively heterogeneous socio-economic support base,

[2] The book analyses the case studies between the years 1980 and 2014–15. The case study of Andhra Pradesh is until 2014, that is, it refers to the united state of Andhra Pradesh. In West Bengal, the Left Front was voted out of power in 2011, which would make the case study of West Bengal valid until 2011.

such as the Congress party in Maharashtra, tend to reform gradually. In contrast, the relatively homogenous socio-economic support base of the Bharatiya Janata Party (BJP) in Gujarat or the Telugu Desam Party (TDP) in Andhra Pradesh, originating in urban middle class and forward class/caste groups, results in the establishment of a more reformist government. The logic of dominant socio-economic support base similarly leads to a pro-labour regime in West Bengal. Deriving on the support base of organized labour, radical bhadralok community, and agrarian interests, the Left Front government pursued a pro-labour policy at the cost of investments and industrial stagnation.

The operation of partisan configuration of the government in determining reforms can be attributed to the rational behaviour of parties to negotiate between ideational and instrumental interests. The relative homogeneity of the socio-economic support base ensures clarity and focus in policymaking towards reforms; whereas, the heterogeneous social base tends to create an ambivalent attitude and contradictory pressures. The creation of particular partisan configurations, that is, homogenous or heterogeneous socio-economic support bases for parties, is dependent on existing structural conditions such as social cleavages and stratification, the extent of competition among groups, and strategic behaviour of competing political parties. In the context of Indian society, configurations of caste cleavage and correlation between caste and class constitute the dominant structural condition. However, the transformation of any particular cleavage into a political identity that fuels partisan mobilization is largely dependent on party competition, understood in terms of both ideology and the number of parties. As such, the partisan configuration is not something static and just as the existing social cleavage influences the composition of the partisan support base, the party system, too, has an important role in shaping the support bases.

In the context of the labour market, the party system or partisan competition operates as a crucial endogenous variable. The party system influences reform preferences of various social groups by providing or constraining policy alternative and electoral choices. The party system provides the wider political context in which configuration of partisan support, dominant political agenda, and the importance of competing interest groups are determined. It is the wider political environment that influences not only how individuals or groups locate themselves in the economic structure but also their opinion on reforms. The prevalent theoretical understanding of the relation between the party system and reform suggests that increasing party competition (fragmentation) impedes reform by encouraging populist policy stance of parties, making mobilization of legislative support difficult, and contributing to political instability (Haggard and Webb 1993).

Interestingly, in the context of the subnational states, contrary to expectation, party competition has a facilitating role in labour market reforms. The escalation in party competition corresponds to an increase in labour market flexibility, indicating that the relation between fragmentation and reform is neither unilinear nor unmediated. The positive relation can be traced back to the peculiar impact of party fragmentation on the composition of socio-economic support bases for parties, the transformation of political discourse that is associated with the emergent parties, and the shifts in the instrumental interest of parties. Such a finding suggests that the specific impact of fragmentation is mediated through political dynamics, which need to be considered in any analysis.

Relevance of Politics and Politics of Relevance

This book highlights the relevance of politics in determining policy reform under conditions of globalization. It reinforces the political character of economic reforms as political salience of economic interests emerges as a critical determinant of policy transformation. The research outcome indicates that policy transformation is essentially a political process reflected through conflicts and bargaining between relevant social groups. Certainly, it seems that unfolding of globalization in any society depends on who governs it. The role of class interest in adjustment process is significant and public policies under globalization continue to be nuanced, if not shaped, by distributive conflicts and the nature of party competition.

The overall theme of the book and the research findings can be positioned within certain strands of contemporary scholarly debate on public policy and politics. At a generic level, the book addresses the issue of policy transformation in transitional economies through a political-economic analysis. This is a necessary intervention due to the dearth of politico-economic research on transitional economies. Much of the existing literature on policy transformation or convergence–heterogeneity debate[3] is based on cross-national experiences of developed economies with a limited focus on transitional economies.

Second, the analysis of political actors and processes in affecting policy transformation contributes to the wider debate on the relation between politics and economic policy under conditions of globalization. The dominant interpretation of policy convergence or heterogeneity highlights structural–institutional factors such as political framework and nature of economy as being responsible for policy variation. The conclusions of this book emphasize on party-oriented explanations for reform variation. In the process, it contributes to literature that highlights negotiations between different social forces as a determinant of reform outcomes (Nayyar 1998; Przeworski 1991). In one sense, the research findings echo Theda Skocpol (Weir and Skocpol 1985: 120) who argued, '[I]t makes no sense to reduce political choices to the dictates of economic circumstances, for economic circumstances do not command so unambiguously, not even at moments of extraordinary crisis.'

At a more specific level, this book contributes to the literature on politics of labour market reforms. The emphasis on the relevance of interest groups, partisan configuration, and party competition builds on the literature on labour reforms in transitional economies such as Alesina (1997), Cook (2007), Deshpande et al. (2004b), and Horton, Kanbur, and Mazumdar (1994). Labour reforms have been identified as one of the most contested and difficult issues of reforms. The study of the variations in labour market contributes to the identification of precise political factors that induce or inhibit reforms.

Finally, the framework of comparative subnational case study provides insights regarding the location of policymaking in a multilevel polity. The book considers the interaction between politics and market forces as a causal explanation for reform variation and locates the space for such an interaction at the subnational level. Such a spatial focus reiterates some recent literature on federalism that highlights the emergence of regional states as important actors mediating the process of structural adjustment through institutional and political innovations (Sáez 2002; Sinha 2005).

---

[3] This refers to the debate among scholars and practitioners about the nature of public policies under condition of globalization. See Chapter 1 for a detailed discussion on this.

Globalization, Labour Reforms, and Politics

The arguments made in this book are based on the politico-economic analysis of labour market reforms in India. Through a study of sub-national variations in the labour market, the book reassesses the existing arguments on the political economy of reforms. The arguments presented emphasize on the continued relevance of politics in shaping public policy despite the structural–institutional constraints attributed to globalization.

The analytical point of departure for this book is the perceived policy shift towards the models of market economy under conditions of globalization. The pressure for such neo-liberal policy convergence can be traced back to developments within economies as well as external politico-economic factors. The foremost explanation for policy convergence has been the facilitation of trade and finance in the new global economic architecture. In this process, international organizations such as World Trade Organization (WTO) and trade agreements play an important role in determining convergence. Domestic considerations like changed political–ideological orientation of governments under the influence of free market ideational discourse also have a role in shaping convergence (Drezner 2001).

The relative importance of the domestic and international factors in affecting policy convergence is determined by macroeconomic conditions such as nature and size of the economy, the condition of balance of payments, and the rate of growth. It is argued that the pressure for policy convergence is especially acute in countries that have foreign debt and face economic crisis, which reduces state decision-making autonomy (Huber and Stephens 2001a). Again, the policy convergence is relatively indiscernible and unremarkable in the existing liberal market economies compared to the welfare states. Clearly, the sources and mechanisms of policy convergence across different economies vary according to the economic, institutional, and political conditions that characterize nation states.

An important, perhaps the most significant, dimension of policy reforms under conditions of globalization concerns market (factors market as well as product market) regulations. Neo-liberal economic policy emphasizes on increased deregulation to remove all 'distortions' in the factor markets to promote efficiency and optimal allocation.

In this context, the labour market constitutes an important agenda for reform because of its consequences on employment, wages, and overall growth. Characteristics of the labour market, such as bargaining coverage and employment protection legislation, have significant consequences for product market interventions. Unsurprisingly, labour reforms have attracted enormous academic as well as policy attention as a crucial component of macroeconomic reforms.

Labour market reform through deregulation, however, remains highly contested across the world. Labour, unlike other factors of production, is not only a resource but also constitutes an important social group capable of political manifestation. As Przeworski (1993) points out, labour reforms towards deregulations are often difficult to implement, as working class is a powerful constituency with potential to resist the reform. Critics have also expressed concern about the distributive aspects of a free labour market on grounds of welfare, social equity, and balanced growth (Chandrasekhar and Ghosh 2000). Unsurprisingly, organized labour or trade unions have opposed and impeded economic reforms in many instances (Cook 2007; Horton, Kanbur, and Mazumdar 1994; Rama 1995; Rueda 2007).

Even though the extent of reform in labour markets has been relatively low compared to the product market, labour is one of the most challenging issues of reform. The study of labour market politics provides an excellent opportunity to evaluate the role of political-agencies in determining policy and outcome under conditions of globalization. An additional dimension of evaluating labour market reforms is the identification of the location of decision-making in a multilevel polity. Decisions regarding economic reforms in large transitional economies are often difficult to locate, as much of the reforms take place informally at the level of practice, rather than policy. The particular study of labour reforms across Indian states reveals how reforms have progressed much more at a subterranean level through administrative fiats and action (or inaction), rather than formal policy transformation.

Politics of Reform Variation: India as a Case

In a politico-economic evaluation of labour reforms, India presents an interesting natural laboratory. Since its economic liberalization, India has been recognized as an emerging economy distinguished by its democratic framework as opposed to the quasi-authoritarian regimes that characterize many East Asian economies. Most of the developing countries, including India, discarded the state-led development approach and adopted a market-led model in the early 1990s, primarily due to internal policy failure and international pressures (Mukerjee 2007). Interestingly, despite similar institutional and structural conditions, the paths and extent of reforms have varied across subnational states of India, which constitutes the case study for this research.

This specific case study is based on four subnational states of India that are similar in terms of economic condition and institutional framework. The states under consideration are Gujarat, Maharashtra, Andhra Pradesh, and West Bengal. Gujarat and Maharashtra are considered among the high growth, high per capita, and comparatively more industrialized states of India. In contrast, the states of Andhra Pradesh and West Bengal have medium growth with median per capita income and moderate industrialization. The respective sets of states, that is, Gujarat–Maharashtra and Andhra Pradesh–West Bengal, are largely similar in their economic structure such as size of the economy, industrial contribution, the composition of industries and economic integration as revealed through foreign direct investment (FDI) inflows. Being provinces of India, these states are also characterized by similar institutional structures such as the organization of bureaucracy, broad contours of labour laws, electoral and political systems, and a level of socio-economic development. Historically, most of the states of India have had a similar experience since Independence, given the state-centred developmental model, and the operation of institutional framework at the pan-India level with minor innovations at the state level.

Despite such structural (economic) and institutional similarities, the labour market outcomes diverge across the states. According to the index of labour market flexibility based on labour market regulations and labour market outcome (wage share, proportion of contractual labour), there exists substantial variation across the subnational states. It is widely recognized that Andhra Pradesh and Gujarat have a comparatively flexible labour market than Maharashtra and West Bengal. Existing literature on comparative assessment of labour market conditions acknowledges West Bengal and Maharashtra as relatively employee-friendly states compared to Gujarat and Andhra Pradesh, which are identified as pro-employer states (Aghion et al. 2008; Shyam Sundar 2008).

Such variations in reforms across subnational states have been addressed in contemporary literature through the ideological nature of particular governments and the power of trade unions across states. However, such explanations fall short on closer scrutiny. Political ideology and interest group explanations for reform variation may appear valid in the case of West Bengal and Gujarat. In terms of the party in power in West Bengal, until 2011, an alliance of Left parties with substantial support from Labour was in government. Similarly in Gujarat, the centre-right BJP with an explicit reform agenda has been in power since the mid-1990s. Apparently, the high labour market flexibility evident in Gujarat and the lack of reforms in West Bengal can be explained through the ideology of the party in power.

On closer inspection, such unidimensional interpretation of reform variation fails to explain the labour market situation in Andhra Pradesh or Maharashtra, where ideological polarity between competing parties is indistinct. (In Andhra Pradesh, the parties which formed the government since liberalization have been the Congress party and the TDP with little ideological divergence on reform, while in Maharashtra, the political contest has been limited to the Congress and the Nationalist Congress Party (NCP) alliance and the BJP–Shiv Sena alliance.) The argument of the strength of trade unions also cannot account for the variations across the selected cases. Available records suggest that the extent of trade unionism is higher in Andhra Pradesh compared to Maharashtra by all counts. Yet labour market flexibility is markedly higher in Andhra Pradesh. Thus, accounting for the political party in power and the relative strength of interest groups (trade unions) does not explain the labour market condition in the states; especially, Maharashtra and Andhra Pradesh.

This book provides an alternative explanation to the variations in labour market policy and outcome across subnational states through political factors that go beyond the limitations of conventional explanation. Using both qualitative and quantitative evidences, it accounts for the relative variation in the labour market by highlighting the role of partisan governments, dynamics of interest group negotiation, and party competition in the states.

Organization of the Book

The arguments presented in the preceding section have been elaborated in the chapters of the book. The book is divided into five core chapters apart from the introduction and the conclusion.

Chapter 1, 'Globalization, Policy Reform, and the Labour Market', frames the broad theoretical arguments regarding globalization, policy convergence, and labour market reforms. The chapter initiates the discussion on globalization and public policy and elaborates on the nature of such an interaction. A major section of this chapter is devoted to the discussion of the factors and mechanisms of policy convergence. Such a discussion is theoretically linked to the issue of the labour market as a site of reform. The chapter sets out the theoretical framework for the analysis of labour market reform and presents an index of labour market flexibility to facilitate subnational comparative study.

Chapter 2, 'Locating the Politics of Reform: Labour Market in the Subnational States of India', presents the case study and the research design. The chapter provides an overview of the labour market in India with its structural and institutional dimensions. This is followed by the subnational comparative model where four states are selected on the basis of their institutional and economic similarities, but variations in the labour market. The selection of the case study is based on the logic of most popular cases, where Gujarat and Maharashtra represent high growth, high per capita, and high FDI, while Andhra Pradesh and West Bengal represent medium growth, moderate per capita, and moderate FDI. The chapter concludes with a discussion of the limitations of conventional explanations of reform variation and alternative political explanation of negotiated reform.

Chapters 3, 4, and 5 constitute the core of this book. Chapter 3, 'Political Economy and Partisan Government: Configuration of Labour Reforms', presents the key argument of the book. It argues and shows that variation in labour reform can be explained through specific political economy of partisan governments. When parties in government have significant business support and a socio-economically homogeneous dominant support base, the degree of labour market reform is greater. However, when the dominant support base of the party is heterogeneous and wide, the pace of reform is significantly muted.

Governments tend to reform slowly, formulate broader socio-economic policies, and maintain a wider network of political patronage. Party configuration, that is, the socio-economic support base of government determines the orientation of policies and the interrelation between government and various interest groups in society. A caste–class analysis of elected representatives of parties (signifying political leadership) and evaluation of electoral support base are presented to substantiate the argument. The chapter concludes with a discussion on the underlying cleavage structure of caste and class, and the nature of party competition that contributes to the creation of divergent electoral support bases for parties.

Chapter 4, 'Partisan Government and Interest Groups', further elaborates on the theme of partisanship by showing that the influence of business groups and trade unions on policy is contingent upon their proximity to the government. The chapter evaluates business groups and trade unions as contending interests in shaping labour reforms across the states and shows that influence of interest group depends more on interactions with the government than the material resources at its disposal or its organizational capacity.

Chapter 5, 'Party System: Partisanship, Interest Groups, and Politics', provides the context to the overall argument. The chapter presents the party system as the macro context of politics and elaborates on the impact of party system on reforms. In the context of labour market flexibility, the party system operates as an intermediate variable, shaping the composition of socio-economic support bases of parties, influencing the instrumental behaviour of parties, and shaping the broader political discourse. In the specific case of labour reforms across subnational states, the party system fragmentation facilitates reforms. The chapter contradicts the conventional notion that party system fragmentation impedes reform by showing how increasing party competition corresponds to greater labour market reforms.

'Conclusion: Political Economy of Reforms' presents the overall findings of the research and highlights the crucial interventions of the book in existing academic literature. The specific case study of labour reforms in India is linked to the wider literature on reforms by emphasizing the claims of relative autonomy of politics despite pressures of globalization. The pressure for policy convergence by forces of globalization is negotiated by local and regional politico-economic dynamics, and politics has a significant role in the process. The chapter summarizes the arguments of partisan orientation, party–interest group dynamics, and party system in shaping overall reforms to highlight the significance of politics.

Globalization, Policy Reform, and the Labour Market

The term, 'globalization' has become the metanarrative of the present time, often used to define as well as explain contemporary events. It has attracted both proponents and opponents with equal vigour, and has been subject to intense scrutiny given its transformative influence on society, economy, and politics. Despite the expansive currency of the term in socio-economic and political discussions, and broad agreement about its role in shaping social, political, and economic outcomes, globalization remains a contested concept. The World Commission on the Social Dimension of Globalization, appointed by the International Labour Organization (ILO), appropriately introduces globalization as a divisive subject that verges on a dialogue of the deaf (World Commission on the Social Dimension of Globalization 2004). To proponents such as Bhagwati (2004) and Wolf (1997), globalization is a positive development that heralds the beginning of a new age of prosperity and well-being for all. Friedman (2007) points out that globalization is the triumph of capitalism and free market over other forms of social arrangement and ideology. To critics like Patnaik (2003), however, globalization reflects the worldwide dominance of monopoly capital and increased social and economic disparity. It is the spread of profit maximizing capital across the world through military and ideological apparatuses to facilitate the global exploitation of natural resources, protect the interests of rich and powerful nations, and sustain cultural homogenization among others (Wallerstein 1974).

Clearly, the concept of globalization elicits a diversity of interpretations that prevent any consensus over a universal definition.

Globalization

The term 'globalization' has been subject to multiple interpretations, ranging from simple economic integration to complex socio-economic transformation that characterizes contemporary interdependence. The problem of defining globalization is compounded by its multifaceted nature and differential impact on societies and economies. A survey of the extensive literature on globalization reveals certain broad features that are associated or attributed to globalization.

First, globalization has been identified with economic and social transformations resulting from technological innovations in the late twentieth and early twenty-first century. Emphasizing on the dramatic technological revolution, Castells (1989) defines globalization as a global network society and an economy based on information and technology revolution.

Second, focusing solely on the economic dimension, Piore and Sabel (1984) characterize globalization as a new stage of production organization (post-Fordism) replacing the earlier Fordist model of mass production. Fordism refers to the industrial system that characterized most developed economies after World War II. It refers to the idea of mass production for mass consumptions, symbolized by the assembly lines in automobile industry popularized by Henry Ford. This framework of production paved the ground for post-War economic growth and material welfare through economies of scale and scope, functional specialization, and minute divisions of labour (Thompson 1998). The standardization of products, production, and work processes increased productivity in large industries, reduced the cost of production, and allowed increase in wages for workers. These transformations in the industrial system also created the grounds for variety of public policies, institutions, and governance mechanisms to mitigate the failures of the market, and reform modern industrial practices (Polanyi 2001).

The onset of globalization has witnessed a transformation in the system of organization of production and consumption with proliferation of flexible production system. This new system emphasizes on reduction in overheads, quality management, inventory control, and production of a higher quality end-product (Piore and Sabel 1984). This new system reflects the declining importance of both scale and scope of production and emphasis on customer preferences and is driven by reductions in communications, logistics, and information costs in smaller firms (Thompson 1998). The transformation in industrial system has consequences for society such as dramatic reduction in the demand for unskilled labour, increased income inequality, and political decline of trade union. Sklair (1995) considers globalization as the global phase of capitalism with a transnational capitalist class that requires increasing production and trade with necessary political condition for global expansion.

Third, scholars like Scholte (2005) have highlighted the spatial dimension of globalization by pointing out the rise of supra-territoriality or trans-border spaces with networks of production, civil society, politics, and information.

Evidently, the word 'globalization' is used to refer to both a process as well as an outcome with three broad dimensions, namely economic, socio-cultural, and political–spatial.

Globalization has a distinct economic connotation. It signifies the increasing economic linkage between states and societies, leading to a worldwide network of production, distribution, and consumption. It has been viewed primarily as external economic liberalization by states reflected through flows of trade, FDI, and portfolio investments (Garrett 1998a; Sikdar 2004). Pascal Lamy (2006), the director general of the WTO, has argued that globalization is a historical stage of accelerated expansion of market capitalism, similar to the one experienced in the nineteenth century with the Industrial Revolution.

Globalization has a cultural dimension. Many scholars argue that increasing interconnection between societies is, in fact, an outcome of socio-cultural transformations. Many features of contemporary nation state systems are derived from worldwide models propagated by 'global cultural and associational processes' which contribute to cultural and ideological standardization (Meyer 1997). As Waters (2001) argues, global integration (or globalization) is conditioned by the extent to which economy and polity are culturalized in the emerging global norms. It is the cultural domain that precipitates globalization of economy and polity.

Finally, globalization has a political connotation. As Keohane and Nye (2002) point out, the process of globalization creates a network of complex interdependence guided by transnational rules and organizations. Although the nation states remain as the major actor, several centres of power have come forth, and no singular hierarchy of power or agenda dominates. International treaties such as the General Agreement on Tariffs and Trade (GATT) and the Agreement on Trade-Related Investment Measures (TRIMs), and organizations such as the IMF, the WB, and the WTO now form the framework of institutional interaction and constrain in varying degrees the policy autonomy of nation states.

All of the stated dimensions find mention in contemporary definitions of globalization. Scholars such as Held and McGrew (2000) and Kellner (2002) have emphasized on all these broad aspects in their definition or characterization of globalization. According to Kellner (2002), globalization is at once a product of technological revolution, and the global restructuring of capitalism in which economic, technological, political, and cultural features are intertwined. Held and McGrew (2000) hold that globalization is manifested through certain policies and practices such as strengthening the dominance of market economy, constricting the role of states, expanding the influence of transnational corporations, and the creation of a 'global culture'.

Importantly, globalization is distinct from internationalization to the extent that it replaces the nation state from the centre of analysis, and confines the powers of the state to conduct effective national policies. As Daly (1999) points out, globalization implies the economic integration of many national economies into one global economy, leading to decontextualization of economic production, harmonization of cost-internalization standards, abrogation of the nation-specific social contract between capital and labour, and loosening of national borders. It is a movement towards a single, cosmopolitan, integrated, and global economy where the unfettered individualism of corporations undercuts the ability of nation states to deal with economic, environmental, social, and political issues. The centrality of the economy is also highlighted by

Dicken (2011: 13) who argues that the creation of 'production circuits and networks' that 'cut through, and across, all geographical scales, including the bounded territory of the state' is an original feature of globalization.

As the preceding discussion reveals, interrelation and interaction between nation states are multifaceted and historical in origin. However, it is anchored by economic interdependence through the global production networks of transnational corporations, mobility of capital, and trade (Daly 1999; Dicken 2011). In fact, contemporary globalization is distinguished from previous stages of interdependence in terms of scale of such interdependence and nature of integration driven primarily by economic interests (Drezner 2001; Garrett 1998a).

Globalization, Public Policy, and Reform

Among the many consequences of globalization, an important one with significance for state politics is the issue of public policy. It is argued, not without evidence, that globalization with systemic changes has implications for policymaking autonomy of nation states (Sklair 1995). States increasingly appear to adopt policies that expand the scope of markets, empower non-state actors, and encourage economic interdependence (Rodrik 1997). As Sachs and Warner (1995) point out, globalization is not merely the integration of national economy with world economy, but also an institutional harmonization with respect to property laws, trade rules, tax systems, and other regulatory arrangements. The increasing similarities in public policy have led to currency of the idea of policy convergence.[1]

Policy congruence or convergence has implications for domestic economy and society, as public policies are expected to reflect the distributive concerns within societies. As policies are increasingly influenced by global norms and decided beyond territorial confines of the

---

[1] Convergence is defined as any increase in the similarity between one or more characteristics of a certain policy (for example, policy objectives, policy instruments, and policy settings) across a given set of political jurisdictions over a given period of time (Knill 2005).

state, concerns have been raised about the decision-making autonomy of state actors and relevance of social control.

A survey of the literature on the theme suggests that scholars are not in agreement regarding the exact relationship between globalization and state policy autonomy. The many arguments can be broadly represented into three distinct viewpoints—hyperglobalizers, transformationalists, and sceptics.

Hyperglobalist scholars like Strange (1996) and Omae (1999) argue that the powers and functions of the state are eroding vis-à-vis global actors such as multinational corporations (MNCs) and intergovernmental organizations due to increasing deterritorialization of production and producers, privatization of economic activity, and dominance of global market rules, among others. The impetus for convergence or reform may be external, such as international organizations and global trade, or internal, such as increasing cost of economic closure and epistemological likeness in economic considerations. Evidently, such view of convergence privileges the economic necessity and contends that the needs of global capital imposes a neo-liberal economic discipline on all governments.

Opposed to the hyperglobalizers, the sceptics contend that globalization does not entail any fundamental change in the state-based international system, and states retain substantial policy autonomy. Rejecting the hyperglobalist assumptions, they contend that contemporary globalization reflects heightened levels of interactions between predominantly national economies. Hirst and Thompson (1996) completely reject the idea of a declining state, and argue that nation states and national economies continue to predominate in the age of interdependence.

Diverging to the two binary classifications of hyperglobalists and sceptics, the transformationalists argue that globalization heralds a new era of rapid changes that reshape existing societies and world order. The process, however, is replete with contradictions and there is no certain causal relation between a policy and globalization. As Rosenau (1997: 4–5) poses that globalization has led to the growth of 'intermestic affairs'[2] through the expanding political, economic, and social space in which the fate of societies and communities is decided.

---

[2] In political parlance, the phrase 'intermestic affairs' is used to highlight the linkage or the entanglement of international and domestic affairs caused by globalization.

Interestingly, underlying the apparent divergence of the contending arguments, one can identify certain similarities in the theoretical positions. All the three approaches reflect considerable normative divergence, and none of them subscribes directly to any traditional ideological positions. For example, within the hyperglobalizers, one can identify neo-liberals who welcome the triumph of individual autonomy and the market principle, as well as the radicals or neo-Marxists for whom globalization represents the coup of an oppressive global capitalism.

Further, all the approaches accept and recognize that states are increasingly adopting similar policies under conditions of globalization, although they vary in their causal interpretation. The hyperglobalist framework attributes homogeneity in policy due to structural and global forces that render domestic political institutions emaciated. The sceptics, while championing the cause of national government, also do not reject the convergence hypothesis. To them, governments are not passive, but they are the primary architects of globalization, and have a central role in the regulation and promotion of cross-border activity. The transformationalists also do not reject the idea of convergence, but deter from reducing the causal dynamics to state–market dichotomy.

The foregoing discussion implies that transformations consequent upon globalization have implications for public policy, as states adopt, voluntarily or otherwise, policies conforming to global norms. Such a development has been characterized in public policy literature as policy convergence. According to the policy literature, the sources or pressures for convergence can be classified into three broad categories, namely structural, political, and ideational factors. The classification of the sources of convergence actually mirrors the existing theoretical differences on the relation between globalization and state autonomy.

The structural theorists, similar to the hyperglobalists, argue that globalization leads to policy convergence due to the external environment that affects political units such as nature of international economy, international regimes, and multilateral agreements. Reforms are attributed to intensified economic competition, mobility of capital, and technological changes that constrain autonomous choices of states and limit their course of action (Mosley and Uno 2007). In this context, the WTO as the foremost multilateral trade organization deserves some discussion. As the natural extension of the GATTs, the WTO is considered both as an outcome and a force of globalization, furthering the liberalization of trade, finance, and service (Coppens and Meester 2005). The WTO, through binding multilateral rules on trade remedies and practices, symbolizes the tension between international regulations and domestic regulatory systems (Lingguang 2001).

Contending the structuralist position, the idea of policy coordination argues that states continue to have some power over the market, and convergence is a conscious political choice. Policy convergence is explained by an increased opportunity cost of isolation or similar but independent responses of different countries to parallel problem pressure (Downes, Gomez, and Gunderson 2004). One of the principle economic policy constraints before nation states is the choice in terms of classic macroeconomic policy/financial trilemma.[3] If a country wants to fix the value of its currency and interest rate policy free from outside influence, it cannot allow free capital flow. If the exchange rate is fixed but the country is open to cross-border capital flows, it cannot have an independent monetary policy. Finally, if a country chooses free capital mobility and wants monetary autonomy, it has to allow its currency to float (Schoenmaker 2011). Empirical evidence suggests that countries that fixed their exchange rate and maintained open capital markets lost much of their monetary autonomy compared with countries that adopted alternative regimes (Borensztein, Zettelmeyer, and Philippon 2001; Obstfeld, Shambaugh, and Taylor 2005). As such, states have to formulate particular trilemma configuration depending on macroeconomic conditions and objectives, which lead to appearance of convergence (Aizenman, Chinn, and Ito 2010).

The world society approach locates the source of policy convergence not in any structural constraint, but in the realm of ideas. The impetus for policy consistency is from the spread of certain models and ideas through 'global cultural and associational processes'. Such global ideational norms are usually facilitated through global scientific discourse, international governmental organizations, mimetic emulation of states,

---

[3] The basic idea of a policy trilemma is that a country must choose between free capital mobility, exchange-rate management, and monetary autonomy, as only two of the three are possible.

and have increased the role of technocrats, scientists, academics, and experts who act as a pathway to elite consensus (Knill 2005).

A critical reading of the literature suggests that policy convergence under conditions of globalization may originate externally or internally, and adoption of policies may be imposed or voluntary. However, such a division is purely analytical, as in reality, the dichotomy between external and internal, or imposition and voluntary choice, is often difficult to decipher. Conventional interpretation of convergence emphasizes on the expanding trade and finance in the new global economic architecture as responsible for convergence. The role of international organizations and treaty obligations like the WTO, the IMF, and the WB often serves as an important source in affecting convergence towards neo-liberal policies. Interestingly, there also exists literature that highlights the role of political elites in affecting convergence through changed political–ideological orientation of governments. In an interesting paper, Drezner (2001) has argued that policy reforms in the Organisation for Economic Co-operation and Development (OECD) countries have been a conscious choice of states under the influence of ideational transformation rather than structural constraints.

Intuitively, one can assume that the relative importance of the intra-national and international factors in affecting policy convergence depends on specific politico-economic contexts. The pressure for policy convergence will be especially acute in countries that have foreign debt or suffer from economic crisis (Huber and Stephens 2001a). On the other hand, convergence towards neo-liberal economic policy is relatively indiscernible and unremarkable in the liberal market economies.

Policy Heterogeneity: Limits of Convergence

Despite the strong theoretical arguments for convergence, the empirical evidence of convergence in public policy has been mixed. The pace and orientation of reforms have varied across states, and along with a discernable convergence, there remain policy divergences. Critics of policy convergence argue that globalization originates out of highly diverse national and regional politico-economic forces that contribute to divergences in policy outcomes. The welfare-state literature points out that policy convergence towards neo-liberal minimum has not occurred uniformly and national specificities remain due to domestic political institutions such as electoral system, legislature, and regime type (Esping-Andersen 1996). An influential theoretical argument, the varieties of capitalism literature, points to the differences in corporate governance, labour market, and labour relations between the liberal market economies (those with capital and labour market flexibility) and the coordinated market economies (those with free market with generous social security provisions) due to institutional comparative advantage and coordination (Hall and Soskice 2001).

In fact, at odds with the argument of policy convergence, there exists literature that doubts convergence and highlights national heterogeneities in spite of globalization. New institutionalism goes to the extent of challenging the general expectation of cross-national convergence, emphasizing important differences in national institutions and opportunity structures, and finds diverging rather than converging policy developments across countries (Knill 2005).

Determinants of Policy Convergence: Structures, Institutions, and Politics

The disagreement between the literature on convergence and heterogeneity can be theoretically resolved if we consider the intermediate variables that mediate between forces of globalization and policy outcome. Forces of globalization are mediated and negotiated through a variety of structural, institutional, and political factors that affect the outcome in terms of policy and its consequences. The argument is reinforced by scholarship that finds greater convergence among states marked by similarity in institutional and cultural factors. It is pointed out that converging policy developments are more likely for countries that are similar in terms of economic, political, or social structures (Knill 2005).

The literature on non-convergence of policies also gives credence to the argument of intermediate variables. Scholars of welfare states as Pierson (2001) present institutional impediments such as constitutional rigidity, electoral compulsion, and unchanging preference as contributory to non-convergence on neo-liberal policy prescriptions through path dependence. Likewise, Esping-Andersen (1990) and Garrett (2000) highlight the ideology of the party in government as responsible for policy variation. They argue and show a general association of greater state control, extensive labour market regulation, and economic closure with leftist parties and free market with neo-liberal ideology.

The role of partisanship has also been highlighted in the context of transitional economies marked by the legacy of state-led developmental strategy. Commenting on heterogeneity in labour reforms across Spanish- and Portuguese-speaking countries of Latin America between 1985 and 1998, Murillo (2005) highlights that labour-linked parties used labour market regulation to satisfy their supporters despite macroeconomic pressures for convergence and a regional movement towards deregulation.

Evidently, policy heterogeneity and varying degrees of convergence can be attributed to factors such as historical trajectory of development, political system, structure of the economy, degree of openness, ideological orientation of government, and institutions of state (Esping-Andersen 1996; Hall and Soskice 2001; Kong 2006; Pierson 2001). Summarizing the potential factors that influence policy convergence, we identify three broad categories of determinants, namely structural determinants, institutional determinants, and political determinants of convergence.

The structural determinants refer to the wider environment that is beyond immediate influence or control of any particular political unit. They stand for all underlying arrangements and organizations that are stable in the long run. In the context of public policy, structural factors imply the international economy, nature of integration of national economy to global economy, and the configuration of the domestic economy. The importance of structural determinants has been reinforced in most studies on policy convergence that suggest liberal economies are more integrated and better equipped to respond to constraints of globalization (Garrett 1998a). In contrast, the developing economies have much weaker bargaining capacity, and convergence is often in response to structural adjustment policy under guidance from donors and international agencies.

Institutional determinants refer to institutions such as legal framework, regime type, and nature of party system that are relatively stable in the short run, but subject to the greater control of domestic actors and conditions. Such factors not only mediate change, but often are the objects of such a change. According to Pierson (1996), the transfer and implementation of policy are significantly constrained by the rigidity of institutions. Empirically, greater degree of convergence can be witnessed in countries characterized by high institutional similarity.

Finally, political determinants can be analytically distinguished as composed of interest groups, social networks, political parties, and groups in society who have a stake in public policy. The political actors operate within the institutional and structural constraints, but have the ability to alter the same through political action. Scholars like Cortazar (1998), Frieden and Rogowski (1996), and Rogowski (1987a) have highlighted the importance of composition and preference of social groups in explaining policy heterogeneity. It is argued that policies involving high distributional conflicts between domestic political actors converge to a lesser degree than policies with comparatively small re-distributional consequences.

The relation between globalization and public policy, particularly the extent of convergence, cannot be reduced to a simple causal relation. Policy outcome measured in terms of the extent of convergence or heterogeneity is conditioned by the dynamic interplay of structural, institutional, and political factors in a multilayered process.

Globalization and Labour

In the discussion on policy convergence under conditions of globalization, the issue of labour reforms occupies an important place. Labour reforms are crucial for liberalization of the factors market. Labour policy is also important for socio-economic development, as wage is a mechanism of transfer of income. Furthermore, unlike other factors of production, labour enjoys a unique position, as it is also a political actor.

Characteristics of the labour market such as bargaining coverage and employment protection legislation have important consequences for product market interventions. As such, the structure and forms of the labour market have implications for employment, wage, and overall growth (Horton, Kanbur, and Mazumdar 1991).

Labour is not only a resource for production, but also constitutes an important social group capable of political manifestation. Labour reforms towards deregulations are often difficult to implement because the working class is a powerful constituency with potential to resist reform (Horton, Kanbur, and Mazumdar 1991; Przeworski 1993; Rueda

2007). Naturally, labour market reforms are one of the most contested and challenging aspects of economic policy reform (Cook 2007).

The labour market has significant economic and political ramifications, and provides a site for conflicts over political economic changes under conditions of globalization. It reflects the inevitable and recurring conflict between capital and labour, and as such labour market reform provides an excellent opportunity to evaluate the political economy of policy transformation.

Labour Market Reforms

Labour market reform towards deregulation is a critical component of the macroeconomic reforms under conditions of globalization. The labour market has significant ramifications for the overall economy and constitutes an important transmission mechanism of resources to the poor who rely on labour earning (Horton, Kanbur, and Mazumdar 1991). As Mazumdar and Sarkar (2008: 5) point out, '[T]he impact of economic growth is delineated through the labour market, and any predictions about the impact on poverty and inequality must be based on some implicit or explicit view of the structure of labour markets and their functioning.' Similarly, Davidson (2000) has argued that the structure of the factors market has significant bearing on the way resources are allocated and the speed with which the economy reacts to policy change. As such the cost and benefits of trade reform may vary according to labour market flexibility. Thus, within the broader question of domestic consequences of globalization, labour occupies a crucial position, and the outcome of economic reforms is significantly influenced by developments in the labour market.

According to the mainstream globalization discourse, liberal trade and deregulation are beneficial for economic growth and welfare, as they ensure optimum resource allocation. Free play of market forces results in employment of resources at the market clearing prices that lead to both efficiency (as almost all resources are employed) and equity (all are rewarded according to their marginal contribution). According to neo-liberal theory, liberalization is beneficial for economies, as it expands the export market, promotes industrialization and consequently employment and lowers consumer prices through increased competition (Davidson 2000).

Accordingly, labour, as a factor of production and as a consumer in the market, is thought to benefit from the flexible market not only from effective allocation and efficient wage rate, but also a competitive market that brings prices down. Interference by collective institutions (law and trade unions) in the market process increases transaction costs, which affect investment and cause unemployment and welfare loss. Although the necessity of some restrictions is accepted, labour market rigidity constrains free play of market, and is detrimental to economic growth by limiting employment generation and wage (Besley and Burgess 2004; Fallon and Lucas 1993).

Such an understanding is theoretically corroborated by the Heckscher–Ohlin–Samuelson (HOS) hypothesis. It argues that in a free-trade framework, capital-abundant countries will export capital-intensive products and labour-abundant countries will export labour-intensive goods. Derivatively, the abundant factors of production will be utilized optimally (including labour), leading to increasing real returns (O'Rourke 2003). The 'factor-content approach' similarly associates increasing real returns to labour due change in trade pattern (Kapstein 2000). In this theoretical milieu, the concept of flexibility emerges as central to contemporary labour market reforms.

Flexibility as a Labour Market Condition

The term 'labour flexibility' is a central concept in labour market reforms that not only illustrates the normative objective of a deregulated and free labour market, but also provides an analytical category to compare the extent of policy convergence in respect of labour market reforms. As such, it will be instructive to briefly discuss the idea of flexibility and highlight some of the key features as outlined in literature.

Labour flexibility, in its ideal form, propagates the free operation of forces of demand and supply to ensure optimal allocation, and factors that impede such an operation like regulations and trade unions are considered detrimental. Conventionally, the concept of flexible labour market includes flexible payment, an increase in productivity through change in production process, cutback in social benefits, differential pay scale, and relaxing legislative and regulatory framework. According to supply-side economics, such a labour market would be efficient and competitive through the free play of market forces.

The concern with labour market reform can be traced back to late 1960s and early 1970s when the focus of mainstream policymakers shifted from general unemployment problem to the optimal allocation of productive resources in the context of macroeconomic stabilization (Mathur 1994). Such an ideational change was accompanied by the technological revolution in information and communication that led to a gradual change in production processes. As Piore and Sabel (1984) point out, the changes in capitalism led to changes in work organization, work method, and skill profile. In the context, the concept of labour market reform and flexibility became a part of broader structural change (Sarfati and Kobrin 1988).

At its core, labour flexibility is a condition of the labour market, underlining the extent of unhindered allocation in the market. The definition of a flexible labour market provided by Solow (1998) as one that interposes no obstacle to the frictionless matching of an unfilled job and an unemployed worker with the appropriate, highlights precisely the free movement of forces of demand and supply. Although Solow agrees to the necessity of some regulation, he argues that the degree of flexibility is to be measured in relation to ideal of absence of regulations in the labour market.

The concept of flexibility can also be observed at the micro level, that is, the firm. Standing (1986) has viewed flexibility in terms of certain qualities like technical division of labour, work organization, and forms of payment. He points out flexible labour practices within firms through a shift from progressive to static jobs, narrowing job content, reduction of on-the-job training, growth in casual employment, and relative absence of regulations in labour market.

Approaching the concept of labour market flexibility from the perspective of company strategy, Atkinson (1984) points out three major types of flexibility, namely numerical, functional, and wage flexibility. Numerical flexibility may be further classified into external and internal with the former referring to adjustment in the number of workers through relaxation of employment legislations or employing contractual workers and the latter referring to adjustment of work time. Functional flexibility refers to the extent employees can be transferred to different activities or departments. This is achieved by measures such as employee multitasking and outsourcing activities. Finally, financial or wage flexibility refers to condition, in which wage levels are not decided collectively, and wages are determined according to rate-for-the-job systems, assessment-based pay system, or individual performance wages.

A comprehensive definition of flexibility is put forth by Kong (2006) who emphasizes both on regulatory as well as qualitative features of the labour market. According to him, a flexible labour market can be characterized as one with flexible labour employment, performance-based remuneration, variation in intensity of work according to the market, increasing proportion of casual labour, and scaling down instruments of economic regulation for more flexibility in bargaining rights, employment security, wage, and benefits for labour.

It is important to mention that the purpose of flexibility is essential to facilitate accumulation of profit by capital. Adjustment of labour-to-market signals is a part of the process. That is why Harris-White (2003) argues that the proper way to understand flexibility is to comprehend the nature of accumulation in an economy. However, locating the exact nature and operation of accumulation process requires micro studies of economic process that are not amenable to macro-comparative studies.

Thus at a macro level, labour market flexibility can be understood in terms of greater decision-making power for employers to adjust quantity and price of labour according to market signals. The elemental features of labour market flexibility are—flexible labour employment, flexibility in remuneration, relaxation in instruments of economic regulation particularly employment, wage, industrial relation regulations and variation in intensity, and functions of labour according to market signals.

Limits of Labour Reform Argument

Despite the claims of benefit of a liberal labour market, critics highlight that the state and its regulations are safeguards against an impersonal market that can fail anytime. Emphasizing the virtues of social control, many scholars and activists argue that labour institutions are safeguards ensuring equity, providing impetus for qualitative improvement and industrial research (Wilkinson 1992). Competing firms are forced to be enterprising and technologically advanced only when the option of reducing unit costs by lowering wages and labour standards is barred. Significantly, protected labour expands demand in the market, and thus, promotes growth as well as employment. The criticism against free market is also directed at the broader aspect concerning equity and distributive justice (Chandrasekhar and Ghosh 2000).

Actually, the H-O theoretical model is based on certain assumptions such as competitive markets, full mobility of factors, inelastic supply of labour, capital, and long-term scale, which are difficult to fulfil in real world. Moreover, the labour market is not homogenous with the existence of skill difference and informal–formal dichotomy.

An important theoretical contribution in this context is the Lewisian transition point (Lewis 1954). The theory suggests that as an economy develops, the surplus labour in agriculture is absorbed in the higher wage manufacturing industry. Consequently, productivity and wages of agricultural labour increase. As surplus labour in the economy diminishes, real wage for both agricultural and unskilled workers in urban industries increases, narrowing the income gap between different types of workers. However, if there is rural surplus labour and labour shortages in urban industries due to institutional impediments or skewed nature of industrialization, the income distribution in the economy worsens, and this leads to social and political instability (Minami, Makino, and Kim 2014). Thus, the actual impact of liberalization of labour market is contingent on existing structural–institutional dynamics.

Similarly, economic theory does not consider the impact of technology in such a trade–labour relation, and hence fails to explain the empirical evidence of decreasing price of skill-intensive production relative to unskilled-labour-intensive industries in advanced economies (Slaughter and Swagel 1997).

In this respect, the model developed by Edwards (1988), of a small open economy with two factors (labour and capital) and three goods (exportable, importable, and non-tradable), yields different predictions. According to the theory, a developing country would experience a fall in demand for goods produced in the formal sector (due to cheap imports), after reducing barriers to trade, resulting in a drop in employment in this sector in the short and long run. Employment in the exportable sector is predicted to increase, while the effect on wages in this sector depends on the assumption regarding wage rigidities. The response of the informal sector hinges on whether it specializes in the production of tradeable or non-tradeable commodities. Reinforcing such a theoretical position, a document on labour reforms and economic growth in Latin

America casts doubt on the negative relation between strong labour standards and employment growth (Galli and Kucera 2003, 2004). It argues that macroeconomic stability is more important in job creation than institutional factors, and flexibility in labour market may actually reduce the competitiveness of industry due to low compensation and little training (Tuman 2000).

Empirical evidence of condition of labour under globalization is also mixed at best. In a large-scale comparative study, Rama (2003) finds that the impact of economic reform on economic growth and employment is positive in a long run but it increases unemployment in the short run. Rodrik (1997) has found that impact of globalization on labour has been heterogeneous and argues that less skilled workers with lower paying jobs have withstood the brunt of the adjustment due to internationalization of trade and investment. Bulk of the employment opportunities created due to restructuring of markets and production system tend to be flexible (irregular and casual) in nature as a means of achieving cost efficiency. Such a trend has led to the expansion of informal economy and the progressive elimination of the formal–informal dichotomy in the labour market (Sato and Mayumi 2008).

Inflows of FDI have been found to improve work condition and wages for certain categories of workers (Garrett 1998a) along with deteriorating labour market conditions due to competition for investment and pressure from MNCs (Drezner 2001; Rodrik 1997). Acknowledging the dual impact of globalization on labour, Mosley and Uno (2007) claim that FDI has a positive impact on work conditions while trade competition has a negative impact (that is, it causes a race to bottom)[4] on labour rights.

Heterogeneity in Labour Reform: Determinants of Convergence

Even as scholars differ on the interrelation between globalization and labour market, the developments consequent upon globalization reveal some sort of policy homogenization on grounds of competition,

---

[4] Race to bottom refers to increasing deregulation of markets, including labour standards and taxes, in order to attract or retain mobile capital under conditions of globalization.

economic growth, and creation of employment. At a macro level, states increasingly promote employment flexibility and relaxation of labour laws to facilitate the global shift towards greater market reliance. Available evidence on contemporary labour market suggests increasing casualization and flexibility through sub-contracting, employment of casual workers, and shrinking space for organized labour mobilization (International Labour Office [ILO] 2004).

Interestingly, despite the homogenizing tendencies in the labour market, identifiable differences continue to exist across economies. A survey of available literature shows that although labour relations in different states reveal a shift towards flexible and deregulated labour market, such shifts have been quite heterogeneous, exemplified by reforms in Germany, Sweden, and Norway in contrast to the UK or South Korea (Esping-Andersen 1996; Pierson 2001).

In the context of East Asian countries, Kong (2006) has shown that in Japan reforms have been more towards functional and wage flexibility while retaining the bottom line of secure employment in contrast to South Korea and Taiwan where employment flexibility has been pursued. Even in the transitional economies such as the Latin American countries, there exist divergences in labour market reform. Cook (2007), in a comparative study of six Latin American countries, showed that despite common pressures for flexibility, reform outcomes varied due to differences in legal and institutional frameworks, linkage between trade union and political party, and the strength of labour organizations.

In short, despite homogenizing pressures under conditions of globalization, there exists no unilinear trajectory of development in the labour market. Explanations for continued heterogeneity in the operation of labour market have often emphasized on structural features of economy and institutional rigidities as being responsible for non-convergence towards neo-liberal consensus (Alvarez, Garrett, and Lange 1991; Hall and Soskice 2001). An important theoretical contribution in this regard, the 'varieties of capitalism' literature argues that differences in between the liberal market economies and the coordinated market economies are due to institutional comparative advantage. They argue that divergences in labour relation can be explained through the organization of the national economy and the structure of incentives for coordination of labour and business.

Another dominant interpretation for labour market variation is the institutional rigidities argument that is derived from the welfare state literature. It argues that the continuation of welfare state, and consequent labour market rigidity, is primarily because of path dependence and institutional rigidities. Economic and political institutions that characterize states are historical products of specific socio-cultural or politico-economic dynamics, and as such diverging sets of institutions that regulate the welfare state create hurdles against their own alteration (Pierson 2001). Scholars such as Rogowski (1987) and Rodrik (1997) have also laid emphasis on existing regulations and institutions of government as important influence on the orientation and outcome of the reform process.

Differences in reform have also been attributed to the composition and preference of social groups (Frieden and Rogowski 1996; Kong 2006) and relative strength of labour movement (Rudra 2008). Political dynamics, especially electoral prospects of a political party, have also found a place in explanation for regional variation. It is argued that incentives generated by political uncertainty often contradict the regional trend towards deregulation, as competition dissuaded politicians from adopting policies deemed necessary to attract capital inflows (Murillo 2009). Emphasizing on partisan government, Esping-Andersen (1990) and Garrett (2000) show a general association of greater state regulation with leftist parties and free market with neo-liberal ideology. Similarly, the nature of party system has also been highlighted, as countries with fragmented party system are argued to find free market reforms challenging due to the greater number of bargaining actors or veto players (Roubini and Sachs 1989; Tsebelis 2002).

Following the classificatory scheme of determinants of policy convergence, we can classify the determinants of labour market reforms into structural–historical, legal–institutional, and ideological–political variables. Following the arguments of reform variation, one can argue that pressure for increased flexibility in the factors market, including the labour market, are negotiated or shaped by structural, institutional, and political variables that are specific to regions. As Sarfati and Kobrin (1988) have argued, the scope and method of achieving flexibility in the general milieu towards labour market reforms depend on the relevant economic, social, and institutional contexts. The global scope of labour reform must not conceal the local realities of labour that make such process very distinct and contested.

Political Economy of Labour Market Reform

As mentioned earlier, the issue of labour reforms towards greater flexibility has divided academics and policymakers into opposing camps. According to the distortionist view, regulations impede adjustment of labour and act as an obstacle to growth and employment because of inefficient allocation of resources. The institutionalists, on the other hand, argue that labour regulations fulfil important redistributive roles in a market economy, provide necessary insurance from adverse market outcomes, and create desirable pressures on the employers to focus on the enhancement of their labour productivity (Jha and Goldar 2008). The theoretical deliberation is compounded by a lack of conclusive empirical evidence.

Evidently, liberalization affects diverse economies and sectors differently, depending on factors such as the composition of domestic economy, composition of exports and imports, institutional framework, trade unionism, and partisan orientation. In the analysis of labour reforms, however, the role of political variables remains fairly under-researched. The emphasis on the study of political variables is guided by certain considerations that merit serious discussion.

First, most of the existing analysis on labour market convergence or heterogeneity has been based on cross-national experiences of developed economies and highlights the role of institutions such as political framework, nature of the economy, and nature of the business organization as being responsible for policy variations. The experiences of economic reforms in transitional economies under globalization and especially the role of political actors have remained relatively understudied. This book redresses such an imbalance through an analysis of policy convergence in a transitional economy from a political agency perspective.

Second, the analysis of political dynamics of policy convergence contributes to the literature on reforms, as globalization was heralded in transitional economies through economic reforms. Analysing the role of political actors and variables in policy transformation contributes towards a more comprehensive understanding globalization. At a specific level, actor-based understanding of reform can help us identify the domestic constituencies of support for particular policies.

The underlying argument for such an approach is to bring back the role of political agency in the increasingly structural understanding of economic reform. The choice of policy by government in a democracy is not only influenced by economic-structural factors and institutional dynamic, but also by the constant interplay between relevant socio-political interests. Public policy is shaped not merely by economic theories, but also by political parties, pressure groups, and socio-political dynamics that need to be considered in an analysis. In the context of labour market reform under condition of globalization, the main political agencies are the governments, unions, businesses, and political parties.

2

Locating the Politics of Reform

Labour Market in Subnational States of India

As a research on the political economy of reform, this book looks at labour market reforms and focuses on the role of political variables in determining outcomes. The importance of such a study is augmented by the relative neglect and superficial interpretations of political actors in reform accounts, especially in the context of transitional economies. A cursory survey of the literature on the theme reveals that explanations for labour reform variation emphasize primarily on structural features and institutional rigidities being responsible for non-convergence towards neo-liberal consensus (Alvarez, Garrett, and Lange 1991; Hall and Soskice 2001).

The relative absence of political variables like socio-economic groups and political parties in affecting labour market reform appears remarkable in light of literature that highlights the role of parties, organized groups, and political competition in explaining policy variations (Esping-Andersen 1996; Frieden 1996; Garrett 1998a; Rudra 2002; Tsebelis 2002). This book attempts to rectify the lack of attention to ideological–political variables in determining labour reforms.

The political variables can be analytically distinguished as composed of socio-economic interests with a stake in the policy such as governments, political parties, and relevant interest groups. In the specific context of this research, the three main political agencies considered are the trade unions, business interests, and political parties that interact within specific structural–institutional environment to influence policies. The focus on the political party and party system, rather than the government as a variable, is driven by the peculiarity of subnational comparison. As the institutional structure of government is broadly similar across the subnational states, the partisan dynamics of government is more relevant for causal analysis.

Politics of Labour: Determining Labour Reform

Political understanding dictates that labour policy is the outcome of interactions between relevant socio-economic interests, namely labour and business, with the government, operating within specific political, economic, and social settings. The principal political actors that have a bearing on the labour market are businesses, labour, and the political party in power.

The relevance of a business as the explanatory variable in labour reforms is obvious in a capitalist system since an entrepreneur or a businessperson owns the means of production and employs wage labour in production process. Businesses have an inherent interest in labour policy and seek to determine labour market outcomes. In consonance with the neo-liberal ideology, businesses emphasize on labour market flexibility to meet challenges of global competition and the changing production system. Corroborating the argument of flexible labour market institutions for investment and growth, corporates are in the favour of dilution of existing labour laws to attain greater flexibility (Hensman 2001).

It is worth noting that not all businesses are affected in a similar manner by forces of globalization. Businesses that are threatened by liberalization may favour protectionism. Yet the attitude towards labour market flexibility is somewhat uniform across businesses. Businesses, understood specifically as private enterprises, generally favour flexibility in the labour market to facilitate the adjustment of factors of production and greater decision-making prerogative.

Consequently, a large private sector increases the pressures for labour market flexibility.

Intuitively, we can assume that the influence of a business as an interest group emanates from its contribution to the overall economy (that is, gross domestic product) and the extent of employment generation. However, factors like organization of a business into association(s) (or the extent of fragmentation or centralization), ideology of the party in government, and connection of business interests to policymakers may also impact a business's influence. As such, the capacity of business, as a socio-economic group, to influence policy is determined by the extent of material resources at its disposal as well as the extent of organization as an interest group; particularly, the degree of centralization and political linkages.

Incidentally, globalization with its emphasis on free market has translated into greater policy space to business through concentration of economic power, access to policymaking, and threat of capital flight (Held and McGrew 2007). Such increased power of business over policy has often been identified as 'government–business' coalition where business is perceived as a partner of government rather than a specific social interest group (Mazumdar and Sarkar 2008; Venkataratnam 1993). The MNCs representing the face of global business add a new dimension to business–policy dynamics. Owing to the enormous economic power, MNCs can influence global governance structures by exerting pressure on the policies and practices of governments in both industrial and developing countries (Dunning 1997).

The power of business to influence policy nevertheless remains structured by the specific politico-economic dynamics such as relative power of labour and nature of party in government. As an association of employees in industrial enterprise, trade unions pursue specific objectives embodying workers' interests. Trade unions, by the very logic of their existence, seek to protect and increase wages, work conditions, and social benefits for workers (Flanders 1970). Scholars working on labour reform such as Garrett (1998b) and Deshpande et al. (2004) have noted an inverse relationship between strength of trade unions and extent of labour market flexibility. Garrett (2000) has found that countries with greater unionization of labour forces tend to be significantly more protective than countries with lesser union density. Likewise, Deshpande et al. (2004) in their study have found that firms with unions paid about 17 per cent more wage than those without unions with lower wage difference between unskilled and skilled workers. In the context of labour reform, observers have pointed out that trade unions use their collective status to fail deliberately or extract compensation for reforms that have implications for wage, employment, and job security (Downes, Gomez, and Gunderson 2004; Horton, Kanbur, and Mazumdar 1991).

Interestingly, empirical evidence suggests that the response of labour to flexibility (liberalization) has not been homogeneous across the world (Kong 2006; Kume 1998). According to the literature on trade unionism and reforms, the response of particular trade unions to labour market flexibility is conditioned by institutional–political dynamics. Developing on the wage demand argument of Nelson (1990), it can be argued that small, fragmented organized labour generates weak pressure and acquiesces to reforms. When trade union is centralized and corporatist, it moderates demands being aware of the greater economic costs associated with labour market rigidity. Only when a trade union is moderately strong at the sectoral or industry level, they exert aggressive pressure for achievement of demands. Likewise, ideological dimension of trade unions with regard to economic reforms has an impact on trade union's behaviour. Generally, leftist trade unions are ideologically opposed to economic liberalization; whereas, the response of non-leftist unions is not determined by ideological imperatives, but instrumental calculations.

At a macro level, such as at the level of business groups, the power of trade unions depends on membership, extent of centralization, institutional framework of industrial relations, trade union–government linkage, and existence of public sector.

First, the capacity to influence policy is positively related to the membership and the degree of centralization of trade unions. This is because trade unions derive strength from their ability to act as a monopoly supplier of labour through collective action (Banerjee 2005).

Second, literature suggests that the relative power of trade unions is greatly determined by prevalent economic condition (Kume 1998). Trade unions have been found to be more assertive during periods of economic boom and accommodative during lean periods. In the trade between wage gains and employment protection, the prevalent economic condition exerts critical influence.

Third, at a structural level a large public sector is argued to augment the strength of trade unions. Heller and Tait (1984) have shown that in less-developed countries, the impact of trade union on overall economy operates through the public sector by mechanism of 'leverage effect' on domestic wage. Moreover, public sector unionism provides avenues for direct access to government with implications for overall worker mobilization.

Fourth, the power of trade union is also determined by prevailing institutional and political dynamics. Industrial relations regulation outlines the powers of trade union and provides the basic framework of capital–labour interaction. Political dynamics such as nature of the party in government, level of union competition, and autonomy of union leaders from the party, and rank and file, influences trade union behaviour (Levitsky and Way 1998). In their analysis of labour reform, Alesina and Spolaore (1997) attribute the differing ability of trade union to influence reforms to access to decision-making, nature (corporatist, fragmented, and centralized) of organization, and independence from state and legal prerogatives.

Although labour and business have distinct interest in the labour market, it is ultimately the government that formulates and implements labour policies. In fact, any reform reflects a change in the set of beliefs and interests of governments determined by the relative costs of the policy alternatives. At a theoretical level, government policies are driven by exogenous concerns of the economy like trade, investment, and intra-governmental dynamics such as the relation between different departments, bureaucracy, and the political agenda of the party in power.

As the focus of this research is on political variables of reform, the roles of institutional and structural constraints are made uniform through a careful selection of subnational case studies. The influence of structural considerations and external compulsions is somewhat uniform in the case of subnational units that are broadly conditioned by the national economic conditions. Similarly, administrative frameworks, such as institutional mechanism to resolve industrial dispute and interaction between executive, legislature, and bureaucracy, are broadly similar across the subnational states given the quasi-federal framework of India. Hence, rather than the government as an institution, this research focuses on political parties in government to understand differences in government policies.

In this context, it is important to mention that the emphasis on political party does not seek to undermine the institutional dynamics of reforms that can be unearthed in a study of government. The roles of institutional framework of government and bureaucracy and judiciary in policy formulation and implementation have been important themes in reform literature (Pierson 2001; Tsebelis 2002). There is literature which emphasizes the importance of bureaucracy both in the expansion of welfare states as well as de facto reforms through non-implementation of policy (Harris-White 2003). Although important and interesting themes in their own right, these issues are not considered as the focus is on inherently political dynamics of reform. The subnational comparative case study of this research makes the impact of broader structural and institutional factors minimal at best.

The nature of the political party in government specifies the partisan dimension of labour policy. As Alvarez, Garrett, and Lange (1991) point out, all governments aim to further partisan interests and preside over re-electable macroeconomic outcomes. Scholars working on welfare state and policy transition such as Esping-Andersen (1996), Garrett (1998a), and Korpi (2003) have found significant differences in the economic and social policies of governments with left representation vis-à-vis secular-conservative representation across Europe. This difference in partisan orientation to reform emanates from differences in the ideological and instrumental interests of parties. As Huber and Stephens (2001b) point out, the orientation of parties to economic reform is conditioned by support base of the party and its ideology. While the former, that is, instrumentalist logic presupposes the electoral motive of parties as a determinant of social and economic agendas of the parties, the ideological argument focuses on the party's ideology as an explanation for the different policies enacted by the parties in power.

It is well accepted that ideology has an important role in partisan policymaking as political parties have definite ideological bias. According to Bello (1994), policymaking is a complex process in which the often-unspoken ideologies mediate between interests and policy. There is evidence to suggest a general association of greater state control, extensive labour market regulation, and economic closure with Leftist parties and free market with neo-liberal ideology (Esping-Andersen 1990). In fact, ideology has featured as the preeminent explanation in strands of literature on the global shift from state- to market-led policies (Naim 2000; Waters 2001).

The literature, especially the political-economic literature, also emphasizes the importance of social configurations in determining reforms. Those who oppose the reform literature argue that the beneficiaries of free trade are dispersed and disorganized, whereas those affected negatively are concentrated and organized. Thus, the negatively affected launch a concerted effort to halt the reform agenda (Frieden and Rogowski 1996). The importance of socio-economic support base is also reflected in the literature that views politics of reform as an exercise in political 'blame avoidance' (Pierson 1994). It is argued that reforms are usually attained through either a broad reform coalition to deflect criticism and opposition or through gradually, incrementally, and strategically tied packages that divide potential opponents by providing them with selective compensation (Jenkins 1999; Williamson 1994). At the level of partisan governments, the support base has significant ramification for policy, as governments have electoral concerns. The welfare state literature suggests that configurations of party support determine the policy orientation of governments. Explaining the reform variation between Japan and Germany, Vogel (2001) attributes the resilience German social welfare policies to the broad-based nature of main political parties that contain both pro- and anti-reform groups. Esping-Andersen (1990) has explained the survival of social security measures in the Scandinavian states through coalition between working class and white-collar workers that has proved historically decisive in the politics of redistribution.

Although partisan differences in terms of left–right ideological division and support base are largely correlated in most western democracies, in transitional economies such clear-cut ideological difference between parties is not present. Consequently, correlation between programmatic orientation and support base also does not conform to left–right classifications. As such, in the context of transitional economies, partisan orientation needs to be addressed in terms of both the ideological programme and the interest of support base of parties.

The discussion on the political actors in the labour market remains incomplete without reference to the wider political context. This is because interest-based analysis is not a static zero-sum game and political actors do not act in isolation. Parties and interest groups

operate in an environment inhabited by contending political forma-
tions and, consequently, their responses are influenced by the logic
of opposition and wider political context. In this context, the nature
and extent of political competition is crucial, exerting influence as an
endogenous variable affecting the operation of interest groups and
partisan interests.

The two dimensions of party system, which are much discussed in
literature, are ideological polarization among parties and the number
of competing parties. The conventional relation between party system
and reforms suggests that fragmentation in the party system prevents
alteration in socio-economic policies by creating a large number of
decision-makers and hence making consensus elusive (Haggard and
Webb 1993; Roubini and Sachs 1989). A one-party dominant system
has different policy consequences than a fragmented coalitional system
characterized by greater bargaining actors. Relatedly, policy changes
are most likely when there is a low level of ideological polarization
among major parties. Horowitz and Heo (2001) point out the presence
of strong far-Left parties and that other identity-related ideological
parties have inhibiting effects on policy reform. Thus, the extent of
ideological polarity between parties acts as an important determinant
of policy transformation in a democracy and thus, the government is
able to implement policies on which there exist low levels of difference,
effectively. It is important to note that features of party system share
a relation of complex interdependence. Intuitively, one can assume
that ideological polarity in party system becomes important when
the extent of party fragmentation is high. Analogously, governments
under conditions of high fragmentation are more likely to successfully implement policies if the level of ideological polarization among
major parties is low.

The concise discussion on the political variables that condition
reforms in particular societies paves the way for an empirical analysis.
In order to scrutinize the role of the political actors in labour reform,
this book looks at subnational variation in labour reform across selected
Indian states. The impact of globalization, structure of national
economy, and historical-institutional factors are fairly similar across
subnational states. As such, the case study enables a comparison of
institutionally and structurally similar units with variations in labour
market to identify the political agencies affecting labour reforms.

Subnational Comparison: India as a Case Study

Before going into the specifics of the case study, it is useful to have an overview of the labour market conditions in India to contextualize the research. As the second most populous country in the world, India has a huge labour market in terms of workforce participation. The country has witnessed massive proliferation in the labour force between 1983 and 2014, as the labour force has increased from 270.6 million to around 496.9 million (Mitra 2008). This massive growth in labour force has been corresponded by growth in employment, particularly since economic liberalization. Interestingly, the period of employment growth is also paralleled by a downward movement of formal sectoral wages and upward movement in the share of contractual labour (Mitra 2008). Thus, the increase in employment has been largely in the informal sector and in non-permanent jobs (Papola 2012). This is corroborated by the current daily status of employment that increased from 6 per cent in 1993–4 to around 8 per cent in 2004–5.

Table 2.1 shows the predominance of self-employment and casual employment in the labour market of India. Notably, the share of casual and informal worker reveals an increasing trend even in the organized sector. According to calculations by Mitra (2008), the share of informal workers in the organized sector increased from 37.8 per cent in

TABLE 2.1   Percentage Distribution of Workforce in India, 1983–2005

Employment	1983	1993–4	2004–5
Rural			
1. Self-employed	61.37	57.96	60.2
2. Hired	38.63	42.04	39.9
(i) Regular	7.15	6.45	7.1
(ii) Casual	31.49	35.59	32.8
Urban			
1. Self-employed	42.05	42.29	45.4
2. Hired	57.95	57.71	54.5
(i) Regular	39.80	39.40	39.5
(ii) Casual	18.15	18.31	15.0

Source: Based on data from National Sample Survey Organisation (NSSO) various rounds; calculation by Karan and Selvaraj (2008).

1999–2000 to 46.6 per cent in 2004–5. Associated with this informaliza-tion has been the rise in proportion of contract workers in the orga-nized manufacturing sector from 13.24 per cent in 1993–4 to 30 per cent in 2006–7.

The declining share of regular employment appears more remark-able in the light of the shifts in the sectoral allocation of labour in the Indian economy. Standard theories of labour mobility contend that with economic development, there would be a shift in labour allocation from low-productivity, low-wage sector to the more formal high-productivity employment (Lewis 1954). In India, the transformation in the sectoral distribution of employment has been rather slow. Agricultural and allied activities still contribute around 52 per cent of the employment and maximum employment generation in the post-reform period has been in the service sector, whose share in total employment increased from around 17 per cent to 25 per cent.

The data on sectoral allocation and distribution of workforce (Table 2.2) shows declining share of agriculture and increasing share of employment in secondary and tertiary sectors. Much of the employ-ment generated in the secondary and tertiary sectors, however, is casual and informal in nature. Clearly, the Lewisian notion of a turning point when surplus labour would disappear from the rural economy, after being absorbed in expanding manufacturing sector, is a distant reality for India. The rural economy (primary sector) remains labour thick and the poverty in rural areas remains much higher than urban areas. Poverty, measured by the population below the poverty line, although declining (around 21.9 per cent in 2011–12), is much higher in the rural areas than urban poverty (25.7 per cent in rural area vis-à-vis 13.7 per cent in urban areas) (Planning Commission 2013).

TABLE 2.2   Sectoral Distribution of Employment in India, 1983–2010

Sector	1983	1993–4	2004–5	2009–10
Primary	69.03	64.38	59.07	53.90
Secondary	13.21	14.89	17.57	20.90
Tertiary	17.52	20.73	23.36	25.30
Total	100.00	100.00	100.00	100.00

Source: Calculated on the basis of data from National Sample Survey (NSS) 38th, 50th, 61st, and 66th rounds and Mitra (2008).

The discord in employment and poverty is also mirrored across subnational states of India. Employment structure and growth in employment have been highly uneven across the subnational states of India and the considerable variation in the rate of decline in poverty can be associated with the divergences in labour market. Karan and Selvaraj (2008) have categorized Indian states according to share of regular employment, which reveals that states like Bihar and Uttar Pradesh have low regular employment compared to states like Maharashtra and Delhi.

Intuitively, the sectoral allocation of labour or the structure of employment is a function of the wider economic situation (historical trajectory and endowments) as well as relevant institutional framework. In this context, the role of the labour market regulations has received a lot of attention, especially in discussions on employment and growth. Scholars like Hasan, Mitra, and Marchand (2006) have found that the impact of trade reforms on poverty alleviation was positive and more visible in states with relatively 'flexible' labour market conditions. Scholars such as Dougherty (2009) and Ramaswamy (2015) have traced high labour costs, incentive to increase informal employment, and low productivity to the rigidity of labour regulations, and traced subnational labour market outcomes to regulatory framework.

The interregional variations in labour market policies and outcome, within the macro framework of Indian polity, provide a natural comparative framework. As a methodology, subnational comparative analysis has received attention as limitations of large cross-national studies have increasingly come to the fore. The existence of historically evolved differences between different nations makes cross-national studies analytically constrained, since classification scheme often overrides historical–political differences. As Snyder (2001) points out, cross-national studies often suffer from incorrect 'part-to-whole' generalizations. In contrast, subnational comparison makes the process of coding relatively simpler. In terms of pure methodological considerations, subnational comparison allows us to increase the number of observations and variations in a small number of cases, and control some of the explanatory variables to focus on specific processes and actors (King, Keohane, and Verba 1994). The value of subnational comparison is also augmented by the fact that theories have observable implications at many levels and study of infra-national variations contributes towards understanding of political process obscured by the national framework of regulations (Sáez 2002; Sinha 2005).

In spite of the potential benefits, subnational comparative study remains limited in its ability to explain macro processes, that is, national or supranational processes. It has to be recognized that national politico-economic dynamics determines the choices available before subnational states and regional politics remains embedded within broader national political economy.

As mentioned earlier, India, being a large transitional economy with subnational states that exhibit significant variations, provides a natural case study. The constitutional division of powers grants regional states some degree of autonomy in framing and implementing policies and the subnational variation in reforms highlights the regional–political economy. Economists and policymakers have identified substantial variations in economic growth, reforms, and policy innovations among the subnational states (Bhattacharya and Sakthivel 2007).

Further, as a stable democracy, India is a model of a successfully negotiated economic reform in contrast to the undemocratic reforms experience of many East Asian and Latin American countries. The stability of the political and bureaucratic institutions has ensured some-what reliable government records on labour condition and a plethora of academic works on the theme. India has an impressive record of collection of statistics among developing countries.

With regard to the availability of data, it is important to mention that labour data is primarily for the formal sector of the economy and a large unregulated informal sector exists beyond the scope of this research. The labour market of developing economies such as India is characterized by its duality with the existence of formal and informal sectors. While the formal sector is organized, characterized by existence labour institutions and rights, the informal sector is characterized by the lack of formal employment status. According to Tendulkar (2004), less than 10 per cent of the 500 million persons who form the labour force in India are organized or have regular employment. Sen and Dasgupta (2009) have found that within the organized sector, small and medium enterprises comprise around 44 per cent of aggregate production and constitute 95 per cent of all industrial units in the country. Not only is this sector vulnerable, the unionization of labour is very poor in this sector, leading to high levels of insecurity and low wages for workers.

Such a situation has led Jha and Goldar (2008) to conclude that over-all, the Indian labour market is very flexible with the absence of social security and employment security regulation for large sections of the working class.

The issue of labour market flexibility at a macro level is inexorably linked to the formal–informal divide in the labour market as informal sector indicates de facto labour market flexibility. However, an analysis of labour flexibility in the formal sector, particularly with reference to the politics of reform, may be undertaken without recourse to the informal sector due to the inherent differences in the two labour markets.

First, the issue of labour market reform towards greater flexibility pertains only to the formal sector, and not to the informal sector that remains outside the realm of the state. Since, by definition, the laws and policies of the state do not apply to the informal sector, the issue of reform towards greater flexibility through regulatory relaxation does not arise in such a sector. Further, by definition, the informal sector is beyond the records of the state and consequently, data is very difficult to gather for macroeconomic research.

Second, labour literature suggests significant differences between formal and informal labour markets in terms of efficiency, wage differentials, information asymmetry, and market elasticity. Based on a case study of the Mexican labour market, Alcaraz (2009) has found a relation between unemployment rate and wage in the informal sector, but no statistical effect of unemployment on formal wages. Thus, the informal sector is more flexible and adjusts according to market forces, unlike the formal sector where questions about flexibility are relevant.

Third, the existence of an informal sector is considered an outcome of greater labour market regulation rather than the other way round. Existing literature suggests that the continuation of the informal sector is due to rigidity in the labour market. Regulations have been argued to impact formal–informal divide in the economy by influencing firm behaviour, increasing the cost of hiring workers, affecting the speed and cost of labour adjustment, and influencing the relative bargaining power of workers and firms (Hasan and Jandoc 2012). As such, the share of informal sector in the economy is a function of labour market flexibility rather than flexibility being influenced by the share of the informal sector. The Indian labour market, characterized by a 'missing middle' with employment concentrated in the small firms (indicating the informal sector) and large enterprises, illustrates the argument (Mazumdar and Sarkar 2008).

Labour Reforms in India

The issue of labour market flexibility gained currency in India after economic liberalization in the 1990s. The Indian state formally signed the GATTs in 1991, signalling the end of import-substituting industrialization (ISI) strategy and dismantling of the licence/permit raj system. The economic reform aimed at growth by improving efficiency through removal of government control in the economy and changes in regulations such as exchange rules, tax policy, banking regulation, industrial policy, and trade policy.

In consonance with the new economic policy, changes were sought in labour laws and industrial relations, regulations on grounds of rigidity limiting competition, and optimal allocation of resources (Basu 2004; Besley and Burgess 2004). Mainstream scholars criticize most of the labour and industrial regulations as responsible for discouraging employers from recruiting workers, diminishing competitiveness, and dissuading investment. The existence of a dual labour market with an organized sector (where labour has secure employment and rights) and an unorganized sector (casual employment with no security), and unemployment is often attributed to the severity of legal provisions in India (Basu 2003).

The labour market institutions in India were adopted at the time of Independence in 1947, and reflect the development orientation of a paternalistic state that regulates both labour and capital and negotiates between economic growth with social equity (Shyam Sundar 2008). Broadly, the major central acts that determine labour relations can be classified on the basis of their objectives and orientations into four categories, namely laws related to work conditions, industrial relations, social security, and wage-related provisions.

The work conditions and matters related to workplace are mostly dealt with by the Factories Act, 1884, and the Trade Union Act, 1926. The Factories Act lays down the conditions of work and rights of the workers. It provides minimum conditions of work safeguards for health and safety, and deals with issues of payment of wage, overtime, and working hours. It covers all factories employing 10 or more workers with use of power and those with 20 or more workers without power. The enforcement of the act is through the state government although the act is a central legislation. The Trade Union Act ensures the rights of workmen to organize and collectively redress their issues. According to the act, at least 10 per cent of the total workforce in a unit or 100 workers (whichever is less) can form a union and seek registration to take part in the collective bargaining negotiations. (Before the 2001 amendment to the act, the number required to form a union was at least seven.) However, the formation of a union does not guarantee the right to participate in negotiation with the management in the absence of clear rules to decide the bargaining agent on behalf of the workers.

Among the social security measures, the major acts are the Employees' State Insurance (ESI) Act, 1948, and the Employees Provident Fund (Miscellaneous and Provisions) Act, 1952. Workers in the organized sector enjoy social security such as provident fund, gratuity, bonus, and post-retirement pension. However, due to fiscal issues, the government has moved from a system of defined benefits to a scheme of defined contribution and market-return-based benefit since 1994, a pertinent development after economic liberalization. The ESI Act provides for certain benefits to employees in case of sickness, maternity, and employment injury, and lays down the procedure for delivery of these benefits.

In the context of wages, there exist mainly two acts in India, namely the Minimum Wages Act, 1948, and the Payment of Wages Act, 1936. The Minimum Wages Act stipulates statutory minimum wages in certain list of activities in which unorganized labour is employed. The appropriate governments update these lists from time and time. The act is a recognition that unorganized workers in a labour surplus economy would be the victims of below-subsistence wages and exploitation. In order to ensure regularity, fairness, and judicious modes of payment, the Payment of Wages Act ensures protection against delays in payment and unreasonable deduction from wages, and fixes the period of payment. It applies to the entire country, and covers persons employed in establishments specified by the central and state governments.

The industrial relations framework of India constitutes the main source of contention in contemporary debates about labour flexibility. With regard to industrial relations, there are two major acts: the Contract Labour (Regulation and Abolition) Act, 1970, and the Industrial Disputes Act, 1947. The Contract Labour Act lays down the conditions under which contract labour can be employed, the rights and benefits of contract workers, and abolition of such contracts under certain conditions. The act is applicable to establishments employing more than 20 workers as contract labour and to contractors enlisting 20 or more contract workers on any day of the last 12 months. The Industrial Disputes Act is the principal legislation for resolving conflicts at the workplace, wherein the state intervenes in any dispute between employer and employees. The objective of the act is to ensure the investigation and settlement of industrial disputes with the purpose of securing good relations between employers and employees and between workmen; preventing illegal strikes and lockouts; providing relief to workers in matters of layoff, retrenchment, and closure; and promotion of collective bargaining. The act stipulates that in case of any industrial dispute, the state, through the office of the labour com-missioner, becomes a mediating and conciliating party and employers or employees are expected to inform the labour commissioner before declaring a lockout or going on a strike. The act also lays down the institutional framework such as works committee, conciliation officers, board of conciliation, court of enquiry, labour court, industrial tribunal, and national tribunal.

Business is especially critical of the restrictive provisions of the Industrial Disputes Act regarding retrenchment, layoff, and redundancy of workers. Chapter VB of the act is applicable to all industrial estab-lishments with more than 100 workers and requires prior government permission for retrenchment. Section 25(G) of the act determines the procedure for retrenchment with the established principle of last come first go for workers being retrenched, a month's notice in a prescribed manner, and due compensation for retrenchment. With regard to clo-sure, the act lays down two broad procedures: Under chapter VA of the act, applicable to industrial establishment employing less than 100 workers, two months' notice from the employer to the government and due compensation to the workers is required for closure. Chapter VB, applicable to firms employing more than 100 workers, prescribes application from the employer to the government at least 90 days before the intended date of closure for necessary permission. If the decision of the government is not communicated within 60 days, the permission for closure is granted automatically. The act also refers to unfair labour practices by both employers and employees, and provides a comprehensive list of unfair labour practices and infringement in section 21(M) to discourage it.

It is notable that despite two decades of economic reform, the changes in labour regulations towards deregulation have not materialized adequately. As late as 2014, with the election of the National Democratic Alliance (NDA) government led by Narendra Modi, the issue of labour reforms has resurfaced as an important agenda. In this latest phase of incremental labour reforms, the Government of India (GoI) considered amendments to the Child Labour (Regulation and Abolition) Act, 1986; the Factories Act, 1948; the Mines Act, 1952; the Minimum Wages Act, 1948; the Apprenticeship Act, 1961; and the Labour Laws Act, 1988 (*The Times of India* 2014). The important changes introduced include the increase in the provision of overtime from 50 hours to 100 hours and from 75 hours to 125 hours in work of public interest, relaxation in the norms for women to work in night shifts in industries, reduction in the number of days an employee needs to work to be eligible for benefits from 240 to 90, and increased the penalty for violation of the Factories Act, 1948. The government also sought to simplify labour law compliance by amending the Labour Laws Act by introducing one return of compliance for all labour laws for industries with less than 40 workers.

Apart from the recent changes, the previous central government, under the United Progressive Alliance (UPA) government led by the Congress party, brought some amendments to social security regulations such as the Unorganised Workers Social Security Act, 2008; the Employees State Insurance Amendment Act, 2010; and the Sexual Harassment of Women at Workplace (Prevention, Prohibition and Redressal) Act, 2013. The Factories Act was amended in 2005 to allow women to work in night shifts.

In 2001, changes were introduced in the Trade Union Act, 1926, which put 10 per cent or 100 workers as a minimum requirement for the formation of trade unions instead of the earlier seven workers under the act. In fact, with a view to reforming the labour laws, the government had constituted the Second National Commission on Labour that presented its recommendations in 2002. In spite of broad reform proposals, no major policy change occurred under successive pro-liberalization governments.

Interestingly, the lack of comprehensive labour reforms at the central level has shifted the focus of labour reform to the subnational states. In the constitutional scheme of things, the subnational states are empowered to bring amendment, subject to certain restrictions. States can and often do make policy changes in areas like trade union registration, recognition, minimum wage laws, defining or redefining limits, or granting exemptions regarding the applicability of legislations. Moreover, the responsibility for implementation of labour regulations is largely delegated to the subnational states. As such, regional states have emerged as the forerunners in implementing labour reform. Scholars like Hensman (2001) and Sharma (2006) have pointed out that labour market flexibility in India is occurring de facto at the subnational level.

Even the current effort of deregulation by the central government is accompanied by major changes in labour laws by the BJP-led government of Rajasthan. The government in Rajasthan amended three key labour legislations, namely the Contract Labour Act, 1970; the Factories Act, 1948; and the Industrial Disputes Act, 1947, and introduced significant flexibility in the labour market. Notably, the amendment to the Contract Labour Act increased the threshold for applicability of the law to establishments employing 50 or more workers instead of the earlier 20 workers. The amendment to the Factories Act doubled the definitional threshold of factory from 10 or more workers using power or 20 or more workers without using power to 20 workers (using power) and 40 workers (without using power). The amendment to the chapter VB of the Industrial Disputes Act 1947 raised the employment threshold to seek prior government permission for retrenchment, layoff, and closure from 100 workers to 300 workers.

Subnational Variation and Labour Reform

The shift in the locus of labour market reform from the national government to the subnational state forms the crux of this research. At a macro level, all subnational states share structural and institutional similarities due to historical dynamics. As Radice (2000) points out, the structure and nature of capitalism have always been institutionalized largely on a national basis. In terms of institutional framework, most subnational states are largely comparable, given the state-centred developmental model and that constitutional authority determined the institutional framework. The dominance of the central government and political dominance of the Congress party for a long time furthered such standardization.

Despite the broad structural and institutional similarity, interstate variations in socio-economic development and policy have persisted and increased particularly since economic liberalization. Bhattacharya and Sakthivel (2007) point out that since the 1980s, as the growth rate of India accelerated so did the regional disparity. They show a fair degree of difference in the coefficient of variation of state domestic product (SDP) growth of states, which increased from 0.14 in 1980s to 0.29 in the 1990s. Out of the 17 major states considered between the years of 1980 and 2000, Gujarat, Tamil Nadu, and Maharashtra were high growth states; West Bengal and Andhra Pradesh were medium growth states; while Odisha (earlier Orissa), Bihar, and Assam were low growth states.

Table 2.3 reveals the increasing divergence in the economic outcome over time. The divergences in growth rate have translated into increasing disparity in economic condition across states. The per capita SDP growth for the period suggests that Goa, Gujarat, Maharashtra, Haryana, and Tamil Nadu recorded higher growth rates; West Bengal, Andhra Pradesh, and Madhya Pradesh recorded medium growth rates; and Assam and Bihar had the lowest growth rates.

The scholars are divided on the causes of such divergences in economic outcomes. Cali and Sen (2009) point out the role of geographical factors and initial resources endowments as an explanation for the variation. Bhattacharya and Sakthivel (2007) support such a view and argue that increasing inequality can be traced back to infrastructural endowments, as regions with better infrastructure attracted more investment. In contrast, Sinha (2005) highlights historical institutional developments and state-specific political dynamics as a causal explanation.

TABLE 2.3   Net State Domestic Product (NSDP) Growth Rate for 15 Major States, April 1980 to March 2015

States	1980–1 to 1992–3	1993–4 to 2004–5	2004–5 to 2014–15
Andhra Pradesh	5.70	5.30	5.58
Assam	3.38	2.98	3.77
Bihar	3.32	4.53	7.92
Gujarat	4.94	5.70	7.89
Haryana	6.11	6.00	6.58
Karnataka	5.52	6.80	5.97
Kerala	4.05	5.20	6.91
Madhya Pradesh	4.28	3.90	6.37
Maharashtra	6.58	5.00	7.65
Odisha	3.58	4.40	3.97
Punjab	5.23	4.20	6.22
Rajasthan	6.50	5.70	8.52
Tamil Nadu	5.33	4.60	4.50
Uttar Pradesh	4.86	3.70	5.39
West Bengal	4.70	7.10	5.76
Average	4.90	5.09	6.20
Standard Deviation	1.07	1.16	1.39

Source: Author's calculation based on 'Net State Domestic Product at Factor Cost: State-Wise (at Constant Prices)', available at http://dbie.rbi.org.in/DBIE/dbie.rbi?site=home, last accessed on 4 February 2016.
Note: Goa and Himachal Pradesh have not been considered here because of their size and negligible manufacturing industry.

The divergences in growth rates have translated into variance in per capita income and NSDP over time. The per capita net state domestic product across the states reveal increasing disparity over the years (Table 2.4).

An important aspect of economic infrastructure that affects growth and socio-economic development is the policy orientation of regional states. Liberalization has been followed by shifts in the federal framework whereby the power of the central government has declined and subnational states have gained importance in mediating the process of adjustment and institutional change (Nayar 2007; Sáez 2002). As such, policy innovation at the subnational level has emerged as an important determinant of growth and development.

TABLE 2.4 Classification of 16 Major Subnational States according to Per Capita NSDP, 1980–2010 (Values in Rupees)

Rank	1980–90		1993–8		2004–10	
	State	Per Capita NSDP	State	Per Capita NSDP	State	Per Capita NSDP
1	Punjab	3,216.27	Maharashtra	13,486.71	Maharashtra	50,188.62
2	Haryana	2,793.36	Punjab	13,203.80	Haryana	49,343.33
3	Maharashtra	2,706.00	Gujarat	11,840.80	Gujarat	43,968.33
4	Gujarat	2,285.27	Haryana	11,840.40	Tamil Nadu	42,590.83
5	West Bengal	1,923.73	Tamil Nadu	10,149.00	Kerala	41,692.33
6	Himachal Pradesh	1,865.91	Himachal Pradesh	8,785.00	Himachal Pradesh	41,020.50
7	Tamil Nadu	1,792.09	Kerala	8,771.80	Punjab	39,894.50
8	Karnataka	1,766.82	Karnataka	8,541.80	Karnataka	35,358.67
9	Andhra Pradesh	1,666.27	Andhra Pradesh	7,980.60	Andhra Pradesh	33,641.33
10	Kerala	1,537.91	West Bengal	7,526.00	West Bengal	27,719.00
11	Rajasthan	1,472.45	Rajasthan	7,399.00	Rajasthan	22,999.00
12	Assam	1,451.09	Madhya Pradesh	6,862.80	Odisha	21,618.67
13	Madhya Pradesh	1,435.55	Assam	5,760.20	Assam	18,973.17
14	Uttar Pradesh	1,423.18	Uttar Pradesh	5,351.00	Madhya Pradesh	18,859.00
15	Odisha	1,406.00	Odisha	5,061.80	Uttar Pradesh	15,340.33
16	Bihar	1,055.09	Bihar	3,101.80	Bihar	9,781.00

Source: Author's calculation based on 'Net State Domestic Product at Factor Cost: State-Wise (at Constant Prices)', available at http://dbie. rbi.org.in/DBIE/dbie.rbi?site=home, last accessed on 4 February 2016.

Notes: (a) These 16 subnational states are selected in terms of size and population.

(b) Goa, Tripura, Sikkim, Arunachal Pradesh, Jharkhand, Jammu and Kashmir, Chhattisgarh, Manipur, Meghalaya, Mizoram, Nagaland, Jharkhand, Chandigarh, Delhi, Puducherry, Uttarakhand, Andaman and Nicobar excluded.

In this context, labour market policies reflecting significant subnational variation have emerged as an important politico-economic issue. Comparative studies of labour policy such as those by Besley and Burgess (2004) and Aghion et al. (2008) highlight variations in labour regulation across states. Regional states of India have been characterized by 'diverse array of market governance patterns' and regional institutional innovations that reflected the distinct political economy of the states (Sinha 2005). The implications of such variation are twofold: First, any comparative analysis should strive to minimize the differences among states so as to allow comparison of most similar case. Second, subnational variations suggest the importance of regional factors in determining market outcomes.

In order to cross-examine the politics of labour policy, this research focuses on a small number of states that are more alike in social and economic indicators. Such an approach is more rewarding than comparison of all regional states, as it would minimize state-specific economic differences that have an impact on labour market. In this regard, the states of Andhra Pradesh, Gujarat, Maharashtra, and West Bengal provide natural examples suited for paired comparison due to their similarity in economic and institutional developments.

The four provinces are advanced industrialized states in India, employing the most number of workers in the manufacturing sector industry (Nagaraj 2004). Planning Commission data on rate of growth of SDP between 1980–1 and 1998–9 reveals that the states of Maharashtra, Gujarat, Andhra Pradesh, and West Bengal have been among the high-performing states in India (Kapila and Kapila 2002). The similarity between the states in terms of per capita NSDP becomes evident through Figure 2.1.

Clearly, in terms of NSDP, the states of Maharashtra–Gujarat and West Bengal–Andhra Pradesh are most alike with the former representing high-income states and the latter, medium-income states. The similarity between the two sets of states becomes more pronounced when economic growth rates and the composition of the economy are considered.

Table 2.5 shows that for the period between 1980 and 2014, Andhra Pradesh had an average growth rate of 5.52 per cent, whereas for West Bengal it was 5.8 per cent. The contribution from industry for the states was 18.75 per cent and 18.05 per cent, respectively. Thus,

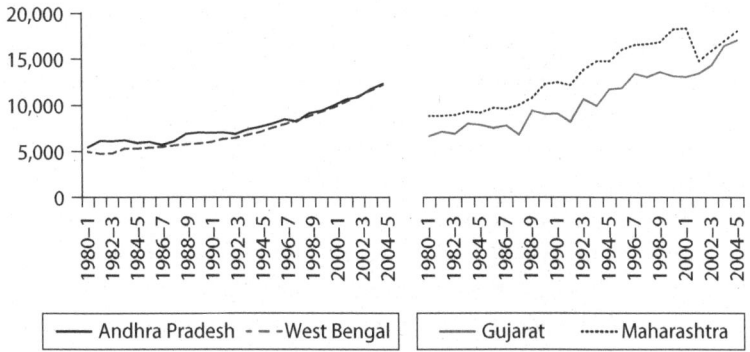

FIGURE 2.1   Per capita NSDP of Andhra Pradesh–West Bengal and Maharashtra–Gujarat, 1980–1 to 2004–5
Source: Per Capita 'Net State Domestic Product at Factor Cost: State-Wise (at Constant Prices)', *Database on Indian Economy*, RBI. Data compiled by Directorate of Economics & Statistics of respective state governments and Central Statistical Organization (CSO). The data is limited to 2005, as the base year for calculation was changed by the CSO in 2004–5.

TABLE 2.5   State-wise Comparisons on Broad Economic Indicators, 1980–2014

State	Growth Rate	Contribution from Industry
Andhra Pradesh	5.52	18.75
Gujarat	6.17	32.95
Maharashtra	6.40	27.33
West Bengal	5.80	18.05

Source: Author's calculation based on Tables 2.1, 2.2, and 'Net State Domestic Product at Factor Cost: State-Wise (at Constant Prices)', available at http://dbie.rbi.org.in/DBIE/dbie.rbi?site=home, last accessed on 4 February 2016.

the two states are broadly similar in terms of economic structure and both were among the middle-growth and middle-income states of India.

Likewise, the states of Maharashtra and Gujarat are largely similar. Considered among the most industrialized states of India, the industrial contribution constituted 27.33 per cent and 32.94 per cent of the SDP in Maharashtra and Gujarat, respectively. Although the industrial sector of Gujarat is more vibrant than Maharashtra, the two states share quite a similar economic growth rate and SDP. The two subnational states feature among the highest-income states of India, accounting for maximum investment, both domestic and foreign.

The four states have also been recipients of significant foreign investment since liberalization. The FDI data can be considered as an indicator of global integration and on that count, all the states are positioned in the top half of the list on FDI recipient states of India. Maharashtra has been the leader in attracting FDI in India. The states of Gujarat and Andhra Pradesh have attracted comparable foreign investment, confirming their status as economically vibrant states. Interestingly, West Bengal, which attracted the least FDI among the selected states, occupies the seventh position in the list of top FDI inflows between 2000–15 in India, with Gujarat in fifth position and Andhra Pradesh in sixth position (Table 2.6).

The standard economic parameters, namely per capita income, growth rate, and contribution of secondary sector to state SDP, reveal the similarity in economic structure among the selected pairs of states. To check the robustness of the similarity in economic structures of the states, I perform a T-test on per capita income and per capita NSDP of the respective pairs of states (Table 2.7).

The statistical analysis of the means of per capita income and per capital NSDP of the states reveals the strong similarity in broad economic structures. Notably, this similarity between the selected states transcends broad economic indicators, and the nature of industrialization is also

TABLE 2.6   FDI Approval for the Period 1991–2001 and Inflow for the Period 2000–15 (in rupees crores)

State	FDI Approval 1991–2001	FDI Inflow 2000–15
Andhra Pradesh	12,615.383	48,536
Gujarat	17,365.511	51,193
Maharashtra	47,491.379	344,449
West Bengal	8,701.293	14,393

Source: *SIA Newsletter*, Annual Issue, Ministry of Commerce and Industry, GoI. Available at http://www.indiastat.com/industries/18/foreigndirectinvestment/17578/rbiregionwiseforeigndirectinvestment19912015/449558/stats.aspx, last accessed on 15 March 2017.

TABLE 2.7 Statistical Test on the Comparability of the Selected Paired States

	Andhra Pradesh	West Bengal	Gujarat	Maharashtra
T	19.847	16.153	17.035	19.632
Mean	7,874.4	7,333.96	10,556	13,228.8
Standard Deviation	1,983.759	2,270.119	3,098.345	3,369.117
Corr. Coefficient	0.847	1	0.989	1

Source: Author's own calculations.
Note: All the results are significant at .001 level.

very similar. This is significant for the study of labour, as contemporary economic processes have led to transformations in industrial structures and establishment of new forms of organizations such as technology-led automation, ascendance of high-growth sectors like petroleum and chemicals, and new production processes. All these developments have implications for future industrial policy and, consequently, labour policy. The industrial structure of the economy constitutes an important dimension of case selection in the study of labour, as states with similar industrial structure are more likely to be subject to similar global market forces.

Disaggregated analysis of net value added (NVA) and employment at the level of industries (the *Annual Survey of Industries* [*ASI*] data on NVA at the two-digit level) provides an overview of the industrial composition. The contribution of the industries in terms of industrial output and workers employed determines their relative importance in the economy of the states. As such, the proportional contribution of each two digit level industry to the total NVA and employment in industrial sector highlight the dominant industries in the respective state.

Table 2.8 shows, the states of Gujarat and Maharashtra are structurally similar in terms of nature of industries with a predominance of petroleum, textile, and machine tools industries. Similarly, Andhra Pradesh and West Bengal have a high degree of similarity in industrial composition with the predominance of agro-industries, machine tools, and steel in the industrial structure. The difference in the nature of industrialization, with high-productivity industries in Maharashtra and

TABLE 2.8   Composition of Industry according to NVA and Employment in the Selected States, 1979–98 (in ASI two-digit format)

Top Five Industry Categories Contributing to NVA				
Andhra Pradesh	20, 21	22	30	33	35, 36
West Bengal	25	37	30	33	35, 36
Gujarat	30	31	35, 36	40	23
Maharashtra	30	35, 36	37	31	20, 21

Top Five Industry Categories Contributing to Employment				
Andhra Pradesh	20, 21	22	40	35, 36	23
West Bengal	25	33	20, 21	37	35, 36
Gujarat	23	24	20, 21	30	35, 36
Maharashtra	23	20, 21	30	35, 36	37

Source: Author's calculations based on the *ASI* (various issues).
Note: The *ASI* classifies industries into codes for enumeration of industrial data. The classification of industries is based on National Industrial Classification (2004) at the two-digit level. Industrial structure is stable in the medium run, which ensures the validity of the classification.

Gujarat and relatively low-productivity industries in Andhra Pradesh and West Bengal, can also be noted in more contemporary data on employment and NVA. The state-wise share of employment and NVA in industries in proportion to India reveals the point.

Table 2.9 makes it clear that the ratio of value added vis-à-vis employment is much higher in Gujarat and Maharashtra compared to West Bengal and Andhra Pradesh, due to a difference in industrial structure with the predominance of high-productivity, high value-adding industries in the former.

TABLE 2.9   Share of Employment and NVA in Industry in Proportion to India

State	Employment Share		NVA	
	2000–1	2010–11	2000–1	2010–11
Andhra Pradesh	10.2	11.4	8.3	6.2
West Bengal	5.0	7.1	3.0	4.0
Gujarat	10.2	9.4	13.3	12.9
Maharashtra	13.4	14.7	20.4	21.1

Source: ASI (2000).

Based on the preceding discussion, it can be argued that the selected pairs of states represent economically and institutionally most alike cases. The similarity goes beyond economic structure, as the states are also positioned closely in terms of socio-economic development. Although difficult to quantify, the variable of socio-economic development has featured in literature as an important determinant of growth and development. The modernization literature suggests that societies with similar levels of technological advancements and economic development share some broad moral and cultural values that can have implications for condition of work, labour, perception of business, and broader social concerns. The literature on convergence also highlights that states with comparable levels of socio-economic development are likely to be affected similarly by the opportunities and constraints of global transformations.

The HDI composite score (Table 2.10) reveals that the selected states are characterized by comparable levels of socio-economic development. The states chosen for our case study are broadly similar in terms of their HDI score as well as their relative position within India.

The nature of the labour market, at any specific period of time, is conditioned by three broad factors, namely historical–institutional developments, political conditions, and macroeconomic dynamics. Given the extent of similarity among the selected states, especially the nature of the economy and broad institutional framework, one can expect their labour markets to be largely similar subject to political

TABLE 2.10   Composite Human Development Index (HDI) for the Selected States, 1981–2001

State	1981		1991		2001	
	Value	Rank	Value	Rank	Value	Rank
Andhra Pradesh	0.298	9	0.377	9	0.416	10
Gujarat	0.360	4	0.431	6	0.479	6
Maharashtra	0.363	3	0.452	4	0.523	4
West Bengal	0.305	8	0.404	8	0.472	8
Overall in India	0.302		0.381		0.472	

Source: State-wise Human Development Index, http://www.indiastat.com/table/economy/8/humandevelopmentindex/14992/30875/data.aspx, last accessed on 13 September 2009.

context. Any perceived difference in the labour markets of the selected states would, however, indicate the operation of political dynamics of labour market.

Subnational Labour Market Variation

Existing scholarship points out significant differences in the labour market policies and outcomes across the selected states. Besley and Burgess (2004) in their study of labour regulations and industrial growth highlight West Bengal, Gujarat, and Andhra Pradesh as pro-labour states and Maharashtra as a pro-employer state. They study the subnational amendments to the Industrial Disputes Act, 1947, to classify the labour market condition in the respective states.

In an important work, Bhattacharjea (2006) has highlighted the limitation of the Besley and Burgess (2004) and other econometric analyses based on labour regulations. He correctly points out that most empirical studies have almost entirely focused on the Industrial Disputes Act (provisions for government permission for layoffs, retrenchments, and closures), ignoring the other important legislations. Another important issue highlighted is the temporal gap between the enactment of rigid labour regulations and the implementation of the provisions. Several provisions of Chapter VB (permission for layoff, retrenchment, and closure) which were amended to increase employment protection were contested in the courts and implemented much later. According to Bhattacharjea (2006), the divergences in the econometric assessment of labour regulations is affected by this temporal gap, as the 1976 and 1982/84 amendments in the Industrial Disputes Act cannot be regarded as events which unambiguously increased labour inflexibility.

Another important limitation of Besley and Burgess (2004) is the methodology of scoring individual amendments and calculating the year-wise score. They classify states on the basis of only the Industrial Disputes Act amendments into pro worker or pro employer, which is often misleading. Further, they assign a score of +1 or –1 each year to the states, which is the cumulative score of all amendments. As Bhattacharjea (2006) points out, a total of 113 amendments are reduced to only 19 episodes of amendment within the period 1958–97. Further, such a methodology considers all amendments as equal regardless of their relative importance or the extent to which they were actually implemented.

In another comparative study of labour regulations, Shyam Sundar (2008) classifies Gujarat as the least regulated state and West Bengal as the most regulated state in India. Contrary to Besley and Burgess, he finds Andhra Pradesh as among the more liberalized states and Maharashtra as among the more regulated states.

The conflicting evaluation of subnational labour market regulation can be traced to the difference in conceptualization of labour regulations. Besley and Burgess (2004) evaluate regulation from a strictly formal-legal perspective focusing on a single labour law. In comparison, Shyam Sundar (2008) embraces a broader idea of regulation incorporating labour judiciary, trade unions, workdays lost, scheduled employments under the minimum wages acts, average minimum wage, number of inspections, average labour cost, and state laws on industrial relations. Naturally, the classification of Shyam Sundar (2008) is more comprehensive.

Given the divergence of opinion on the nature of subnational regulation in India, I independently assess labour reforms across the states. Notably, my focus is not only on regulations, but overall labour market reforms in the context of globalization. The conceptualization of labour reform under economic liberalization incorporates unimpeded operation of the market forces in terms of supply, use, price, and allocation of labour. All these conditions are conceptualized through the idea of labour flexibility.

Labour flexibility is a quantitative and qualitative condition of the labour market. A survey of the existing literature on this topic suggests that different aspects of labour market have been used to understand flexibility. A dominant approach has been to assess the labour market regulation against some ideal neo-liberal prescription or the ILO framework of labour rights. Rama (1995) has evaluated labour market rigidity/flexibility on the basis of qualitative classification of labour market regulations, fixing the lower bound and upper bound of regulations. The lower bound reflects a position close to perfect competition, whereas the upper bound reflects the greatest degree of regulation.

Although instructive, the limitation of measuring flexibility purely through regulations is such that it ignores the actual operation of the labour market. Most of the measures constructed have been based on the experience of developed economies with well-developed institutions and high state capacity. In contrast, most developing countries are characterized by 'restricted state capacity', implying a gap between regulation and their implementation. As Forteza and Rama (2006) point out, the labour law scenario in India is most rigid on paper but most flexible in practice. As such, implementation data on labour regulations needs to be assessed to analyse the extent of flexibility.

Another much-used method to study labour flexibility has been the evaluation of minimum wages across sectors, wage structure, cost of dismissal, and other areas of labour cost. Márquez (1998) constructed an index of labour market flexibility with components of labour regulation like length of probation period, advance notice period, cost of dismissal, reinstatement of worker after cause is deemed unjust, and cause of dismissal. However, in the case of India as in many developing economies, data on wage structure and internal work practices of industry are either not available or suffer from a certain level of incomparability of data.[1] As such, any index of labour flexibility for India must take into account the specificities of labour market as well as availability of data.

The index developed for the specific purpose of subnational comparison across India incorporates both regulatory aspects of the labour market as well as the actual operation of labour market to account for all specificities. The data is derived from the GoI publications, namely *ASI; Statistics on Closure, Retrenchment and Lay Off; Indian Labour Yearbook*, and NSSO data. The data on labour regulations and their amendments is collected from the law books. Also, some secondary data is used, for which due credit and citation is provided, which provides data on implementation of labour laws in the various states. It is important to mention that comprehensive regular data on labour is available only regarding the organized sector and even then, the scope is very limited. The *ASI* data covers only firms under the Factories Act and noncompliance or fudged records are rampant in this data, since firms often do not provide timely or correct information. As such, the index of labour

---

[1] Incomparability of data due to methodological and ideological differences in data collection. Data on some of indicators such as annual leave with pay, universal minimum wages, and probation period are not readily available in most developing economies due to lack of uniform industrial development.

market flexibility is at best reflective of broader trends and exact quantification is extremely difficult, if not impossible.

The index of labour flexibility is composed of the following dimensions:

1. **Data on casual or contractual workers:** Casualization of labour has been one of the foremost features flexible labour markets (Ahsan 2006, 2008). A casual worker has limited or no job tenure, very narrow and static job content, little social security benefits, and lower wages compared to a regular worker. Hence, the proportion of contractual workers is an indicator of the labour market flexibility. The *ASI* records the number of casual workers in the factories sector across the state, and the proportion of contract worker to total workers is considered to evaluate the extent of casualization.

2. **Evaluation of labour law amendment:** Given the federal framework of India, labour laws are framed both by the Union government (applicable to the whole of India) and the subnational state governments. I consider the state-level amendments to the major Union-level labour laws that have implications for work condition and social security. As subnational governments bring about amendment to suit regional requirements, an evaluation of amendments can indicate the comparative levels of regulatory flexibility. The laws considered for evaluation are: (a) work regulation: Factories Act, 1948, and Contract Labour (Regulation and Abolition) Act, 1970; (b) social security: Employees State Insurance Act, 1948, and Workman's Compensation Act, 1923; (c) industrial relation regulation: Industrial Disputes Act, 1947, and Trade Union Act, 1926. The index classifies regulations through a careful reading into pro labour, pro employer, neutral, and pro state. The classification of regulations improves and builds upon the analysis of Besley and Burgess (2004) through an in-depth reading of greater number of laws. Each amendment is carefully read and coded either pro labour (if the amendment strengthens the position of labour), pro employer (if amendment gives greater power to employer), or neutral (if amendment does not clearly favour any one or expands the powers of the state).

3. **Data on implementation of labour laws:** The existence of labour regulations is limited by their implementation. The reform by stealth hypothesis contends that informal deregulations and non-

implementation of laws is a process of reform (Jenkins 1999). The literature on state capacity also emphasizes the importance of institutional factors like bureaucracy in determining the success or failure of any policy (Rodrik 2007). The data on labour law implementation reflects the capacity of state to implement policies and also partly the intention to implement labour regulations. I look at the data on inspection of the Factories Act for analysis, as it includes all productive units in the formal sector of the economy. The proportion of factories inspected under the Factories Act in a particular year is considered as a measure of inspection.

4. **Data on wage and wage share:** Flexibility in wage is an integral part of labour flexibility. In India, it is difficult to get any comprehensive assessment of wage, as organized sector wage is industry specific and typically higher than the minimum wage. As such, a comparison of share of wages to total value added is used for subnational comparison. Wage share reflects the relative share of labour in total value produced and a flexible labour market is characterized by very low or decreasing wage share.

5. **Data on retrenchment:** Data on industrial retrenchment is an indicator of labour market flexibility. The prevalent industrial relations regime under the Industrial Disputes Act requires prior government permission for closure or retrenchment. The removal of prior permission clause has been one of the main demands of business to allow a quick adjustment of labour (Ahuja 2006). As such, the number of firms reporting retrenchment broadly highlights the attitude of government to labour reallocation. However, it is to be borne in that such a data is hugely underreported and can only reflect broad trends.

The suggested variables considered together provide an index of labour market flexibility that can be used for a comparative assessment of labour market condition in subnational states of India. The index provides an ordinal measure through the most relevant variables for which government data is available in India. Measured through the index of labour market flexibility, it is clear that the states of Andhra Pradesh and Gujarat have a comparatively flexible labour market than Maharashtra and West Bengal. The descriptive statistics of the different measures of labour market flexibility makes the point apparent and clear.

Data on Contract Workers

The proportion of contractual workers is an indicator of labour flexibility and, in the Indian context, all subnational states record an increasing incidence of contractual labour. However, the data on proportion of contractual workers employed in industry reveals a clear picture of subnational variation. The proportion of contractual workers (Figure 2.2) in total factory employment is highest in the state of Andhra Pradesh hovering around 50 per cent of all industrial employment. In contrast, the increase in proportion of contractual workers in West Bengal has been relatively less pronounced from a low value of around 3 per cent in 1994–8 to around 25 per cent in 2008–12.

The proportion of contract workers also registers an upward increase in Maharashtra and Gujarat. However, the latter clearly has a greater share of contractual workforce historically. In absolute

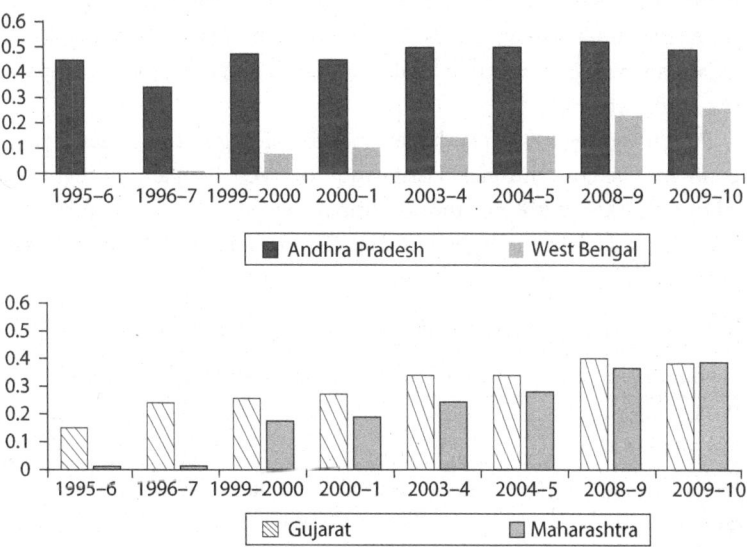

FIGURE 2.2   State-wise Comparison of Proportion of Contractual Workers, 1995–6 to 2009–10

Source: ASI (various issues).

Note: The tables represent the average proportion of contract worker in the states for the periods 1994–7, 2000–03, and 2008–11. Proportion of contractual workers is determined from *ASI* data on total workers and contract workers employed across states.

terms, the proportion of contract workers is significantly higher in Andhra Pradesh, followed by Gujarat and Maharashtra, where the proportion of contractual workers increased to around 40 per cent in 2012. West Bengal employs the least proportion of contractual workers, which increases from marginal levels to around 25 per cent during 2008–12.

Legal Amendment

The evaluation of labour law amendments across the state into pro labour (more restrictions) and pro employer (greater flexibility) presents some interesting outcomes (Table 2.11).[2] In order to maintain parity and congruity with legislative reforms (some labour reforms require consent from the Union government), I have chosen only those reforms, which have been officially notified in the government gazette before the year 2014 (for details, please check the annexure list on state-level amendments). This is because in the year 2014, the state of Telangana was carved out of Andhra Pradesh that altered our comparative framework.

At an aggregate level, the evaluation of legislative amendments confirms the conventional classification of West Bengal as a regulated labour market with the most number of pro-labour amendments. West Bengal, with the legacy of Left dominance, clearly has the most

TABLE 2.11 Labour Law Amendments across Subnational States, 1972–2014

Labour Amendment	Andhra Pradesh	Gujarat	Maharashtra	West Bengal
Pro Labour	11	2	9	22
Pro Employer	5	3	5	0

Source: Author's classification from Malik (2009), and http://india.gov.in/my-government/actsrules, accessed in February 2015.

[2] Restriction and flexibility apply to the labour market. A pro-labour amendment restricts the power of employers to fire workers and undertake adjustment of wages or employments. In case of pro-employer amendment, it translates into greater flexibility for the employers granting them more power in determining employment, wages, working conditions, and readjustment of labour.

number of pro-labour amendments and not a single amendment that can be considered pro employer. Andhra Pradesh comes next in terms of pro-labour amendments; however, unlike West Bengal, it has some pro-employer amendments, which occur after economic liberalization. The state brought amendments to introduce labour flexibility such as relaxation of Contract Labour Act to allow contractual employment in perennial jobs, variable dearness allowance for contract workers, integrated registration and furnishing of returns of labour laws, and mandatory insurance to pay gratuity to workers.

Gujarat records the least number of amendments in labour laws, but the direction of such amendment has been largely pro employer. For example, in a major reform the Gujarat government passed the Gujarat Labour Laws bill that introduced out-of-court settlement for labourers and employers by paying fine (violations can be negotiated through monetary payment and not state intervention), gave power to the government to prohibit strikes in public utility services, reduced the time period available to workers to file complaint against employer, allowed change in nature of job of workers without notice, and allowed outsourcing under the Contract Labour Act (*The Indian Express* 2015).

Interestingly, Maharashtra also contemplated many changes in labour laws, but no major reforms have been introduced till date. Maharashtra is the most interesting case, as the proportion of pro-labour and pro-employer amendments is highest amongst the state. Remarkably, both types of amendments appear to happen simultaneously as if the government sends signals to both labour and capitalists about its concerns. Table 2.11 presents an amendment index. The construction of the composite index broadly follows the methodology of Besley and Burgess (2004). Neutral amendments are classified in the complete list. Each amendment is considered distinct and sum total of all amendments are presented.

Although a simple aggregation of amendments is not enough to capture the extent or gravity of legislative reform, it provides a good indicator of the extent of regulation and orientation of the state governments. Based on a comparison of pro-labour (regulation) and pro-employer (deregulation) amendments, it would be safe to argue that West Bengal is the most regulated state while Gujarat is the more deregulated state among the cases considered. Andhra Pradesh and Maharashtra have an intermediate position between the two extremes in terms of regulation.

Inspection of the Factories

The effectiveness of labour market regulations is contingent on implementation of labour laws. As Jenkins (1999), Mukherjee (2007), and
others have argued, reforms in India have occurred largely through
the back door such as patronage to the potential opposition, reforms
in the guise of continuity, and non-implementation of laws. As such,
data on implementation is a potential measure to capture the extent
of withdrawal of the state from the labour market to promote de facto
reforms. However, it would not be very prudent to compare the states
in terms of inspection, as the data is not very regular (many states do
not provide timely records), leading to issues with missing data points.
Moreover, there is inconsistency in data, as states often follow different
norms for industrial monitoring such as bureaucratic inspection, self-
certification, and declared random inspection policy scheme that may
lead to incorrect assumptions.

The data on inspection (Figure 2.3) clearly shows the secular decline
in the rate of inspection over the years across the states. The high rate
of inspection in Gujarat and Maharashtra can be partially attributed to
the self-certification schemes introduced in the states. Importantly, the
trends in inspection fit with the comparative cases with Andhra Pradesh
and West Bengal, recording similar inspection rates. The declining
trends in inspection are corroborated by scholars like Shyam Sundar
(2010), who find decreasing instances of inspections under various
labour laws across subnational states.

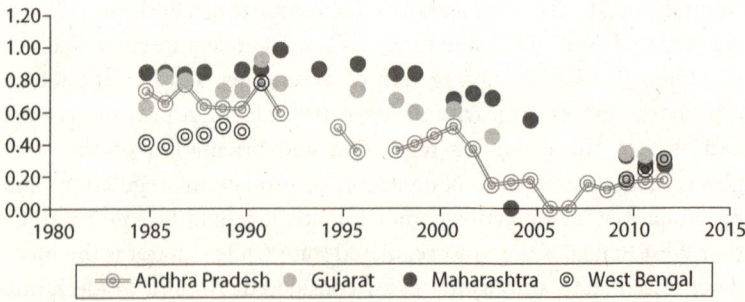

FIGURE 2.3   State-wise Data of Factories Inspected, 1985–2012
Source: Statistics on Factories (various issues), Labour Bureau, GoI.

Wage Share

An important dimension of labour flexibility is wage adjustment. Wage and its various components reveal the extent to which the price of labour can be matched according to market signal, thus indicating flexibility. Wage share, that is, the wage as a proportion of NVA, indicates the relation between productivity and compensation for labour. Higher wage share means higher returns to labour (lower flexibility) and lower wage share mean higher returns to capital (higher flexibility).

The data on wage share (Figure 2.4) recorded in the *ASI* reveals significant divergences among the states within the overall trend of declining wage share. Across the period, the labour share of value (wage share) is highest in West Bengal, followed by Andhra Pradesh, Maharashtra, and finally Gujarat, which has the lowest wage share.

The overall decline in labour share across the states (Table 2.12) indicates the operation of market forces such as increasing capital-intensive

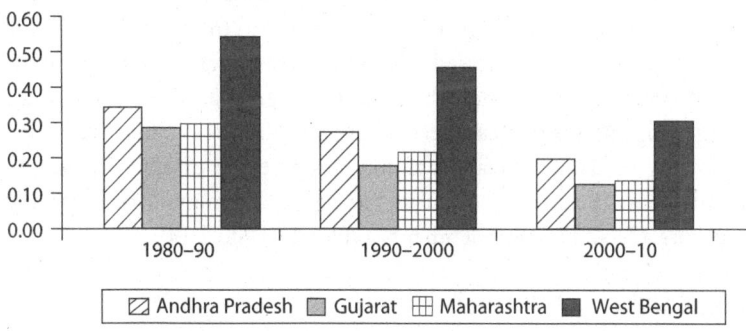

FIGURE 2.4   Wage Share across States, 1980–2010
Source: *ASI* (various issues).

TABLE 2.12   Decadal Rate of Change in Wage Share, 1980–2010

Year	Andhra Pradesh	Gujarat	Maharashtra	West Bengal
1980–90	−0.01	−0.02	−0.01	0.01
1990–2000	−0.01	−0.03	−0.03	0.00
2000–10	−0.04	−0.11	−0.05	−0.02

Source: Author's calculation based on wage share averages taken from *ASI* (various issues).

production and increasing use of contractual workers, particularly since liberalization. What is important is that the rate of decline appears to be lower in the states of West Bengal and Maharashtra compared to Andhra Pradesh and Gujarat.

Retrenchment

An employer's prerogative to hire and fire has been a crucial issue of labour market reform. The Industrial Disputes Act, 1947, under chapter VB, stipulates that all firms employing more than 100 workers have to seek permission from the government for retrenchment and layoff in the firms. Thus, data on retrenchment can provide some indication of the government intent and employer's ability to undertake workforce restructuring across the states. However, as mentioned previously, such data is not exact due to under- and non-reporting given the socio-political implications. Nonetheless, data on retrenchment can provide some broad trends.

The data on the proportion of firms undertaking reporting retrenchment across the states (Figure 2.5) reveals that in the post-liberalization period, Gujarat has witnessed most retrenchment and West Bengal the least. Overall retrenchment has declined significantly over the years suggesting either significant restructuring of industry or massive under-reporting of data. To elaborate and compare the extent of retrenchment across the states, I calculate the aggregate number of firms and workers affected by retrenchment (Tables 2.13 and 2.14).

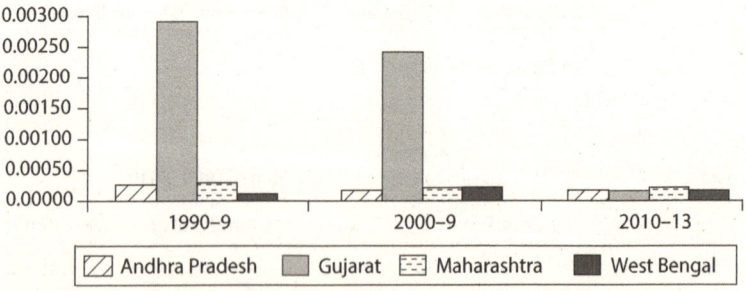

FIGURE 2.5   Proportion of Firms Undertaking Labour Retrenchment in the States, 1990–2013

Source: Author's calculation of firm undergoing retrenchment as a proportion of total working factories from *Indian Labour Yearbook* (various issues).

TABLE 2.13   Total Number of Firms that Were Allowed Retrenchment,
1980–2013

Year	Andhra Pradesh	Gujarat	Maharashtra	West Bengal
1980–90	114	1,164	982	153
1991–9	56	445	69	10
2000–9	4	432	11	7
2010–13	2	1	8	4
1991–2013	62	878	88	21

Source: *Indian Labour Yearbook* (various issues).

TABLE 2.14   Total Number of Workers Affected by Retrenchment, 1980–2013

Year	Andhra Pradesh	Gujarat	Maharashtra	West Bengal
1980–90	3,838	22,716	11,802	2,739
1991–9	709	4,647	1,220	193
2000–9	105	4,160	660	37
2010–13	194	37	889	16
1991–2013	1,008	8,844	2,769	246

Source: *Indian Labour Yearbook* (various issues).

As the data in Tables 2.13 and 2.14 suggests, at an aggregate level, Gujarat has witnessed most retrenchment both in terms of firms as well as workers affected followed by Maharashtra. Andhra Pradesh records third highest numbers on both counts, which, when normalized by total number of firms or workers, puts it before Maharashtra. West Bengal records the lowest retrenchment among the states. Although data on retrenchment is hugely under-reported in government records, the data reveals important subnational trends.

Aggregating the discussion on the various dimensions of labour market reform, a clear trend towards increasing labour market flexibility can be established. The secular decline in wage share and inspection reveal steady de facto liberalization of the labour market. The increasing proportion of contractual workers and definitive legislative amendments towards greater free play of market forces further reinforces the argument. Labour is intrinsically a part of the productive process like capital and it is subject to forces of market that cannot be completely constrained by governments or domestic interests. Significant pressure for policy convergence under conditions of globalization appears to be valid as labour flexibility increases secularly across states.

However, perceptible variations in the extent of flexibility can be noted across the selected states. An ordinal arrangement of the states according to the various indicators of labour flexibility suggests that Gujarat has the most flexible labour market while West Bengal has the most rigid labour market. Intriguingly, the labour market of Andhra Pradesh is more flexible than Maharashtra.

This variation in the extent of labour market flexibility can also be approached through unemployment data. The mainstream argument of rigid labour market inhibiting employment generation corroborates the situation in the four subnational states.

Table 2.15 shows that West Bengal has high unemployment rates while Gujarat has the lowest unemployment rates. Interestingly, Maharashtra, despite its industrial advancement, has higher unemployment rates than Andhra Pradesh. The variations in the urban unemployment rates across the states are particularly relevant in the context of labour market regulations. Ideally, labour market conditions should have been somewhat similar across the selected pair of cases given their structural and institutional similarities. This suggests the operation of political dynamics in shaping labour market reforms in the subnational states.

Politics of Labour Reform

The divergences in labour market flexibility across the subnational states point to the operation of political dynamics in the reform process. This is because of the absence of credible structural or institutional arguments explaining reform divergence.

The issue of labour market outcome and policy is inevitably related to the prevailing condition of labour market, especially the supply of labour. The situation of the labour market in the selected states broadly mirrors the pan-Indian features such as higher employment in the agricultural sector, greater unemployment in urban areas, and higher unemployment for women. Moreover, most of the employment growth has been contributed by the unorganized, informal sector and employment growth in the organized sector has been mostly in the categories of casual and contract labour (Papola and Sahu 2012).

TABLE 2.15   State-wise Urban Unemployment Rates by Sex and Location for Select Years between 1983 and 2005

State /Year	1983–4			1993–4			2004–05		
	Male	Female	Persons	Male	Female	Persons	Male	Female	Persons
Andhra Pradesh	4.5	3.4	4.2	2.9	3.8	3.2	3.6	3.8	3.6
West Bengal	8.1	12.8	8.8	6.3	15.1	7.9	5.6	8.4	6.2
Gujarat	4.4	3.0	4.1	3.0	4.6	3.3	2.3	2.9	2.4
Maharashtra	5.3	3.7	5.0	4.2	4.7	4.3	3.5	4.1	3.6
Overall India	5.0	5.2	5.1	4.1	6.6	4.6	3.8	6.9	4.5

Source: NSSO *Survey on Employment and Unemployment* (various rounds); statistics released by the Planning Commission of India, GoI.

The selected states have broad similarities in urban labour market participation rate (that is, the share of people who are either employed or actively looking for work in the urban sector). The trend overtime shows that workforce participation rate (WFPR) has been above the all–India average for all the states. The WFPR rates are highly similar for males with minor divergences for females. The actual divergence in the rate of participation across the states is in the rural sector and for females. In this regard, West Bengal records the lowest WFPR rate across the period while Andhra Pradesh has the highest rate (Table 2.16). Since the focus of the study is manufacturing and industrial sector primarily concentrated in urban centres, the immediate concern is with the urban labour market.

Evidently, with regard to employment pressures in the urban sector (that is, workforce participation), there is little to distinguish among the states.

To interrogate the issue of labour market participation, we also look into the migration as a potential factor in influencing labour supply. In most countries, large-scale rural–urban migration has corresponded industrialization and economic development. In India, interstate and rural–urban migration is unrestricted and a fundamental constitutional right (Art. 19 of the Constitution provides freedom to practise any trade and reside in any part of India). The interregional variation in migration, however, has little influence on the formal labour market, as migrants are engaged largely in the informal sector. Migration in India, especially rural–urban migration, is fairly low compared to other developing societies (Srivastava and Sasikumar 2003) (see Table 2.17).

According to Table 2.17, employment among males and marriage among females are the main reasons for migration (Mitra 2008). Interestingly, interstate immigration is higher from the developed states while poor states have low rates of overall as well as male immigration. Patterns for inter-censal migration between 1991 and 2001 suggest that economic migration (employment and business) is higher from urban to rural rather than rural to urban (Srivastava and Sasikumar 2003).

In the context of our case study, as the WFPR suggests, migration has little effect on the overall share of people willing to work in the economy. Table 2.18 shows variation in the migration rates across the states with Maharashtra and Gujarat experiencing high in-migration possibly due

TABLE 2.16 State-wise WFPR by Sex and Sector in India for Select Years

State	1993–4		2000–01		2004–05		2011–12	
	Male	Female	Male	Female	Male	Female	Male	Female
			Urban WFPR					
Andhra Pradesh	54.4	19.9	55.8	18.5	51.1	17.8	54.14	19.1
West Bengal	55.0	14.3	60.5	15.1	56.7	11.7	56.84	15.4
Gujarat	53.5	14.2	54.7	10.7	53.6	13.5	57.18	11.4
Maharashtra	52.6	16.9	56.2	15.4	53.2	13.7	55.16	16.8
Overall India	52.1	15.5	55.3	14.4	51.8	13.9	53.76	15.4
			Rural WFPR					
Andhra Pradesh	63.1	52.1	59.0	41.8	60.5	47.8	58.4	44.6
West Bengal	55.7	18.5	58.5	16.7	53.4	16.0	57.2	19.4
Gujarat	57.4	39.6	63.5	39.5	58.4	41.3	57.1	32.0
Maharashtra	55.1	47.7	56.4	44.6	53.1	43.4	56.7	42.5
Overall India	55.3	32.8	55.2	28.8	53.1	29.9	53.0	30.0

Source: NSSO survey (various rounds); figures are based on usual status approach and include principal status and subsidiary status workers of all ages.

TABLE 2.17   Share of Migrant Population to Total Population in India, 1981–2001

Migrant Population	1981	1991	2001
Total Migrants	31.2	27.4	30.6
Male	17.6	14.6	17.5
Female	43.9	41.2	44.6

Source: *Census of India* (various issues), Registrar General & Census Commissioner, New Delhi.

TABLE 2.18   Inter-censal Migration Data, 1991–2001

State	1991 Population	2001 Population	Population Growth Rate	Inmi-gration	Outmi-gration	Migrant to Total Population
Andhra Pradesh	66,508,008	76,210,007	0.146	428,281	637,360	1.4
West Bengal	68,077,965	80,176,197	0.178	983,728	730,226	7.0
Gujarat	41,309,582	50,671,017	0.227	1,140,618	451,458	5.1
Maharashtra	78,937,187	96,878,627	0.227	3,280,006	896,988	8.0

Source: *Census of India*, Table D, 1991 and 2001.

to economic opportunities in the states. In contrast, the net migration is low in West Bengal and actually negative in Andhra Pradesh.

The literature on labour market suggests that migration can influence labour market by reducing employment standards and increasing competition (Devitt 2009; Lillie and Greer 2007). Intuitively, states may be inclined to greater regulation of labour market to assuage concerns of trade unions or in the absence of such pressures facilitate incorporation of migrant labour by relaxing regulatory restrictions. Clearly, the regulatory response of the states to migration does not corroborate the actual condition of the labour market. As the discussion on labour market variation suggests, Maharashtra (high migration) and West Bengal (low migration) have comparatively lower reforms than Gujarat (high migration) and Andhra Pradesh (low migration). Thus, the absolute flow of migrant labour does not seem to correspond to the policy response of the states.

This non-correspondence appears more remarkable in the context of the relative position of the trade unions in the states. The strength of organized labour across the states may be a potential reason for the variation in labour reform. However, explanations of variation through trade unions appear stylistic, as the extent of unionization across the states does not correspond to the levels of labour flexibility. Trade union density, that is, the number of trade unions normalized by the number of industrial units, is a measure of unionism indicating the likelihood of worker organization facilitating collective action. Even after taking into account the trade union density, the situation of labour flexibility and policy response to migration does not corroborate expectations (Figure 2.6).

As the figure reveals, density (per factory) is greatest in West Bengal, although the period since the late 1990s shows a declining trend. Among the other states, union density is high in Andhra Pradesh followed by Maharashtra, and both show an increasing trend since the 1990s. Gujarat has the lowest levels of union density, indicating a weak trade union presence. The data on trade union density, although indicative due to its limitations, reveals the non-correspondence between unionization and labour market policy. Even though the strength of trade unionism may account for low labour flexibility in West Bengal and high in Gujarat, it fails to explain the situation of greater labour flexibility in Andhra Pradesh and lower reforms in Maharashtra.

In this context, the foremost explanation appears to be the nature of the party in power. It can be argued that greater labour reforms in Gujarat are due to a reformist BJP in government while in West Bengal, the Left party government has ensured low reforms. Another set of explanation for variation emphasizes on broader political–social dynamics namely

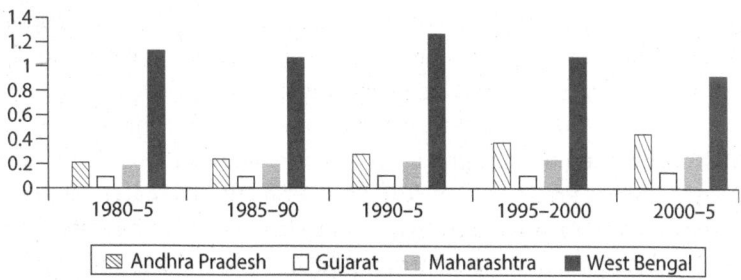

FIGURE 2.6   Average Density of Trade Unions across the States, 1980–2005
Source: Author's calculation based on *Indian Labour Yearbook* (various issues).

the distinct political culture of the states. Historically, Maharashtra and West Bengal were under direct colonial rule and sites of initial industrial development. Gujarat and Andhra Pradesh came into existence only after the linguistic reorganization of states in the 1960s. Such differences in historical origin have often been held responsible for differences in political culture, accounting for variation in labour and other social movements. There is a body of literature that emphasizes on cultural or normative conditions as powerful explanatory variable in comparative analysis (Misra 2006). It is noteworthy that culture is not an all-encompassing explanatory variable but an inherent part of the socio-political reality. As an endeavour in political economy, this book focuses on the political agencies and considers normative–cultural values as a subsidiary but significant factor.

The reasons are twofold: First, the causal arguments presented in the book would remain valid even if we considered culture as important in determining the behaviour of political actors. The fact remains that an analysis based on cultural and social norms usually improves upon existing materialist analysis by providing clarification to existing gaps. Second, cultural or social norms are habitual practices of groups and communities that have historical origins. Political norms are part of the dominant culture and are generated, maintained, and altered through interactions between political actors and environment, between actors themselves, and internal characteristics of actors (Misra 2006). Thus, any effort to analyse and understand political actors within specific environment encompasses cultural elements.

Explanations based on partisan ideology or the party in power are also limited as clear-cut left–right ideological division of parties (visible in developed democracies) is often not present in India. Evidently, in the context of the present case study, partisan explanation of reform cannot account for the divergences in labour reform across Andhra Pradesh or Maharashtra where ideological polarity on reform issues between major parties (the Congress party and the BJP–Shiv Sena alliance in Maharashtra and the Congress party–Telugu Desam Party [TDP] alliance in Andhra Pradesh) is unclear. Programmatic differences between parties as an explanation for variations also fail to account for state-level reform variations in Maharashtra and Gujarat where Congress and BJP have been the dominant parties. Gujarat is marked by political contestation between BJP and the centrist Congress party while Maharashtra is characterized by political alternations between the Congress–NCP and the BJP–Shiv Sena alliance. The extent of labour reform in Gujarat and Maharashtra manifestly varies under Congress party as does in the case of BJP. Thus, despite the similar nature of parties in competition, variations across states in reforms pose questions about simple party-based explanations.

Thus, existing political-actor-based explanations for reforms variation, particularly in the case of the labour market, suffer from limitations, which necessitate further interrogation and more nuanced analysis.

3

Political Economy and Partisan Government

Configuration of Labour Reforms

As the preceding discussion suggests, variation in labour reforms can be noted across structurally (economically) and institutionally (rules and regulation) similar political units that are not amenable to simplistic interpretations. These variations can only be accounted through region-specific political dynamics. The argument of the regional political economy is intuitive and widely accepted. (Sinha [2005] is a notable work in this regard.) Variations in reform have often been attributed to the ideology of the party in government and strength of interest groups in society with labour market reform, can conveniently be associated with the nature of the political parties in power, namely the Left Front in West Bengal (1977–2011) and the BJP in Gujarat.

The chapter argues that subnational variation in reform can be explained through the regional political economy, taking into consideration the partisan composition of governments and the nature of party competition. The argument builds on a multilevel understanding of reform process (state level and regime level), whereby historical–institutional specificities and partisan politics interact to shape reforms. This chapter shows that the extent of a business group's presence within the governing party has a positive relation to the extent of labour reforms in the state. That is, higher the representation of business within partisan government, higher is the likelihood of labour reforms in the state. However, this relation, that is, the ability of a business to influence policy, is conditional on the extent of 'inclusivity' of a political party. Even though all political parties claim to and have support from a wide cross-section of society, every organization has a dominant core group. By 'inclusivity' of the political party, the chapter specifically refers to the composition of the dominant groups within the party leadership. It shows that if the dominant support base of the party consists of homogeneous groups, then business presence is most effective, unlike situations where business presence is counterbalanced by competing claims of heterogeneous groups. Partisan orientation is conditioned by the composition of the support base, and specific interests have a greater likelihood to emerge dominant when the support base is relatively homogenous in composition.

The core argument can be conceived as an evaluation of partisan governments along a two-dimensional plane, where the vertical dimension measures the extent of business presence in party leadership–government and the horizontal dimension measures the extent of other groups in the party leadership–government. The finding broadly mirrors the power resource hypothesis, which contends that political representation and organization of specific interests significantly influences the policy and outcomes of governments. In terms of the specific case study, greater labour market flexibility in Andhra Pradesh and Gujarat can be attributed to the support base of the party in government, characterized by the predominance of business castes (endogamous occupational groups within Hindu society). In contrast, the lower reforms in Maharashtra can be explained through the socio-economically wide support base of regime parties where business influence within parties cannot become hegemonic. The situation in West Bengal can be explained through a regime with virtually no representation of business interests in party leadership–government. The regime derived ideological and political support from relatively weaker sections of society such as labour and peasant.

I prefer business as the key social group in analysing partisan policies, since in a capitalist system, a business owns the means of production, employs wage labour, and plays a crucial role in the accumulation process. Emphasizing the centrality of business in the context of economic globalization, Hall and Soskice (2001) write that firms act as 'key agents of adjustment' and therefore constitute the centrepiece of analysis. Despite the recognized importance of business in politics under capitalism, there is a lack of theoretical work on the linkage between business and public policies; particularly, in the context of transitional economies.

In generic terms, the findings suggest that political salience of economic interests determines policy under conditions of globalization. Such an outcome is important to counter the argument that under conditions of globalization, the role of government and politics is emaciated; especially, in matters of economic policymaking. As the case study reveals, the extent of labour flexibility has an important causal relation to partisan orientation depending on relative presence or absence of socio-economic interests. This chapter expands on the argument of the political economy of partisan orientation and demonstrates the relationship to labour market reform. The first section presents the theoretical model of partisanship and reform. The second section provides a detailed state-wise discussion on the regional political economy and partisan government that explains the variation in labour market reforms.

Political Party and Policy Reform

That political parties and political system have implications on policymaking is well acknowledged in the literature. The importance of political parties in socio-economic analysis has been theoretically endorsed from a structural–functional perspective as parties act as foundational structures of the liberal democracy, mediating between the state and diverse societal interests. Political parties reflect and mediate social demands; act as channels of communication between the state and society; have a pivotal role in mobilization, governance, formulation, and implementation of policy; and perform functions of political socialization, formation of governments, interest representation, and social integration (De Souza 2006; Hasan 2002; Morehouse 1973; Schonfeld 1983). The importance of a political party is magnified in the labour market, as the government plays an important role in industrial relations and government intervention often alters the outcome of bargaining between capital and labour. Such government intervention is particularly significant in the context of the public sector. In India, the importance of a political party is further augmented due to historical–institutional developments that led to the creation of what is characterized in literature as the 'interventionist state'. The adoption of a state-led strategy of economic development contributed to the institutionalization of state in mediating social and economic interests (Chatterji 2001). Political parties and the broader political system played a crucial role in not only determining the regulatory structure, but also the relative dominance of organized interest groups over policies.

The conventional relation between political parties and socio-economic policies derived from literature reveals two broad strands of arguments, namely instrumental and ideological arguments. While instrumentalist logic presupposes the electoral motive of parties as determining the social and economic agendas of parties, the ideological argument focuses on the party ideology as an explanation for the different policies enacted by parties in power. The distinction between ideological and instrumental interests is more analytical than real. Study of political parties has emphasized almost universally the alignment of social cleavages (religion, class, ethnicity, and region) with a programmatic orientation of parties that is relatively stable. However, the analytical is necessary to extrapolate the causal linkage that shapes partisan behaviour towards labour market reforms.

Ideology of Political Parties

Political parties in their simplest form are organizations seeking to utilize the power of the state to pursue objectives determined by their ideological orientation. As such, ideology of party in power has had an important role in determining policy. The differences in political parties based on ideological positions reflect variations in policy choice by government, and a method to attain a socially desirable outcome. In the specific context labour policy, governments have distinctive objectives based on their ideological orientation. Esping-Andersen (1996) and Garrett (2000) have found general association of greater state control, economic closure, and extensive labour market regulation with leftist party-led governments. Left parties generally favour employment growth and follow expansionary macroeconomic policies, since being pro poor and welfare is an integral part of left ideology. On the other hand, parties to the right of the ideological spectrum prefer to reduce inflation and budget deficit even at the cost of immediate employment.

The ideological explanations for government behaviour have been questioned from an instrumental perspective, as well as structural context as pressures emanating from global and national economic forces have further constrained ideological interpretations. Questions have been raised about the importance of ideological distinctions, as, in the new politics perspective, socio-economic transformations are conceived as emanating largely from economic and technological changes of post-industrial society. Inglehart (1997), in his study of politics across 43 developed countries, found a shift towards postmodern values leading to transformation of political agendas. Contending such 'end of ideology' and new politics arguments, Korpi and Palme (2003) have found that cuts in insurance programmes in OECD countries can be largely explained by composition of partisan government based on ideology. Based on a comprehensive study of social insurance in 18 OECD economies, they find that the risk for major cuts has been significantly lower with Left party representation in cabinets, while the opposite holds true for conservative-centrist governments.

Partisan Support Base of Political Parties

In democracies, political parties are guided not only by ideological objectives, but also by the instrumental objective of re-election and expansion of electoral support. The support base of parties refers to categories of individuals or groups who are relatively stable in their support to a particular party based on programmatic or other factors. Research on party system has revealed that stability of the party system is dependent upon a secure mass base that changes rather slowly. Despite the wide segment of society that political parties claim or seek to represent, all political parties have some dominant support base in all societies (Hazan and Rahat 2006). The identification of white Christian males with the Republican Party or minorities with the Democrats in the USA, although stylistic, has real basis.

This group alignment of parties assumes importance in the context of contesting policy implications for groups in society. Alternatively, policy disputes often reflect competition among socio-economic groups manifesting in partisan competition. As such, analysis of social basis of parties can reveal the instrumental logic of party behaviour in the choice of policies. Social groups like business who control economic resources tend to favour market distribution, but groups like workers and poor, who are disadvantaged in economic resources, seek to alter economic outcomes through political redistribution. Naturally, the choice of policies is bound to vary if there are significant differences in the composition of the support base.

There is considerable literature on the politics of reform that focuses on domestic class configuration or social networks to explain policy choices and outcomes (Frieden and Rogowski 1996). The importance of support base is reflected in the literature that views politics of reform as an exercise in political 'blame avoidance' (Bonoli 2005). According to the literature, reforms create winners and losers; successful reforms require either a broad reform coalition to deflect opposition, or incremental and strategically tied packages that divide potential opponents by providing them with selective compensation (Williamson 1994). Thus, government policies, particularly with regard to economic reforms, can be found to vary according to the nature of socio-economic support base of the party in power. The role of social groups' linkages to political parties, popularly known as partisanship, has also been a recurrent theme in policy literature. In their study of taxation in the USA, Quinn and Shapiro (1991) find support for partisanship thesis with lower taxes associated with the Republican governments and higher taxes for the Democratic regimes.

It is necessary to point out that the distinction between ideological and instrumental imperatives of political parties is not merely analytical. Admittedly, there exists broad correspondence between ideological orientation and nature of support base of political parties. The literature on party system also suggests that stability of party system is dependent upon mass base and party commitments (ideology) that change rather slowly, ensuring stability in the competing balance of parties (Petrocik and Brown 1999). However, there is a body of literature that depicts ideology and parties as disparate entities, due to a range of exogenous and endogenous changes, such as globalization and rise of postmodern values, to demonstrate the decreasing relevance of ideology to party politics. Even in the case of India, the ideological position of many of the parties is often unclear and shifting (the initial position of BJP regarding swadeshi or the Congress party's idea of economic sovereignty have been replaced by ideas of economic integration for growth).[1] In sum, the necessity of disaggregating ideology from the support base is necessitated by the changing political milieu under conditions of globalization that has often led to absence of clarity on political-ideological differences between parties.

Disentangling Partisanship: Ideology and Caste–Class Support

Clear from the preceding discussion is the role of ideological and instrumental interests in determining party behaviour and the necessity of examining specific interests to elaborate the role of partisan government in labour market reforms. An interrogation of partisan difference at the subnational level should focus on the twin dimensions of ideology and support base of the principal political parties or coalitions (forming government during the period) in the respective states.

To determine the ideological position, the chapter follows the much-accepted methodology of looking at the party constitution and policy statements of the major political parties. As the issue of labour reforms does not occupy major policy concern of most mainstream parties, except the Left (Communist parties), it becomes imperative to consider the broader attitude towards economic reforms. The dominant idea regarding ideological orientation suggests that the Left parties are ideologically opposed to economic reforms and labour flexibility. The ideological distinction among the parties other than the Left in matters of economic policy, however, appears very marginal. Evaluating the 2004 election in India, Suri (2004b) opines that although economic reforms were an electoral issue, the differences among major political parties, namely Congress and BJP, were regarding implementation and not against economic reforms as such. Mehta (2004) in his analysis of the 2004 election that led to the defeat of the NDA argues the electoral

---

[1] For the shift in BJP's economic policy from rejection of both communism and capitalism in favour of a revival of swadeshi, to free market see Abraham (2014), Arulanantham (2004), and Nayar (2000).

reversals should not be interpreted as opposition to reforms, since there is consensus among parties on the basics of reform programme.

To make matters more complicated, ideological orientation is found to vary according to the logic of political convenience and compulsions of governance. Regional parties like the TDP in Andhra Pradesh that came to power on the plank on opposition to reform have, in course, become champions of reform. The Left Front in West Bengal (an alliance led by the Communist parties) accepted the idea of private investment-led growth in the early 2000s and promoted large-scale private investment under the stewardship of Chief Minister Buddhadev Bhattacharya. It seems that under the conditions of globalization, ideological distinctions on economic policy matters largely lose their edge when parties are in power. Although structural pressures emanating from broader economic transformation may account for such behaviour of parties when in government, such an explanation is limited by non-incorporation of instrumental understanding. Structural pressure argument does not elaborate or explain how political parties implement reforms that may come into conflict with their support base. As such, it is necessary to investigate the nature of support base of parties in any partisan evaluation of reform.

There is a large body of literature on reform alliances that highlight the creation of broad reform alliances or strategic division of potential opponents necessary for implementation of reforms. The literature on nature of partisan support base in India is wide and extant (Hasan 2002; Palshikar 2004; Roy and Wallace 2007; Yadav 1996; Yadav and Palshikar 2006). Parties represent different social cleavages that constitute the support base of parties and party system is organized along dominant social cleavages (Sinha 2005). The salience of such social cleavage is dependent upon a number of factors such as degree of intersection of cleavages in society, social stratification, and ideological position of parties. In most literature on partisan politics, the dominant explanatory categories have been either 'caste', 'class', or both, which, according to Heath and Yadav (1999), represent the most important aspect of socio-economy in India. In the examination of partisan support base, the chapter adopts both 'class' and 'caste' as conceptual categories to interrogate the support base of parties.

Both the categories of class and caste have been the subject of theoretical and empirical debates. To maintain a clear unprejudiced basis of selection, the chapter adopts a simple definition of the two categories. It defines class by occupation, leading to a threefold classification of business class, professional middle class, and agriculturist class. The proposed classification, admittedly very narrow, is suitable for the purpose of identification of political leadership across the states, as the data on elected representatives provides these threefold professional categories.

In terms of caste, the chapter follows the standard classification of fourfold division of castes, which even if not nuanced, conforms to conventional divisions. To the uninitiated, caste is a hereditary and ascriptive form of stratification, which defines communities into thousands of endogamous hereditary groups called jatis. According to Hindu religious texts, the jatis are categorized into four broad hierarchical varnas, namely Brahmans, Kshatriyas, Vaishyas, and Shudras, followed by non-caste untouchables. According to Béteille (1965), the significant characteristics of caste are its hereditary nature, the pursuit of traditional occupations, hierarchical rank, and endogamy. According to scholars, caste has evolved into an important socio-political category with deep imprint on politics due to policies adopted by the Indian state, both under the colonial rule as well as in independent India (Brass 1984; Jayal and Mehta 2010; Mukherjee 1999). At the level of political mobilization and interest, articulation caste plays an important role in the choice of candidates, poll promise, and aggregation of support for parties; especially, at the local and regional levels (Brass 1984; Kohli 2001; Yadav and Palshikar 2006).

Despite the divergences in the etymology of caste and class, the former being a socio-religious category and the latter primarily economic, there is some correspondence between the two. In short, caste as a hierarchical system of social stratification has economic implications. As Mukherjee (1999: 1760) points out, although the jati division of society is viewed in the realm of 'cultural' norms, such as inter-dining, inter-marriage, and purity/pollution,[2] in economic terms 'the landlords, traders, moneylenders belonged essentially to the high castes, the bulk

---

[2] The philosophical essence of caste is in the distinction of purity and pollution, where Dalits are considered impure and the upper castes are considered pure. Any interaction between the two can make the latter impure. That is why inter-dining and inter-marriage are not allowed under the caste system.

of self-sufficient peasants, small-scale artisans, petty traders, belonged to the middle castes and, those at the lowest echelon, such as the marginal peasants, landless workers, belonged overwhelmingly to the lowest castes and the tribes'. In an empirical study of 27,000 respondents, Vaid (2012) has found tentative congruence between castes and classes at the extremes of the caste system and a slight weakening of the relation over time. She has found correspondence between manual/non-manual employment divide, with high castes dominating white-collar work and avoiding manual work. This overlapping correspondence of caste with class can be noted evidently in particular business groups in India.

In the context of business castes/classes in India, Damodaran (2008) has highlighted the historical patterns of social stratification that create broad correspondence between business groups and specific castes. Notably, the industrial class generally emerges from the trading and business castes or groups that have had historical control over capital or land. Thus, caste and class as categories of stratifications share some broad congruence at the societal level. As such, analysis of support base in terms of caste configuration broadly highlights the socio-economic profile of support base of parties.

To determine the electoral support base of political parties, the chapter relies on existing literature such as Chhibber (1997), Heath and Yadav (1999), and Yadav and Palshikar (2006), which analyse voting across socio-economic groups for different political parties. However, to go beyond the electoral base (which is often wide) and identify the dominant social group within parties, it looks at the caste composition and profession of elected party representatives across the states.

Implicit in the methodological argument is the division of party support base into electoral support base that includes all voters for respective parties and dominant support base that is limited to social groups in the decision-making positions of the parties. Such a methodology is supported in the literature on political parties that suggests candidate selection by parties reflects their support base both at the level of ideas, as well as identity (Hazan and Rahat 2006). The rational choice argument suggests that political parties reduce the 'transaction costs' of electoral participation by choosing candidates that reflect the political belief and share similar descriptive characteristic to their voters (Jones and Hudson 1998; Mueller 2007). There is also evidence that interest groups and activists are key actors behind candidate selection that justify policy implications of elected members (Bawn et al. 2012). In the context of the study, such a methodology is supported by socio-political specificities, such as historic association of business activities with specific ethnic or religious communities. As Damodaran (2008) has pointed out, the historical patterns of social stratification in India have led to broad correspondence between occupational groups and caste structures within society. As such, an analysis of the caste identification of elected representatives (members of parliament [MPs]) could potentially indicate the nature of support base of parties.

To examine the dominant support base of parties, this section specifically examines the caste and occupation of MPs across the states over the period of 1980–2008. The choice of MPs as the object of study in place of the members of state legislative assembly (MLA) (decision-makers at the subnational level) is a carefully considered choice.

Labour is a concurrent subject on which both union (parliament) and state legislature can make laws (in case of conflict between the two, the union law shall prevail). Although the subnational states can amend the central labour legislations, such amendments cannot be against the letter of the central act. Naturally, any discussion or alteration of labour regulations at the subnational level is circumscribed by the parliamentary regulations where MPs have a role. The MPs in the federal structure represent the highest elected representatives of parties, constituting publicly responsible leadership of the party. As such, the attitude of MPs on issues of labour is likely to represent that of the party and similar to that of MLAs from the party at the state level. This argument is reinforced by literature on candidate selection that suggests nominated candidates share broad characteristics of their voters. As political parties nominate candidates for both legislative and parliamentary elections, characteristics of candidates for the roles of MP and MLA should be somewhat alike.

The choice of MPs also has some methodological advantages. As the members of the lower house of Parliament (the Lok Sabha) are directly elected across the states during the same time, it helps us overcome state-specific political conditions with temporal (occurring simultaneously) and political similarities (issues and agenda). The number of elected MPs is significantly smaller than MLAs (for example, West Bengal has 294 MLAs and 42 MPs), which makes collecting and collating data for four subnational states over the 20-year period manageable.

Further, the data on profession of MPs is available and verifiable, as the Lok Sabha Secretariat publishes list of members titled *Who's Who*. The evaluation of the composition of MPs in terms of caste and occupation enables us to identify the dominant support groups of regimes across the states, as well as indicates the share of proprietary classes in the political system in each state.

Partisan Ideology and Labour Reform

All political parties claim to have well-defined ideologies which guide their actions and policies. The literature on policy reform suggests an important role for ideological orientation of the party in power. According to the literature, the ideological orientation of government in terms of left or right economic programmes has significant relation to macroeconomic characteristics, such as employment levels, monetary growth rates, income distributions, and growth strategies (Quinn and Shapiro 1991). Intuitively, it can be expected that ideological difference between parties may account for the policy variation across the states.

The impact of ideological orientation on policies, however, cannot be reduced to a straightforward unitary relation. In fact, the relation is complex and bidirectional, as parties operate in a dynamic environment. An example is the dilemma of business and Left governments under conditions of liberal economy. Theoretically, a business should exert more influence in economies with higher share of private sector investment contributing to growth and employment. However, business decision to invest is also influenced by government policies and capitalists may be less likely to invest in domestic economy when it confronts a strong labour movement and Left government (Alvarez, Garrett, and Lange 1991).

In the context of the selected subnational states, roughly, since the 1980s, political competition has been characterized by continued bipolarization of the party system. In Andhra Pradesh, the main contending political parties have been the regional TDP and the centrist national party, the Indian National Congress (INC or simply the Congress), while in Gujarat political contestation is between the rightist BJP and the Congress. West Bengal and Maharashtra are also characterized by bipolar political contest, albeit between stable political alliances. In West Bengal, the Left Front coalition (a coalition of Left parties with the

Communist Party as the main constituent) was in power between 1977 and 2011 with Congress (since 1999, the All India Trinamool Congress (AITC), which is a breakaway faction of Congress) acting as the principal opposition. In Maharashtra since the early 1990s, the Congress–NCP (centrist-regional) and the BJP–Shiv Sena (right-regional) have been the two principal forces dominating political space.

Given the distribution of the parties across the states, the political orientation of government evidently corroborates the higher labour flexibility in Gujarat due to the reform-oriented BJP government and lower labour flexibility in West Bengal under the Communist party-led government.

The mainstream Left parties in India (the Communist Party of India [CPI] and the Communist Party of India, Marxist [CPI(M)]) have been explicit in their opposition to globalization. The political-ideological report of 18th party conference of the CPI(M) resolved that globalization is a natural development of capitalism brought about by the concentration of capital and need for profits. The process leads to jobless growth with deteriorating job security and service conditions (CPI(M) 2005). The party congress took resolution opposing the deregulation of labour market and public sector enterprises, arguing that public sector was a bulwark against efforts to undermine India's economic sovereignty and labour regulations were instruments to pursue socio-economic equality.

In contrast, the mainstream national parties, namely Congress, BJP, and the regional TDP, seem to have reconciled to economic liberalism. A cursory glance of the Congress election manifesto or policy document, titled 'An Expanding Economy—A Just Society: Freedom from Hunger and Unemployment' (Congress 2004) clearly demonstrates the modification of economic policies from socialist pattern of society to economic liberalism. The official party statement suggests that 'Congress policies were modified in response to the changing world of the '50s and '60s to the '70s and then to the '80s, and more dramatically in the '90s'. The party believes in the potential of economic liberalism for increased growth and acclaims 'we can grow at a high rate leading up to 10 per cent a year and abolish unemployment, abolish poverty, hunger, illiteracy, and ensure universal coverage of primary health care throughout the country'. Interestingly, there is also a strong emphasis on social development: 'at the same time we can make our farmers prosper, and build capacities of our Dalits, backward classes (BCs), tribals, and underprivileged minorities to secure greater opportunities and be enriched, and empower our women'. The party prides itself as the party responsible for substantial reorientation of economic policies to further the objectives of economic growth along with social justice. The Congress's opposition to the BJP on the issue of reforms is not so much in terms of content as in terms of implementation. As the document states, '[U]nlike the Congress, the BJP had neither the heritage of modernising India nor of championing the all-round progress of the economy that benefited all cross-sections of our people.' Although not explicitly stated, a careful reading of the policy document suggests that the Congress party is not opposed to labour market reforms. On the question of labour market flexibility, the party programme advocates a balance between requirements of capital and social needs of the marginalized, including labour.

The BJP, although critical of reforms undertaken by the Congress, has been an advocate of free economy and supports economic liberalization. According to the BJP, the economic policy of state-led development rendered Indian industry, services, and agriculture non-competitive and disadvantaged. The party has been a critic of socialist pattern of development and planning, and argues for a liberal economic regime. As the BJP policy statement states, the party is 'opposed the inefficient State capitalism that came about as a result of the collusion between the politicians, bureaucrats, and businessmen and was promoted at the cost of entrepreneurial classes' (BJP 2010). Interestingly, the party is critical of liberalization introduced during the 1990s by the Congress government as surrendering to foreign interests and reorients its position vis-à-vis the Congress as the party of indigenous capital espousing swadeshi (made by national companies) against goods made by foreign companies. The criticism of the economic policy of Congress primarily stems from internationalization of the economy and BJP calls for calibrated globalization. In terms of economy policy, BJP seems to adhere to liberal economics with emphasis on fiscal rectitude, moderate inflation, credit availability to industry, and disinvestment of the public sector. Such an attitude of the party is also reflected in their policy towards industry and labour where the party emphasizes relaxation of labour laws and a healthy capital market with the objectives of increasing capital investment in the corporate sector (BJP 2010).

Unlike the national parties, the ideological position of the regional parties like the NCP and the TDP is rather restricted. Interestingly, the issues of labour and labour regulations do not form an important part of party objective. In case of the TDP, there is a superficial mention of labour in the manifesto with emphasis on development of the informal sector and public sector employees. However, issues of cultural nationalism, agriculture, rural development, and health and poverty alleviation through state support are part of the principle policy position of the party (TDP 2009). The most striking policy interventions by the party appear to be in the form of social subsidies like pucca houses to the poor, rice at 2 rupees per kg, and clothes to the poor at half the price. Overall, the policy orientation of the TDP reveals emphasis on rural development, welfare, social justice, and good governance.

A brief survey of the ideological position of the political parties reveals that apart from the Left parties, labour does not have any stated political importance. In case of Congress party and TDP, the concern is for socially marginalized groups that are reflected in distinct state-mediated social welfare orientation. The BJP, on the other hand, appears to rely more on market forces for overall welfare and favours liberal market model. As such, we can infer that labour market flexibility should be higher in states ruled by BJP and lower in Left-party-ruled states. This assumption is widely held and empirically corroborated. However, the position of centrist parties such as Congress and TDP remains somewhat inconclusive from such a textual analysis. To complicate matters, the policy stance of parties is often found to vary between in-office and out-of-office situations, owing to political and administrative exigencies.

The major political parties in India such as the centre-left Congress party and the centre-right BJP have quite similar positions on economic reforms, but the outcome of subnational partisan governments is visibly different between the Congress-led government of Maharashtra and the BJP-led government of Gujarat. The variations in government orientation can also be identified across subnational states irrespective of political party in government. A case in point is the Congress-led governments in Maharashtra and Andhra Pradesh, which exhibit divergent outcomes in investment incentives and labour market reform (Sáez and Mahmood 2016). This divergence in the behaviour of parties across regions can be noted in two important indicators, namely legislative amendments and labour policy adopted by government. Labour regulations and their amendments brought by different parties as well as policy interventions constitute the fundamental method of government intervention.

The composite data on labour law amendments (actual or proposed) under the various partisan governments across the states between 1980 and 2015 (methodology and details in the previous chapter) corroborates the conventional evaluation of the BJP in Gujarat as pro reform and the Left Front in West Bengal as anti-reform (Table 3.1).

The labour amendments across the state regimes provide for a very interesting reading. In terms of state orientation to issue of labour reforms, Andhra Pradesh and Maharashtra do not provide a clear signal (pro labour vis-à-vis pro employer) as in the case of Gujarat and West Bengal.

In Andhra Pradesh, except for one amendment in 2006, all the labour law amendments were brought forth by the TDP government. Here a clear temporal difference in government attitude can be noted as most of the pro-labour amendments were brought in the 1980s emulating the extensive pro-labour regulations introduced by the Left Front government in West Bengal. In 1980, the Left Front brought nine pro-labour amendments, followed by one in 1983, three in 1986–7 and two in 1989. In 1987, the TDP government brought eight pro-labour amendments. All the pro-employer amendments can be traced to the post-liberalization period. The TDP evidently reoriented its position as the party in 2003 brought four pro-employer amendments facilitating labour flexibility.

TABLE 3.1   State-wise Labour Law Amendments Proposed or Passed across Parties, 1972–2014

Amendment type	Andhra Pradesh		Gujarat		Maharashtra		West Bengal	
	Congress (I)	TDP	Congress (I)	BJP	Congress (I)–NCP	BJP–Shiv Sena	Left Front	AITC
Pro Labour	0	11 (1)	0	2 (1)	9	0	22	0
Pro Employer	1	4 (2)	0	3 (7)	5	0 (2)	0	0

Source: Author's classification from Malik (2009), and http://india.gov.in/my-government/actsrules.

Note: Figures in parentheses represent amendments yet to be operationalized or awaiting president's/governor's approval.

In contrast, the Congress party government in Maharashtra brought both pro-worker and pro-employer amendments almost simultaneously since the 1980s. The difference noted is that during the 1980s, pro-labour amendments dominated, but, since liberalization, more pro-employer legislations were brought to increase flexibility of labour market. Notably, the almost simultaneous correspondence of pro-labour and pro-employer amendments by the Congress party reflects a pattern whereby the government sends a signal to both employers and employees about its concerns. A typical example would be the amendment of 2006 to the Contract Labour (Regulation and Abolition) Act, 1970, that expanded the definition of contract labour by introducing significant flexibility in the labour market. At the same time, it also expanded the definition of a worker in terms of to include more people under the scope of the law.

Another indicator of partisan orientation to labour reform is the government policy towards privatization. Privatization or disinvestment of public sector firms is a mechanism to withdraw the state from the economy and constitutes a major aspect of structural reform. It not only increases the share of private business in the economy, but also has consequences for wages in the economy (government as the ideal employer influencing floor-level wage) and power of unions (public sector unionism is likely to be more powerful). The data on disinvestment of state public sector companies after liberalization also substantiates the partisan difference across states and regimes (Table 3.2).

TABLE 3.2   State-wise Comparative Picture of Public Sector Reforms as of 2003

State	No. of State Public Sector Firms Undertaking	No. of State Public Sector Firms Privatized	Percentage of Public Sector Reform	Workers in State Public Enterprises
Andhra Pradesh	128	13	67	150,965,000
Gujarat	50	3	48	94,967,000
Maharashtra	66	0	20	230,578,000
West Bengal	82	10 (partial)	15	153,071,000

Source: Uba (2008).

Evident from Table 3.2 is variation in the reform intent of the partisan governments. The BJP government in Gujarat and Left Front government in West Bengal diverge significantly in their attitude towards privatization that can be attributed to partisan ideological disposition. However, the orientation of government in Maharashtra and Andhra Pradesh does not correspond to the declared ideological position of parties (Congress in Maharashtra and TDP in Andhra Pradesh, respectively). The attitude towards privatization fits with the categorization of labour market flexibility across the selected states. Efforts towards privatization are comparatively lower in West Bengal and Maharashtra, and higher in the states of Gujarat and Andhra Pradesh.

The attitude of the government reflected through amendments or disinvestment does not correspond to clear political–ideological identification of parties. Ideological explanations of reform cannot account for the situation in Andhra Pradesh and Maharashtra. The governments under Congress and TDP in Andhra Pradesh appear to favour flexibility although the extent and orientation vary significantly. In Maharashtra, however, the Congress government exhibits a cautious approach to labour reforms. Clearly, ideological explanation of government behaviour is inadequate to explain the extent or variation in reform across the selected states.

Partisan Support Base and Labour Reform

The preceding discussion reveals that conventional explanation of variation through ideological differences of political parties is too simplistic and cannot explain the relative variations in flexibility in states like Andhra Pradesh or Maharashtra. To explain the relative variation, it is imperative to move beyond the simple unilinear explanation and focus on the instrumental logic of party behaviour, that is, satisfaction of demands of partisan support base. The importance of socio-economic groups in affecting government policy choices is well accepted in reform literature (Frieden and Rogowski 1996; Hankla 2006). Economic liberalization in India has facilitated increased participation of the private sector in the economy, contributing to greater policy space to business. From the perspective of interest groups, it is plausible to link the demand for business-friendly policies such as labour flexibility with an increasing relevance of business in policymaking (Furlong 1997; Yackee and Yackee 2006). The literature on partisan government suggests that governments represent the interests of the partisan support base and, theoretically, a greater representation of business castes/classes among elected representative should lead to greater business influence and vice versa (Sáez and Mahmood 2016).

Further, interest group representation is not a zero sum game and the influence of specific groups on policy is determined by wider political dynamics, including the presence of competing interests and influence of caste/class on partisan orientation. The influence of business classes/castes within a party is contingent upon the broader support base, that is, existence of other numerically significant groups or castes. In order to examine the dominant support bases of political parties across states, the chapter evaluates the caste/class composition of political leadership.

Political parties in modern democracies seek and represent a wide cross-section of society, without which electoral success becomes difficult. Yet, it is possible to identify some social groups within all political parties who dominate or enjoy over-representation within parties. The socio-economic groups that form the dominant support base participate in leadership, important party positions, and usually have a critical voice in decision-making. Theoretically, it can be assumed that parties with relatively homogenous dominant support base with the presence of business will promote greater reform. Conversely, if the support base is wide and heterogeneous, governments will find it difficult to pursue reforms, despite business representation, due to the contradictory pressures from the support base.

The argument stems from a broader logic relating to pressures on partisan governments to cater to diverse constituents and a relatively homogenous social support base is likely to be characterized by absence of contradictory demands making policy formulation somewhat easier. When the socio-economic support base of government is wide, concerns of redistribution and welfare tend to dominate, due to the pressures exerted by the disparate social groups within the support base. The creation of socio-economically homogenous or heterogeneous support base is conditioned by social–historical factors, particularly pre-existing social cleavages and organization of political parties. In the context of India, the configuration of caste divisions and its broad correspondence to class and occupation provides the basis of partisan support base. To put simply, the prevalence of caste as a political cleavage and party strategy of alignment according to caste in specific cases lead to the creation of relatively homogenous support base.

The discussion of labour market variation across the subnational states will show that greater labour reform in Andhra Pradesh and Gujarat and lower reforms in Maharashtra and West Bengal can be explained through partisan support base. States where governments are supported by business castes and relatively homogeneous dominant support base (Congress and TDP in Andhra Pradesh and BJP in Gujarat) are marked by greater reforms. When governments have marginal presence of business and socio-economically homogenous support base, market-friendly reforms are least likely. The low labour flexibility in West Bengal can be attributed to the support base of non-business and marginalized classes concentrated amongst the rural populace, which enables the government to pursue a pro-poor and pro-worker agenda. Maharashtra provides the intriguing situation where governments, in spite of business presence, proceed gradually with reform due to the wide and heterogeneous support base. The case study reaffirms the arguments and reveals that the extent of labour flexibility can be explained through the socio-economic support basis of the regimes.

Partisanship: Business Representation and Composition of Support Base

The literature on partisan orientation hypothesis contends that policy choice by governments is conditioned by demands and preferences of support base of parties. In the context of labour market, reform or flexibility corresponds to the relative presence (or absence) of business classes and homogeneity (or heterogeneity) of caste groups within the support base of parties. An analysis of partisan representation across the states based on social composition of elected MPs confirms the partisan orientation hypothesis. The findings suggest that the impact of economic interest groups is a function of their political relevance. The state-wise analysis of support base of regimes across the subnational states from a historical–political perspective elaborates on the relation between support base and policy preference. An interesting aspect that emerges from the discussion is not only subnational variation, but also party-wise variation in the extent of reforms according to dominant support base of regimes.

Case Study: Andhra Pradesh

The high levels of labour market flexibility in the state, particularly since liberalization, can be explained with reference to the nature of dominant support base of the two main contending parties in the state, namely Congress and TDP. Politics in Andhra Pradesh has been conventionally analysed in terms of the dominant castes which is useful for our frame of analysis (Kohli and Bardhan 1988; Roy and Wallace 2007).

Studying the political economy of Andhra Pradesh, it is evident that industrialization in the state occurred mainly under the auspices of state planning and, until the 1970s, the regional elite were not keen on industrialization due to their association with land. It was after the green revolution, particularly in the fertile region of the state, that there emerged an agriculturist-turned-industrial class along with a sizeable urban middle class (Alivelu 2009). Due to specific historical–social reasons, the emergent agriculturist-turned-industrial class was largely dominated by few castes, notably Reddis and Kammas, and partially Kapu (a backward caste). Such a development marked the emergence of a regional business class and increasing participation of private sector in the economy.

In the political scheme of things, the Reddis (the landowning and industrial caste) dominated the Congress party although the electoral base of the party was a broad catch-all. In terms of electoral mobilization, Congress relied heavily on the patronage network based on a stable alliance of Reddis and scheduled castes (SCs). Given the historic rivalry between Kamma and Reddi caste groups, the Kammas could not really find space in the Congress-dominated political regime and largely supported the opposition parties. As long as Congress had the support of the backward castes, it could win elections in the state. According to Kohli and Bardhan (1988), the decline of Congress and the rise of TDP in the state could be traced to the rising caste conflict between the Kammas and the Reddis, and the increasing disenchantment of the backward castes with Congress who reoriented themselves with TDP in the 1980s.

According to Suri (2004a), such an analysis of politics through caste competition is rather simplistic, as Kammas do not constitute a numerically large caste. Rather, the emergence of TDP could be traced to the growing anti-incumbency with Congress, the assertion of regional bourgeoisie, the rise of new educated middle-class elites, and the alliance between the Kammas and the numerically large peasants and backward castes who reacted against the pro-Dalit programmes of the Congress. The economically dominant Kamma caste along with educated middle class formed the backbone of the TDP support. That is why the emergence of TDP during the early 1980s marks a sharp increase in the representation of business and professionals in the politics of the state.

An analysis of the support base of parties based on elected representative in the state corroborates the dominance of Reddis and Kammas in the politics of the state (Table 3.3).

Clear from Table 3.3 is the predominance of Reddi, Kamma, and (to a lesser extent) Kapu caste groups in the politics of the state (where SC and ST seats are constitutionally reserved) in terms of representation within the major political parties. Overall, Reddi and Kamma represented 42.6 per cent of the total number of MPs from Andhra Pradesh from 1980 to 2008. Around 45.7 per cent of the Congress party MPs were either members of the Reddi or the Kamma caste groups. Likewise, 42.2 per cent of the TDP MPs came from these two caste communities. Since these castes also constitute the major business communities in the state, business interest within support base of both Congress and TDP is dominant. The chi-square test of independence, to examine the

TABLE 3.3   Cross-Tabulation of Caste and Political Affiliation of MPs in Andhra Pradesh, 1980–2008

Caste	Congress	TDP	Communists	BJP	Others	Total
Brahmans	9 (9.26)	5 (5.95)	3 (0.72)	1 (0.79)	0 (1.25)	18
Reddi	45 (39.11)	20 (25.14)	4 (3.07)	1 (3.35)	6 (5.30)	76
Kamma	19 (20.58)	18 (13.23)	1 (1.61)	1 (1.76)	1 (2.79)	40
Kapu	12 (16.47)	17 (10.58)	0 (1.29)	1 (1.41)	2 (2.23)	32
Velama	5 (6.17)	3 (3.97)	0 (0.48)	2 (0.52)	2 (0.83)	12
Goud	6 (8.74)	6 (5.62)	2 (0.68)	3 (0.74)	0 (1.18)	17
SCs and STs	22 (19.55)	14 (12.57)	1 (1.53)	1 (1.67)	0 (0.18)	38
Muslims	4 (5.65)	1 (3.63)	0 (0.44)	0 (0.48)	6 (0.76)	11
Others	7 (7.19)	3 (4.63)	0 (0.56)	2 (0.61)	2 (0.97)	14
	140	90	11	12	19	272

Source: Sáez and Mahmood (2016), and calculation based on *Who's Who* of Lok Sabha.
Notes: The figures represent observed frequencies (f_o) and expected frequencies (f_e) in parentheses. Degrees of freedom $(d_f) = 28$, chi-squared $(\chi^2) = 97.57$.
ST = scheduled tribe.

relation between political party affiliation and caste in Andhra Pradesh, statistically corroborates the relation. The relation between caste and party is statistically significant with χ^2 (28, N = 272) = 97.57, p <.01.

As such, business groups in Andhra Pradesh, by virtue of their dominance in the support base of major parties, can be argued to have greater influence over public policy. Competing business castes constitute an important support base for political parties ensuring a pro-business orientation across regimes. The assertion of this regional bourgeoisie became decisive during the post-liberalization period and reflected in the leadership change in the TDP when son-in-law Chandrababu Naidu displaced N.T. Rama Rao (NTR), the founder leader. Observers of politics of Andhra Pradesh, such as Suri (2004), have argued that the leadership contest between NTR who represented 'opposition to reforms' and Chandrababu Naidu who favoured increased reforms signified a wider social contestation where the business classes played a crucial role.

An important difference between the two competing parties, Congress and TDP, is the relative variance within the support bases. In terms of the number of constituent social groups in the support base, Congress is relatively more heterogeneous compared to TDP.

Figure 3.1 shows the apparent similarity between the support base of the parties and domination of Kammas, Reddis, and Kapus in the politics

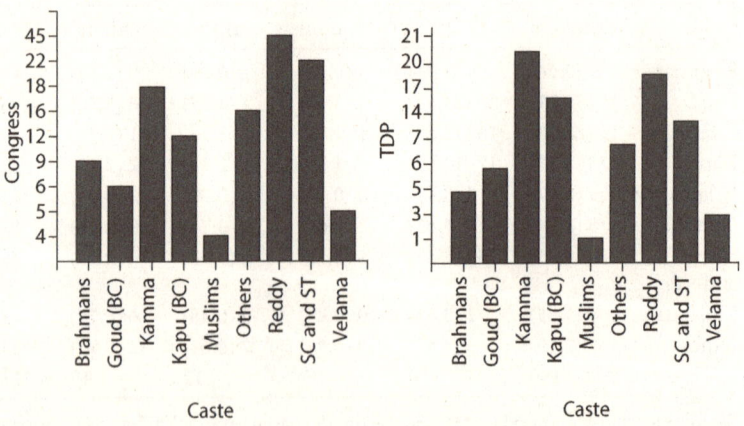

FIGURE 3.1   Caste and Party Affiliation of MPs in Andhra Pradesh, 1980–2008
Source: Author's calculation based on *Who's Who* published by the Lok Sabha secretariat.

of the state. This similarity in the social basis of the Congress and the TDP in terms of social and economic categories has also been noted by scholars such as Heath and Yadav (1999). However, in a comparative evaluation, the support base of the TDP is relatively more homogenous than that of the Congress. In other words, the presence of different social groups within the support base is greater in Congress compared to TDP. A simple measure of deviation in the relative share of different castes in the support base shows that support base of Congress is more heterogeneous than that of TDP. The relative difference in the extent of homogeneity of the support base explains the extent of reforms observed across regimes. A relatively homogenous support base with business representation within TDP explains greater reforms under it, as compared to the Congress regimes. Contextualizing the extent of labour market flexibility with political developments in the state, we can corroborate such an argument.

Historically, electoral mobilization of the Congress relied on the patronage network based on a stable alliance of Reddis and SCs that made the support base wide (Kohli and Bardhan 1988). The wide and disparate social support base meant competing claims on the government and while the interests of dominant industrial and agrarian elites were preserved, the government had to symbolically cater to the social support base. The relatively wide support base of the Congress ensured a gradual-ist approach to reforms, including labour flexibility.

The impact of the TDP governments on labour flexibility across the period represents contradictory images with the TDP under NTR, marked by increased protection for labour and the TDP under Chandrababu Naidu, marked by increasing labour flexibility. Under NTR, during the pre-liberalization period, the TDP reflected the dominant interests of the regional bourgeoisie, agrarian backward castes, and urban middle class which supported the welfare state. The TDP had a regionalist appeal in *telugugauravam*, or 'Telugu pride', in its discourse and sought to create a broad platform by stressing on the twin theme of populism and regional nationalism. The opposition to Congress, both at the state and the centre, contributed to a political stance that highlighted centre–state disputes and welfare programmes aimed at overall development of Telugu people (Reddi and Ram 1994).

After liberalization, the dominant sections within the TDP reori-ented policy priorities towards reform which is reflected in the rise of

Chandrababu Naidu.[3] According to Roy and Wallace (2007), Naidu ush-
ered the policy realignment by discarding populist policies of NTR and
focused on attracting investments. The TDP became completely reform-
oriented and sought removal of subsidies, privatization, reduction in
welfare expenditure, and deregulation which catered to the dominant
interests. Importantly, this shift was made possible due to the congruity of
interests expressed by the support base which explains why the period of
the TDP rule since 1994 witnessed significant increase in labour flexibility.
Clearly, variations in labour flexibility over time and across governments
correspond to the political context and the social basis of the parties.

Case Study: Gujarat

Partisan orientation in the context of labour market reforms in Gujarat is
difficult to disentangle given the historical dominance of business community in the politics of the state. As Sinha (2005) points out, the regional
bourgeoisie in the state consists of a class of capitalist farmers who
later turned into industrial class (Patidar Patel), the class of artisans and
traders (Bania), and the Brahmans. This regional business class developed and gained in strength even during the pre-liberalization period
of state planning due to policy choice of regional political elites. The
policy of promoting the private sector and lack of public sector investments was directed to strengthen the business classes by ensuring a
larger share of the economy (Sinha 2005).

Analysing the politics of the state, it is evident that the state has witnessed a stable two-party competition between Congress and BJP since
the mid-1980s. BJP has been in power in the state since the mid-1990s,
and given the reformist economic orientation of the government it is
but expected that labour market flexibility in the state would be quite
high. However, it is interesting to note that labour flexibility was promoted and appears to increase even prior to economic reforms when
Congress was in power. Thus, the correspondence between reformist
government and increasing labour market flexibility cannot be interrogated at the level of the parties, as dominance of business appears
hegemonic in the politics of the state.

---

[3] For more information on the shifting contours of the Andhra Pradesh
politics, refer to Suri (2002, 2003).

The continued business-friendly policies of the state can be explained through the particular configuration of the support base of the major parties that facilitates domination of regional bourgeoisie in politics. Congress, which dominated state politics till the mid-1970s, drew on support from all castes and classes, specifically the regional bourgeoisie consisting of capitalist farmers turned industrial class (Patidar Patels), the artisan-trader (Bania) class, and the Brahmans. According to Sinha (2005), the pro-development coalition of upper castes, agrarian capitalists, and disenfranchised social groups created the institutional frameworks for industrial development of the state. All of these groups acquired political and economic stakes in the rapid expansion of labour-intensive industrialization. The process was facilitated by the near-complete hegemony of the ideological positions as party competition was primarily between the centrist and centre–right parties, with the prominence of Gandhian ideology of alliance between capital and labour.

After the split of the Congress in 1969, the caste coalition broke down as the Patels remained with the old Congress and later supported the Janata Party. The Congress (I) in a strategy of mobilization developed the KHAM, a coalition of backward castes—Kshatriyas, Harijans, Adivasis, and Muslims—to counter the dominance of the coalition of Banias, Brahmans, and Patels. Interestingly, the period of Congress rule based on electoral support of the economically and educationally backward sections was marked by business-friendly policies and increasing labour flexibility. Scholars like Breman (2002) and Shah (2002) have carefully documented the decline and informalization of organized textile industry in the state during this period. As such, the Congress government exhibited a business-friendly mindset even when the official economic dogma was 'socialism' and support base was primarily among backward castes. Sinha (2005) attributes such a policy orientation to the benefits of dispersed industrial growth that provided crucial revenue to the government and employment to the masses.

Although there is some merit in the argument, it is partial as it considers developmental strategy as a class-neutral project based on enlightened self-interest and ignores the conscious neglect of labour. The analysis of dominant support base of the Congress party suggests that even though its electoral base relied on marginalized sections and the poor, Patidar Patels (regional bourgeoisie) remained a significant influence within the party. The emergence of the BJP as the dominant political party in the state in the 1990s signalled the reemergence of the socially and economically dominant Brahman–Bania–Patidar coalition (Shah 2007). The support base of the government concentrated in the upper class–upper caste social strata consolidated the interests of professional class, and agrarian and industrial capitalists.

In the study of electoral support, Heath and Yadav (2002) have found that the support base of the BJP has been more concentrated among upper castes, and middle and upper classes, while it is weakest among Muslims and the underprivileged. Corroborating such a partisan support base, Chhibber (1997) has traced the electoral success of the BJP in the 1990s to its ability to forge a coalition between majority of religious communities and middle classes and traders. Such a support base has enabled the government to identify itself with a pro-reform, business-friendly image, and facilitated implementation of reforms with relatively fewer contradictory demands emanating from the support base. Thus, it is the hegemonic dominance of the regional bourgeoisie (Patidar–Bania–Brahman coalition; see Table 3.4) that has ensured representation of business interests in the developmental orientation of the state, irrespective of political parties.

Table 3.4 reveals the predominance of certain castes, particularly Patidar Patels and Kshatriyas in the politics of the state. Between 1980 and 2008, 68 per cent of MPs from the Congress party were from the Kshatriya and Patel caste groups. Thus, the dominant support base of

TABLE 3.4   Cross-Tabulation of Caste and Political Affiliation of MPs in Gujarat, 1980–2008

Caste	Congress	BJP	Others	Total
Brahman	5 (7.91)	11 (7.91)	0 (0.18)	16
SCs and STs	17 (12.35)	8 (12.35)	0 (0.14)	25
Kshatriya	40 (30.15)	21 (30.15)	0 (0.69)	61
Patel	20 (54.49)	32 (54.49)	2 (0.61)	54
Kayastha	0 (2.97)	5 (2.47)	0 (0.05)	5
Charan	3 (3.46)	4 (3.46)	0 (0.07)	7
Ahir	2 (1.48)	1 (1.48)	0 (0.03)	3
Others	0 (2.47)	5 (2.47)	0 (0.05)	5
Total	87	87	2	176

Source: Sáez and Mahmood (2016), calculation based on *Who's Who*.

Notes: The figures represent observed frequencies (f_o) and expected frequencies (f_e) in parentheses. Degrees of freedom $(d_f) = 14$, chi-squared $(\chi^2) = 58.1$.

the Congress party has had significant representation of business castes although there is greater representation of BCs and SCs. The representation of business castes in the dominant support base is even higher in the case of the BJP. This corroborates commonplace characterization of the party as the party of Banias. The Brahman, Patel, and Kayastha groups, the core of the state's bourgeoisie, together constitute around 45 per cent of all elected members. Together with the Kshatriya caste group (some sections within the caste having business interests), this share increases to nearly 75 per cent, indicating the dominance of business groups/castes in the politics of the state.

To evaluate the relation between political party affiliation and caste in Gujarat, a chi-square test of independence is performed which validates the linkage. The relation between caste and party is significant, χ^2 (14, N = 176) = 58.1, p <.01. The case study of Gujarat affirms partisan orientation in terms of business domination.

The condition of labour market flexibility in the context of political developments makes it apparent that adjustment of labour market towards greater flexibility occurred even before economic liberalization or the ascendance of the reform-oriented BJP. Regional bourgeoisie in Gujarat has been successful in persuading developmental policies due to their political representation, both under Congress as well BJP. The caste-wise disaggregated analysis of dominant support base of the two parties clearly illustrates this point (Figure 3.2).

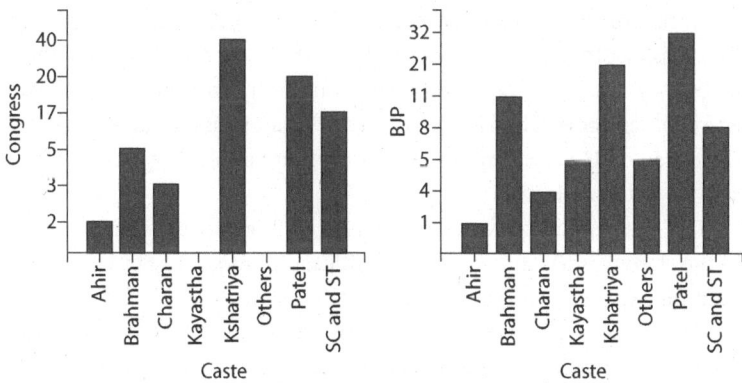

FIGURE 3.2   Support Base Derived from Caste and Party Affiliation of MPs in Gujarat, 1980–2008

Source: Author's calculation based on *Who's Who* (various issues).

The graphical representation of the caste-wise distribution of elected members (dominant support base) shows the marked difference between BJP and the Congress party. The Congress party, although marked by significant presence of Patels and Brahmans, is dominated by the Kshatriya caste with a greater presence of Ahirs, Charans, SCs, and STs, who constitute the socio-economically marginalized groups. This heterogeneity in the dominant support base of the Congress meant contradictory demands from the support base. The policy response of the Congress government reflected this contradiction as the government sought to address the demands of socio-economically marginalized through caste reservations for the Other Backward Classes (OBC) (Wood 1984) and proceeded with protection of business interests. In contrast, the relatively homogeneous support base of the BJP, marked by the dominance of Patel–Brahman–Kayastha group and relative absence of marginal castes, has translated into a reformist regime and greater labour reforms.

A related and important question in this context is the absence of redistributive pressures on the government, especially the BJP, as it pursues the interest of the dominant socio-economic sections. Although it cannot be denied that industrialization and economic growth have had benefits, social and economic disparity and deprivation have not disappeared. According to Mahadevia (2005), development in the state has been highly uneven in terms of regions, sectors, and social groups, and while certain sections of the population have benefited and become more prosperous, others have been marginalized. The concern for redistributive demands is essential in the context of discussion on labour, as issues of wage and work condition can potentially be part of such demands. The lack or absence of labour issues in the political discourse of Gujarat appears even more remarkable given the expansion of industrialization.

The answer can be found in the historical weakness of Left parties in the state that has influenced its political discourse. The political competition between centrist and centre-right parties, historical dominance of pro-industry, pro-capital ideas, and hegemony of capitalist classes in the state provide a contextual explanation. With the rise of the BJP, the demands of the disaffected sections of society and social tensions have increasingly coalesced into a majority–minority communal discourse that has marginalized the social groups such as tribals, gender, and labour. According to Shah (2007), the period of anti-reservation riots during 1985 was a crucial point when the BJP began to reap the rewards of its mobilization strategy as caste agitation against reservation transformed into religious riots. The rise of communalism and economic reforms appears to reinforce itself in Gujarat as the authoritarian style of governance has been helpful in implementing reforms, while communalism has aided retaining power and muting redistributive pressures.

Case Study: Maharashtra

Maharashtra presents the most interesting case study in the context of labour market reforms. The state has been historically one of the frontrunners in terms of industrialization and economic growth among the Indian states. Given the large and vibrant industrial sector, labour market reforms can be expected to be on the higher side in the state (business should be comparatively more influential). However, as this case study reveals, Maharashtra is marked by comparatively lower labour market flexibility; lower than Andhra Pradesh, for instance. Evidently, even though business constitutes an important and powerful social group in the state, it has not emerged as a hegemonic group, as has been the case in Gujarat.

The peculiar situation in the state, specifically low labour flexibility despite a vibrant private sector, can be attributed to the political dynamics, specifically partisan support base. Scholars and observers of Maharashtra politics have pointed out that politics in the state is dominated by the Maratha-Kunbi caste, a numerically dominant traditional agrarian group. This predominance of the agrarian caste in politics has ensured that business interests, although powerful, do not emerge as hegemonic. As Palshikar and Deshpande (1999) point out, the preeminence of the Congress party in the state has been based on an alliance between the numerically dominant Maratha-Kunbi caste and the non-Brahman, non-Dalit castes politically enumerated as Bahujan Samaj.[4] Interestingly, even though political power is concentrated in these social

---

[4] The term 'Bahujan' literally means majority and was introduced in Maharashtra through the Satyashodhak Samaj, a lower caste social and religious reform movement to refer to the majority of Hindu caste, including untouchables who were neither Brahmans nor merchants (Chandra 2004).

groups, the interests of the regional bourgeoisie, industrial, and urban middle classes have also been preserved by the government through an elaborate patronage network. The interests of socially dominant Brahmans and urban industrial interests have been accommodated due to the historical importance of industrial capital in the state and the non-hegemonic position of Maratha leadership unlike the Bania–Patidar–Brahman alliance in Gujarat.

The dominance of the Maratha-Kunbi caste in the politics of Maharashtra is evident in the analysis of the support base of partisan governments, more in the case of the Congress alliance than the BJP–Shiv Sena (Table 3.5).

As Table 3.5 reveals, the Maratha-Kunbi caste enjoys disproportionately large representation among the elected members of national legislature. From 1980 until 2008, 38 per cent of Congress MPs from Maharashtra came from the Maratha-Kunbi caste group. Comparably, 31 per cent of BJP MPs from Maharashtra came from the same caste group.

TABLE 3.5   Cross-Tabulation of Caste and Political Affiliation of MPs in Maharashtra, 1980–2008

Caste	Congress	BJP	NCP	Shiv Sena	Others	Total
Brahman	20 (30.76)	13 (8.52)	2 (2.50)	12 (8.52)	6 (2.67)	53
SC and ST	39 (33.08)	6 (9.17)	0 (2.69)	7 (9.17)	5 (2.37)	57
Kshatriya	7 (6.38)	3 (1.76)	0 (0.52)	0 (1.76)	1 (0.55)	11
Vyasya	0 (1.74)	0 (0.48)	0 (0.14)	2 (0.48)	1 (0.15)	3
Patidar Patel	5 (2.90)	0 (0.80)	0 (0.23)	0 (0.80)	0 (0.25)	5
Ahir	6 (3.48)	0 (0.96)	0 (0.28)	0 (0.96)	0 (0.30)	6
Dhangar	5 (6.38)	3 (1.76)	0 (0.52)	3 (1.76)	0 (0.55)	11
Maratha-Kunbi	70 (73.13)	16 (20.27)	13 (5.96)	24 (20.27)	3 (6.35)	126
Lingayat	11 (6.96)	1 (1.93)	0 (0.56)	0 (1.93)	0 (0.60)	12
Muslim	7 (4.06)	0 (1.12)	0 (0.33)	0 (1.12)	0 (0.35)	7
Mali	8 (6.96)	1 (1.93)	0 (0.56)	3 (1.93)	0 (0.60)	12
Others	6 (8.12)	8 (2.25)	0 (0.66)	0 (2.25)	0 (0.70)	14
Total	184	51	15	51	16	317

Source: Sáez and Mahmood (2016), calculation based on *Who's Who*.

Notes: The figures in parentheses represent observed frequencies (f_o) and expected frequencies (f_e). Degrees of freedom (d_f) = 44, chi-squared (χ^2) = 76.1.

Just as in the case of previous states, a chi-square test of independence was performed to examine the relation between political party affiliation and caste, which is statistically significant, $\chi^2 (44, N = 317) = 76.1, p < .01$.

Thus, Maharashtra represents a case of political dominance of agrarian middle caste in politics that has not allowed business interests to predominate (compared to Andhra Pradesh and Gujarat). However, the agrarian middle caste is not hegemonic in the state, as upper castes (Brahmans) remain socially preponderant and political representation of Maratha-Kunbi is much less hegemonic than the business caste / class groups of Andhra Pradesh or Gujarat. Thus, the dominant support base of major parties / alliances in Maharashtra is relatively heterogeneous that leads to a slower pace of reform. A wide and heterogeneous dominant support base is likely to exert contradictory interests and claims on the government, which makes policy choices a set of measured compromises leading to a gradualist approach.

Considering the argument in terms of specific dominant support base for contending parties, it is evident that the Congress party has significant representation from Lingayat, Mali, Brahmans, Kshatriya, Muslims, and SCs in addition to the Maratha-Kunbi castes. The upper castes (Brahmans) usually concentrated among urban and professional classes also have sizeable representation, which expectedly is greater within the BJP. Such a heterogeneous support base has meant that industrial interests cannot emerge as central to policymaking, and have to be negotiated with other contending interests. The BJP, which relies largely on Brahmans and Maratha-Kunbi castes for support, is comparatively more homogeneous. However, the alliance with the Shiv Sena that derives support from marginal castes, such as Dhangar and Mali, provides the alliance with heterogeneity in dominant support base.

Figure 3.3 shows the absolute domination, in terms of representation of the Maratha-Kunbi caste in the politics of the state. The support base of the Congress party is heterogeneous with representation from Lingayat, Mali, Brahmans, Kshatriya, Muslims, and SCs. The dominant support base of the BJP–Shiv Sena largely consists of Brahmans and Maratha-Kunbis, but also has representation of marginal castes such as Dhangar and Mali providing the alliance greater heterogeneity. In the context of this dominance of Maratha-Kunbi agrarian caste in politics and heterogeneity in the support base of parties, business interests could not emerge as dominant influence in the state.

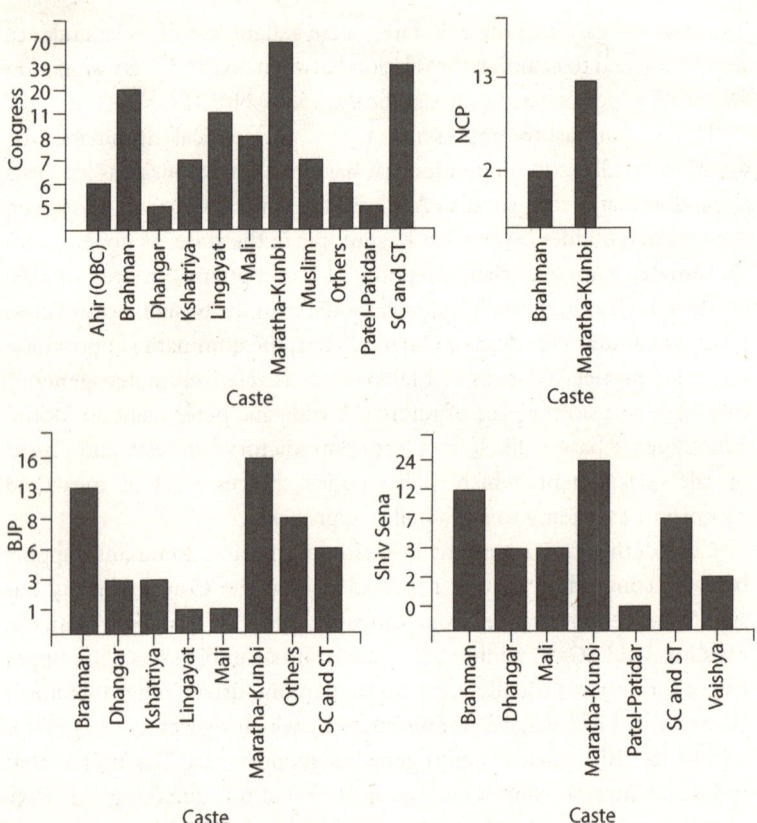

FIGURE 3.3   Support Base Derived from Caste and Party Affiliation of MPs in Maharashtra, 1980–2008
Source: Author's calculation based on *Who's Who* of Lok Sabha (Various issues).

Contextualizing the political dynamics with developments in the labour market further illustrates the argument. The Congress regime in the pre-liberalization period, on the one hand, increased legislative protection accorded to labour and, on the other hand, promoted partial liberalization and industrial restructuring in the state (closure of textile mills). The period between 1985 and 1990 marked the immediate aftermath of the Bombay Textile Mill strike which challenged the hegemony of the Congress-led Rashtriya Mill Mazdoor Union and, given its transformative potential, was dealt strictly by the Congress government, often with intimidation and repression (Omvedt 1983). Thus, the behaviour of the Congress government in the state was characteristic of the dominant support base that included diverging interests and the government made periodic-symbolic gestures towards different constituencies. The Congress party sought to maintain its support base by assuaging urban industrial interests and rural support base by addressing redistributive demands through caste reservations and development boards for backward areas. Like Gujarat, the ideological predisposition of the Congress party significantly influenced the outlook towards redistributive demands from the society. The historic presence of public sector, organized labour, and dominance of the Congress trade unions implied some protection for labour.

In terms of the labour market, such a situation created conditions for lower labour market flexibility. In the 1990s, with economic liberalization and the decline of the textile industry, industrial–urban interests became ascendant in economic policymaking. According to Palshikar and Deshpande (1999), the increased importance of the industrial sector in the state economy meant agrarian interests became less effective than before. In spite of developments favouring flexibility, the Congress government, due to its relatively wide and heterogeneous support base, progressed with reforms gradually.

The election of the BJP–Shiv Sena government in 1995 led to some increase in labour market flexibility, which is expected, as the dominant support base of the BJP consists primarily of upper castes and industrial–urban professional classes who have been the bedrock of support for reformist governments (Heath and Yadav 1999). However, as pointed out in the case study, the pace of labour reforms in Maharashtra is comparatively low and even during the BJP–Shiv Sena government the pace of labour reforms was lower than expected in terms of quantitative increase associated with explicitly pro-reformist government as in Gujarat. The relatively gradual and slow reform under the BJP–Shiv Sena government was due to the wide social basis of the Shiv Sena, the big partner in the alliance (Heath and Yadav 1999). As a regional party, the Shiv Sena built upon groups disenchanted with the Congress such as OBCs and sections of Maratha-Kunbi castes which made the support base of the alliance wide (Palshikar 1996).

Maharashtra presents a situation where labour market flexibility has increased over the years across regimes; however, the increase has not been as pronounced as Gujarat or Andhra Pradesh and labour enjoys relatively better position in terms of wage and legislative protection.

Case Study: West Bengal

The situation of labour market flexibility in the state of West Bengal corroborates the conventional expectation of reforms under a Left government. The state is marked by the lowest labour flexibility among the selected cases that can be attributed to the marginal influence of business interest groups in the politics of the state. According to Sinha (2005), the state acquired a distinct political trajectory with the ascendency of Left politics that can be explained through the overwhelming dominance of the bhadralok community (largely Bengali-Hindu upper-middle-caste professional class) in the politics of the state and marginalization of the industrial elites from the political scheme. The social position of the bhadralok, in the urban governmental professions and middle-class status with historical legacy of cultural renaissance, nationalist fervour, and Marxism-induced ideas radicalized the ideational discourse that represents a stark contrast to the other states particularly Gujarat. The absence of an indigenous business community in the state further facilitated the marginalization of business interests.

The caste-wise representation data reveals that Brahmans and Kayasthas (upper castes) constitute nearly 50 per cent of all elected representatives in the state. The poorer marginalized sections of society— represented by SCs, STs, and Muslims—constitute the other dominant section, which is about 40 per cent of the elected members. Business has practically no presence measured in terms of proportion of businessmen elected as MPs. The distribution of the dominant support group of the parties becomes somewhat comprehensible in the light of the fact that the state had been ruled continuously for 34 years (1977–2011) by the Left Front—an alliance of Left parties dominated by the CPI(M). The social basis of support for the Left regime was based on the alliance between urban and rural upper middle classes (bhadralok), industrial proletariat, poor, and the rural peasantry, especially middle peasants, small farmers, and landless labour (Chaudhuri 1987). As such, upper class (specifically business) had marginal presence in politics.

The caste-wise disaggregate data on the caste composition of the elected MPs (Table 3.6) shows that Brahmans, Kayasthas, Muslims, and SCs and STs constitute the dominant support base for the Left Front. The Congress–AITC have similar dominant support base with some representation of Mahishya caste known to have business interests. The

TABLE 3.6   Cross-Tabulation of Caste and Political Affiliation of MPs in West Bengal, 1980–2008

Caste	Congress	Left Front	BJP	AITC	Total
Brahman	12 (12.22)	69 (60.82)	1 (0.96)	8 (7.07)	93
Vyasya	0 (1.18)	7 (5.88)	2 (0.09)	0 (0.68)	9
Kayastha	9 (6.17)	30 (30.73)	0 (0.48)	4 (3.57)	47
Mahisya	1 (2.10)	9 (10.46)	0 (0.16)	6 (1.21)	16
Muslim	11 (5.25)	27 (26.15)	0 (0.41)	2 (3.04)	40
SC and ST	3 (9.73)	38 (48.39)	0 (0.76)	2 (5.63)	74
Kshatriya	1 (1.05)	3 (5.23)	0 (0.08)	0 (0.60)	8
OBC	1 (0.13)	0 (0.65)	0 (0.01)	0 (0.07)	1
Others	0 (0.13)	1 (0.65)	0 (0.01)	0 (0.07)	1
Total	38	189	3	22	289

Source: Sáez and Mahmood (2016), calculation based on *Who's Who* (various issues).
Notes: The figures represent observed frequencies (f_o) and expected frequencies (f_e) in parentheses. Degrees of freedom (d_f) = 40, chi-squared (χ^2) = 159.09.

statistical test to examine the relation between political party affiliation and caste confirms that caste is significantly associated with parties (chi-square test of independence shows significant relation, χ^2 (40, N = 289) = 159.09, p < .01). The strong representation of non-business caste groups in West Bengal's politics creates the conditions for negligible interests by business groups. The electoral dominance by an alliance of Left parties with pro-labour, pro-poor agenda further marginalized the interests of business in the state. It is not only the preponderance of Left politics in the state, but also the peculiar alignment of caste and partisan support base that lead to the irrelevance of business interests in politics.

Figure 3.4 shows the broad correspondence between the support bases of the main political alliances in the state.

In terms of the labour market, the 34-year-long rule of the Left Front translated into significant regulatory and political protection for labour. Until economic liberalization, wage share was relatively high and contract workforce was low in the state. The pro-labour policy orientation was part of the broader pro-poor politics of the Left parties (primarily, CPI(M)) that emerged as a dominant political force largely through land movements in the rural sphere and radical labour movements in the urban industrial sector. Given the ideological orientation and support

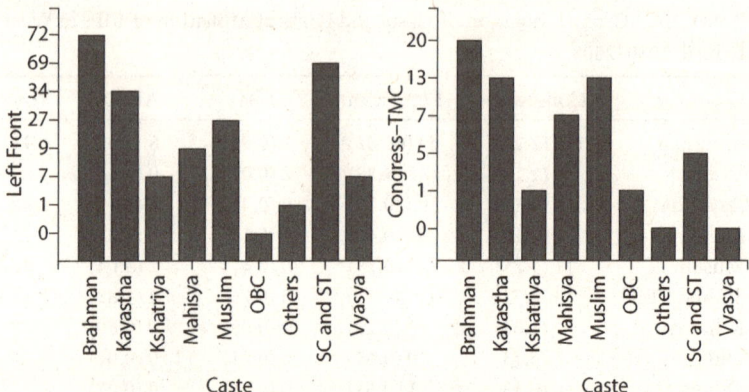

FIGURE 3.4   Support Base Derived from Caste and Party Affiliation of MPs in West Bengal, 1980–2004
Source: Author's calculation based on *Who's Who* published by the Lok Sabha secretariat.

base among the weaker sections of society (Heath and Yadav 1999), the Left Front government could pursue an agenda of social transformation that improved the condition of labour and rural peasantry. The major government programmes of land redistribution, revitalizing local government institutions, support public sector and welfare state specifically catered to this homogeneous constituency of support.

Intriguingly, such political dynamics does not seem to safeguard the benefits accorded to labour in the post-liberalization period. After 1991, a sharp increase in labour flexibility can be noted with declining wage share, declined along with increasing contractual workforce. Although the extent of flexibility in West Bengal is the lowest in India, the increasing trend poses some important questions about the policy autonomy of market regulation under conditions of globalization.

With regard to pro-labour policies, it is important to consider that organized labour in West Bengal became vulnerable during this period due to industrial stagnation. West Bengal had been suffering from industrial decline since 1965 (Dasgupta 1998) and the pro-labour stance of the government did not attract investment (Fallon and Lucas 1993). West Bengal's level of employment in the factory sector in 1987–8 was even lower than the 1970 census of sector employment (Chaudhuri 1987). Although there is a debate regarding the causes of industrial decline, with scholars such as Banerjee (1998) and Dasgupta (1998) highlighting centre–state relation, overall economic recession in India, declining demand for jute, and big engineering as contributing to industrial decline, the issue of industrial decline and employment necessitated change in policy orientation.

The CPI(M), in its 15th state party congress, declared its policy of acceptance of private investment and multinationals in investment. Economic liberalization of the 1990s offered new space to the state government for industrial investment free from central bureaucracy (Das and Mahmood 2015). However, under conditions of economic liberalization, this meant providing incentive to capital, including a certain labour market condition, which is reflected in the increasing labour flexibility.

Such an explanation for increase in labour market flexibility due to structural constraints necessitates discussion on the instrumental impetus for the Left Front government to realign policies towards industrial investment. Sinha (2005) has argued that the Left Front in West Bengal could win elections despite the gradual economic decline and pursue a policy of confrontation with the central government at the cost of investment due to the political dynamics of the state that rewarded subnational tendencies and offered little space to industrial interests in the politics. As such, one needs to interrogate the potential changes that guided such policy transformation.

In this context, the transformations in the dominant social base of the Left Front, especially CPI(M), is especially relevant. The Left Front emerged on the basis of a homogenous support base of small and marginal farmers, industrial working class, and professional middle class. Over the years, this support base expanded in the rural sector with expansion of middle peasants and incorporation of bigger peasantry, while in the urban sector, industrial stagnation significantly reduced the labour constituency of support (Chakrabarty 1998). Thus, there was a shift in socio-economic support base of the Left in terms of spatial orientation. A cursory glance of the electoral records reveals that since the mid-1980s, the bulk of Left victory was accounted for by the rural support base. The limitations of agrarian expansion and the socio-economic transformation in the support base during the 1990s combined to create the conditions for change in the industrial policy.

A handicapped industrial situation with declining employment for the educated youth created pressures on the government. This was aided by the emergence of the new middle class with rising global aspirations within the bhadralok community. The electoral verdict of the 2001 assembly elections that was projected as the referendum for industrialization marks the shift in policy thinking of the Left Front (Das and Mahmood 2015). Analysing the electoral verdict, Das (2001) shows that urban constituencies, especially middle class, demonstrated their new found support as the Left Front won in 30 out of 64 urban constituencies, as against 13 and 18 seats in the 1998 and 1999 parliamentary elections, respectively. In the industrial segments, the Front won 42 of 81 such seats which were significant, as in 1996 the Front won only in 22 industrial seats. The reorientation of the Left Front in economic policy matters that led to the land acquisition and eventual defeat of the alliance in 2011 has to be understood not only in terms of economic constraint, but also in terms of the transformation in the bhadralok dominant support base of the party.

Partisan Support Base and Reform

The preceding discussion highlights the role of partisan governments understood through the dominant support base of parties, in explaining labour market reforms. As the discussion suggests, reform and flexibility across the subnational states in India are conditioned by the extent of representation of socio-economic interests in politics. The subnational variations in labour market reforms are a function of political dynamics, specifically the representation of business castes in the support base and the composition of the dominant support base. The existence of assertive and dominant business caste/class within the relatively homogenous support base of the major parties in Andhra Pradesh and Gujarat has led to greater pro-business orientation. In contrast, the near complete absence of business classes in the politics of West Bengal has meant marginal influence of business in public policy. Maharashtra, on the other hand, shows that mere presence of business interests within political parties is not a sufficient condition to guarantee adequate business influence. Rather, the ability of business castes/classes to emerge as the foremost in the dominant support base of regimes is crucial for influence. Parties with a relatively homogenous dominant support base with business presence find reforms easier to implement than parties with a heterogeneous support base. The differences can be attributed to two interconnected factors: First, a homogenous support base allows parties to formulate coherent and focused policies with relatively fewer contradictory pressures emanating from the support base. Second, parties with a narrow and homogenous support base are more likely to resist interest group pressures compared to parties with a heterogeneous support base.

Broadly, regimes with a relatively heterogeneous socio-economic support base exemplified by the Congress in Maharashtra are likely to reform gradually. Similarly, given the predominant socio-economic base of BJP and TDP originating in urban middle class and upper class/caste sections, both the parties appear more reformist and labour flexibility is significantly higher during their regime. In West Bengal, the initial pro-labour policy, in spite of industrial stagnation, was driven by the support base of labour, bhadralok community, and agrarian sections. It was the transition in economic structure along with support base that led to pro-capital postures by the Left government. Thus, the role of class-based interest in the reforms process appears to be significant and public policies under globalization continue to be nuanced if not shaped by distributive conflicts between major socio-economic groups.

Given the analytical significance of the socio-economic support base of parties, it is necessary to discuss the formation of partisan support bases. In the case of the subnational states, the formation of socio-economically homogeneous or heterogeneous support bases is a function of both existing caste cleavage and nature of political competition. The divergences in caste configurations across subnational states and the specific correlation between caste and occupation influence the nature of support base across states. There is extant literature on party system in India that highlights the regional variations in caste domination of politics (Brass 1991; Yadav 1996). As such, region-specific caste cleavages and their interrelation with politics create relatively homogeneous or heterogeneous support bases for parties.

A socio-economic support base is homogeneous if the nature of assets that individuals or groups control lead to similar rewards from collective action, similar effects in case of transformations in the market, and subject to similar outcomes due to asymmetric effects of democracy (Korpi and Palme 2003). We interrogate the socio-economic supprt base through caste and occupation to arrive at the support bases of parties. To put simply, homogeneity or heterogeneity is determined by the assets under the control of groups (socio-economic position) and expectation from public policies. It is not surprising that homogeneity is determined by similar castes and class. Importantly, this association between caste/class and political parties, that is, partisan orientation, is not static and the nature of existing parties, that is, party system, has an important role in the construction of partisan support base. The association of caste cleavages with parties is a product of historical–political dynamics.

In this context, the transformation of middle classes across the states and gradual marginalization of labour deserve special mention. An important constituent of social basis that seems to influence the extent of reforms is the professional middle class whom Bardhan (1984) considered one of the proprietary classes. This class has undergone significant transformation with the structural changes in the Indian economy, leading to the emergence of a new middle class who is the beneficiary of globalization. According to Corbridge and Harriss (2000), the transformation in middle classes and the emergence of backward castes as the centre of social mobilization have resulted in tectonic socio-economic shifts in India. As a result, the historic alliance between white-collar and blue-collar workers has been ruptured and explosion of identity-based politics has further fragmented labour movement constricting political role of trade unions.

Another important aspect that emerges is the apparent regionalization of parties in India and its effects on reforms. As the case study suggests even national parties in India like the Congress party exhibit regional differences due to variations in socio-economic dynamics. The effect of the Congress regime in Andhra Pradesh and in Maharashtra or the BJP regime in Gujarat and Maharashtra seems to vary due to regional specificities, particularly composition of social castes and classes. As such, it is important to situate interest groups, socio-economic classes, and political parties within prevalent party system in order to capture the gamut of political influences on policy.

The analysis of business presence in the support base of political parties (that is, the partisan representation across states) also reveals some important dimension of interest–politics linkages across the states of India. Interest groups in India have developed along pluralist lines and were often divided along nature of capital, regional concentration, and even caste. The post-Independence legacy of dirigisme had meant that the influence of interest groups dependent on their capacity to influence parties in government and electoral outcomes. As such, the relevance of business within electoral support base for parties emerged as critical to determining its influence. The assertion challenges the conventional notion of variegated influence of interest groups like business across subnational states by highlighting the role of caste in explaining variations in policy. The relative power of business across the states appears to vary due to the relation between business and government, which in turn is structured by the salience of business castes as an electorally relevant group.

The findings show the continued relevance of political dynamics, especially the relevance of class interests, in the support base of parties in the determination of policies. Such a claim does not reject the conventional relation between economic liberalization and pressures for market flexibility, but presents a nuanced understanding of reforms being conditioned by both transformations in the economy and the relative balance between socio-economic classes. Although liberalization of the economy has somewhat reduced state autonomy, domestic politics continues to influence the process. It is the relative balance between social classes both in the sphere of economy and politics that determines the pace and extent of reforms.

4

Partisan Government and Interest Groups

Chapter 3 argued that variation in labour market reform, understood through flexibility, can be accounted through the configuration of the support base of partisan governments. The argument evokes 'partisan politics' hypothesis in explaining reforms by establishing the relation between the dominant support base of parties and policy choices. Such an argument, however, remains limited without the incorporation of interest-group analysis in policy formulation. This is because interest group influence over policy has been a consistent theme in policy analysis. This chapter analyses the role of interest groups, namely business groups and trade unions in shaping labour market reforms.

Contrary to explanations that highlight the role of interest groups in accounting for reform variation, the chapter foregrounds partisan government as a more robust explanation for variation. It goes on to argue that the ability of interest groups to influence policy is in fact conditioned and mediated by their interaction with the partisan government. As this chapter's case study reveals, the capacity of business groups or trade unions to influence labour market policies and outcomes depends on the party in power. In the context of business, even if the private sector increases pressure for reforms, the actual level of flexibility is determined by business representation within parties. Likewise, the strength of trade unions in influencing the labour market is significantly predisposed by its linkage to the party in power.

Interest Groups and Labour Reform: Business and Labour

Business and labour constitute the contending actors in the political economy of the labour market. Business refers to firms and industries that are privately owned and administered by motivations of profit for the owners. The use of the term 'business' (rather than 'capital') is a conscious choice made to underline the role of agency of interest groups. Generically, the term 'capital' is understood as a factor of production that is required in the production of other goods and production of more wealth. Business, however, specifies agents involved in trade or production activities for profit. As such, business as a category is more suited for interest-based analysis.

In the context of the labour market, business is predisposed towards labour market flexibility to meet the challenges of production system and ensure managerial prerogatives (Hensman 2001). The pressure for flexibility is enhanced under conditions of globalization due to competitive pressures for investment-friendly climate. Globalization has strengthened the relative bargaining position of business through capital market mobility, creation of economic and political regimes such as the WTO with reduced tariffs, and reduced foreign ownership restrictions (Held et al. 1999). Intuitively, the increased labour market flexibility noticed since economic liberalization can be associated to the increasing policy relevance of business.

On the other hand, trade unions occupy an important position as the organized face of labour. Economic reforms, particularly deregulation and liberalization, curtail the established rights and privileges of organized labour. Unsurprisingly, literature on reforms has highlighted protective legislations and trade unions as major hindrance to economic reforms (Crouch 1990; Horton, Kanbur, and Mazumdar 1991; Papola 1994). Successful implementation of labour reforms is inversely related to the strength of the labour movement, and it is argued that trade unions in India have been able to stall major reforms due to their absolute numbers and control over key economic resources (Varshney 1999). However, it is likely that the factors leading to ascendance of business such as mobility of capital and technocratic production methods should correspondingly contribute to the gradual marginalization of trade unions. The ILO reports have noted waning influence of labour in most countries of the world over the period (ILO 1996).

Evidently, the relative strength of labour and business can be theoretically associated with labour market policies and outcomes. In the context of the case studies though, the influence of business or labour is conditioned by wider political dynamics especially linkages to political party in power. Despite the pressures from the expanding private sector of the economy for reform, labour reforms depend on representation of business castes and groups within parties. In the case of trade unions also, the ability to influence policies is significantly augmented or limited by the union–government relations. The argument is in line with the recent literature that highlights the growing distance between political parties and unions as a factor in declining importance of labour. Burgess (2004) has argued that in the twentieth century, the trade unions were the dominant instruments of collective action and development strategies due to their alliance with political parties. The advent of globalization with mobility of capital, expansion of service sector, changes in production method, and increasing heterogeneity of skills has led to a decline in the traditional base of trade unions. As such, the relevance of interest groups in influencing policies and outcomes depends on party–interest group interaction.

Business, Globalization, and Labour

Globalization has been a beneficial process for business in general. The dominance of the market economy, economic and technological changes, curtailment or reduction on state functions along with the ideational reorientation has enlarged the bargaining capacity of business relative to other social groups (Held et al. 1999; Stiglitz 2002). Theoretically, the process of globalization increases the political power of business vis-à-vis other social groups as well as the state through increased concentration of economic power and access to policymakers. The increased currency of the terms 'government–business' coalition and 'public–private' partnership that incorporates the role of business interests in policymaking is cited by scholars to highlight the increasing policy relevance of business (Mazumdar and Sarkar 2008). Furthermore, as Dunning (1997) points out, globalization erodes the power of the state to the extent that MNCs can bargain favourably in relation to the state.

The accrued benefit of globalization for business is, however, not evenly distributed. Business, understood as the private sector of the economy, although homogenous as a social group, is marked by a heterogeneous set of interests based on the type, volume, and location of firms. The term 'business' covers both trade and industry and consists of small-scale traders, medium-sized firms, and big industries. Intuitively, we can assume that not all businesses are affected in similar manner by the process of globalization. The response of individual business or business sectors in a reforming economy may vary according to perceived or actual outcomes. If incumbent private business firms are threatened by increased imports, it is likely that they will oppose reform. Likewise, firms that are favoured during phases of import substitution industrialization may favour protectionism as against export-oriented units (EOUs) that are likely to support liberalization (Katzenstein 1976).

Studies such as the globalization report recognize that employers are poorly organized and fundamentally heterogeneous in their response to liberalization (World Commission on the Social Dimension of Globalization 2004). Such differences in approach to external liberalization have been noticed in business organizations with the Federation of Indian Chamber of Commerce and Industry (FICCI), the apex business organization of indigenous private capital, expressing unhappiness with the privileges accorded to MNCs. This reaction from FICCI during the early days of liberalization was natural, given that they represented more traditional and national business enterprises that faced prospects of greater competition. In comparison, the response of the Confederation of Indian Industries (CII) was generally more favourable towards external economic liberalization, given the larger representation of MNCs and EOUs (Kochanek 1995).

The variations in business's attitude, however, should not be interpreted as opposition to globalization and liberalization per se. Actually, the phenomenon of globalization, in the transitional economies, involves two broad dimensions, namely internal liberalization and external liberalization. Internal liberalization encompasses deregulation and the privatization of economic activity, leading to increased importance of the private sector, greater managerial prerogative, and prominence of private business in policymaking. Naturally, private business firms are likely to support such a process. External liberalization, however, involves broader issues such as economic sovereignty, protectionism, and state promotion of export industries. This form of liberalization has evoked mixed responses from private business, particularly around questions of protecting domestic incumbents from international competition (Sáez and Mahmood 2016). In this basic dichotomy, labour market flexibility represents a form of internal liberalization.

Unsurprisingly, there is a broad agreement among businesses on the issue of greater labour flexibility. As Martin and Swank (2004) point out, private sector firms resist any policies that interfere with their profitability by increasing tax burdens, raising the wage floor of collective bargaining, or interfere with managerial control. This agreement on the question of labour market flexibility is enhanced in the context of a competitive market economy that requires adjusting the factors of production according to market signals. Although the necessity of some social regulation is accepted, strict labour regulations and trade unions that impede market corrections are considered detrimental to the growth of a business (Besley and Burgess 2004; Fallon and Lucas 1993).

In India, the adoption of market-led development policies under economic liberalization has amplified the structural pressures for business-friendly policies and labour market flexibility. Being a labour-surplus and capital-scarce economy in the global system, in the contemporary global system, the country is constrained to provide incentives to capital for investment. Such a developmental model is reinforced by the proliferation of trade and investment regimes, leading to the creation of global norms based on a liberal market model (Sáez and Mahmood 2016). The repeated assertions about unfavourable business climate, institutional impediments like rigid labour laws, and bureaucratic control in hindering investments and economic growth by the business organizations as well as the governments reflect this altered politico-economic reality. As such, it can be assumed that a large private sector would share significant correspondence with a flexible labour market due to a mixture of economic reasons.

Business and Labour Reforms

The subject of labour market reform has shadowed the process of economic liberalization in India. Businesses have consistently argued for greater flexibility in the labour market by reforming the archaic and rigid labour regulations. B.P. Pant (2010), the Director of Labour Employment and Skill Development Division of FICCI, sums the attitude of business towards labour regulations: '[L]aws are incompatible with the changes in economy, which has made production process more capital and skill intensive. The present labour regulations and industrial relations are not enabling for business due to excessive restrictions and interventions by trade unions and government.' Scholars working on labour and industrial relations have pointed out that employers in India have responded to these restrictive regulations in many ways such as subcontracting, increasing capital intensity, expansion of leasing-in capacity of small firms, setting up of production in states where labour is not organized or militant, and the increasing resort to corruption and bribery in order to avoid the legal consequences of retrenchment (Datta Chaudhuri 1996; Ramaswamy 1988).

Formal labour market reform reflects the capacity of business to influence public policy. As an interest group, this influence of business may emanate from a number of factors. The capacity of business to influence public policy as an interest group is conditioned by economic considerations. Interest-group literature also highlights that power of any interest group is significantly determined by wider political dynamics, such as countervailing interests in society and linkages to government (Dahl 2005). Consequently, the relative strength of trade unions and linkages to government are important in shaping business influence, especially in countries like India, which have a legacy of state presence in economic policymaking.

The literature on business and politics highlights four broad ideological–political perspectives on the relation between business and policymaking in liberal democracies (Godbole 2004):

1. The theory of 'structural dependence of the state on capital' is derived from the neo-Marxist view that considers politics under capitalism as being dominated by an interconnected elite of financiers and business directors. The dependence of governments on the

performance of the voluntary transactions of business for growth and employment creates the necessary conditions for business incentives in liberal democracies. The privileges of businesses are not challenged because restrictive government policies decrease investment, employment, government receipts, and economic growth (Lindblom 1977).

2. The 'class organization hypothesis' considers business as a central and crucial segment of society. It argues that a business's influence on politics is dependent upon the resources at the disposal of the business. As Lucas (1997) points out, previous development strategies emphasized the importance of interventionist state capable of dominating social groups, including businesses, as it was commonly assumed that business classes were weak and rent-seeking. However, contemporary trends privilege the role of the private sector, as economic liberalization and international competition have shifted the balance of power between business and state.

3. The 'partisan electoral view' considers business influence on policy as a function of business–political party linkage. The literature suggests that the power of a business is much restricted under the Left party, while it is more under parties subscribing to liberal and neo-liberal ideologies (Alvarez, Garrett, and Lange 1991; Garrett 1998b). This is because political parties draw their support from different socio-economic groups, and the power of such groups fluctuates with the fortunes of their allied parties.

4. The 'political institutions' argument suggests that government policies and institutions shape the relative influence of interest groups over politics. According to Quinn and Shapiro (1991), institutions of government have a significant degree of autonomy and policies that are at odds with prevailing conceptions or objectives are unlikely to be pursued.

As an analysis of business influence on labour market outcomes in subnational states of India, the role of structural and institutional factors in policy is arguably similar, if operational. The argument of structural dependence, if valid, should be similar across all subnational states, as the structure and nature of capitalism is historically institutionalized on a national basis (Radice 2000). The role of political institutions is similarly similar across the state given the quasi-federal nature of India with a legacy of state-led development.

Also, it is important to consider the problem of identifying the mechanisms and sources of business influence, as such influence may be on an individual or at a collective level, and can either manifest or be latent. Further, the effectiveness of the interest group's influence over policy also depends on the type of policy. As Godbole (2004) points out, the three major categories of public policy—distribution, regulation, and redistribution—develop their own characteristic political structure, political process, and group relations.

The influence of business over policy emanates from its control over capital and, in turn, the forces of production. In liberal democracies, governments pursue re-electable macroeconomic outcomes. As such, governments must ensure economic growth and accordingly, must provide incentives to businesses to help foster that growth. Therefore, the extent of private ownership of productive resources in the economy should provide some understanding of business power. It can be argued that greater control of productive resources (for example, capital, technology, and industries) by a business will lead to greater influence of the business and vice versa. Further, the inflow of FDI is likely to increase the power of the business to influence policies, given that MNCs have become critical drivers of technological innovation, learning, and economic growth that affords them a 'privileged position' in domestic policy.

Accordingly, the increasing concentration of investment, foreign as well as private, should greatly expand the power of business under globalization. States with a greater share of private sector of the economy, that is, class organization of business should be marked by greater labour market flexibility. In the context of the subnational states, macroeconomic conditions such as the share of industry to the NSDP, the share of public–private ownership of firms and the extent of FDI reflect the relative share of material resources at the disposal of a business that can explain the variations in the business's influence over labour policy. Further, the number of EOUs in the economy can highlight any perceived differences in business's orientation based on nature of the industry.

Material Resources of a Business and Labour Flexibility

As discussed in the previous section, the control over economic resources, namely capital and employment, constitutes the fundamental source of a business's influence over policies. The share of the industrial sector to the NSDP is an important indicator of the extent of business presence in the economy.

Figure 4.1 suggests that business presence is greater in Gujarat and Maharashtra. In contrast, the contribution of the industrial sector is not dominant in West Bengal or Andhra Pradesh. The figure shows the contribution of industry to NSDP is highest in Gujarat. Since economic liberalization in 1991, industrial sector contribution in the state has increased to more than 30 per cent of NSDP. In the case of Maharashtra, the contribution of the industrial sector has varied little over the observed period, hovering at around 30 per cent of the state's NSDP. The disaggregated data on NSDP shows that since the 1980s, the share of service sector in the economy has accounted for most of the SDP growth, which is consistent with the transformation of Mumbai from being the industrial to being the financial capital of India. In the

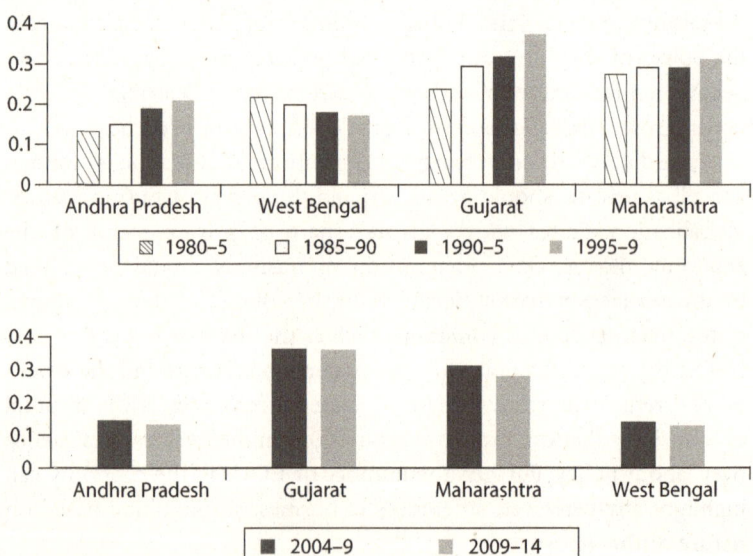

FIGURE 4.1   State-wise Share of the Industrial Sector's Contribution to NSDP, 1980 to 1999 and April 2004 to March 2014
Source: Table on NSDP, RBI (various issues).
Note: Due to change of base year in computation of NSDP, the two datasets are not comparable.

case of West Bengal, the contribution of the industrial sector has actually declined over time, while Andhra Pradesh shows an expanding industrial sector until 2014.

In terms of resources at the disposal of a business, it is difficult to get comprehensive state-level data on the distribution of public and private sources of capital. As such, this chapter examines the share of public and private employment, a data more readily available, to determine the share of public and private sectors in the economy. The importance of business stems from both industrial investment and employment generation, and greater levels of employment in the private sector indicate greater leverage for the business sector (Sáez and Mahmood 2016).

Figure 4.2 shows that during the period 1980–2010, employment trends across the four selected states in India have remained more or less stable, with increasing share of private employment since economic reforms. Private employment is lowest in Andhra Pradesh (around 30 per cent as a proportion of total employment), while it is highest in Gujarat, reaching nearly 60 per cent of the total employment for the period 2000–10.

It is evident from the data on NSDP and employment that there is a greater presence of businesses and resources at the disposal of businesses (private sector) in the economies of Gujarat and Maharashtra, as compared to West Bengal and Andhra Pradesh.

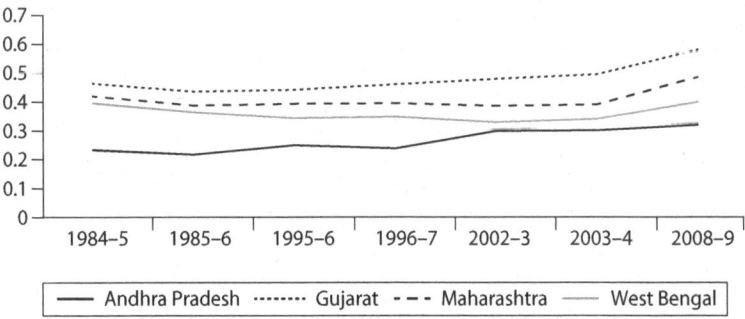

FIGURE 4.2   State-wise Share of Employment in Private Sector in Proportion to Total Employment, April 1984 to March 2009

Source: Sáez and Mahmood (2016), calculations based on *Statistical Abstract* (CSO, various issues) and *Indian Labour Yearbook* (Ministry of Labour, various issues).

Another important factor in determining the influence of business under conditions of globalization is industrial investment, including FDI. The choice over the location of investment with consequences for employment and growth provides leverage to businesses in influencing policies. The number and value of industrial entrepreneur memoranda (IEMs); documents that signal the intended investment in states by potential private investors; the number and value of FDI approvals; and the number of EOUs that have emerged, primarily after the adoption of economic liberalization, together reflect the choice of business over · location and potentially the political-economic orientation of states towards business (Table 4.1).

Table 4.1 shows the preeminence of Maharashtra in attracting investments, particularly FDI and EOUs. Gujarat and Andhra Pradesh attracted high levels of investment following Maharashtra. In the case of Gujarat, industrial investment is relatively greater than FDI inflow or EOUs. Among the four states, West Bengal has the lowest amount of FDI approvals as well as the lowest number of EOUs. If measured in terms of IEMs, Gujarat has been at the forefront of attracting businesses, while West Bengal has been a laggard in courting business.

Thus, at an aggregate level, the data corroborates the conventional notion of greater business presence in Maharashtra and Gujarat compared to Andhra Pradesh and West Bengal. Resources at the disposal of businesses are highest in Maharashtra, followed by Gujarat and Andhra Pradesh, while they are lowest in West Bengal (Table 4.2). Clearly,

TABLE 4.1   State-wise Distribution of EOUs, IEMs, and FDI Approvals, 1991–2012

State	EOU Units	% of India	IEM Value (Rs Cr)	% of India	FDI Approved (USD Mn)	% of India
Andhra Pradesh	256	10.78	847,972	8.84	5,389.34	5.22
Gujarat	244	10.28	1,139,257	11.88	4,446.74	4.53
Maharashtra	361	15.21	928,397	9.68	24,393.58	19.27
West Bengal	58	2.44	642,681	6.70	4,145.41	3.46

Source: Sáez and Mahmood (2016), calculated from *SIA Annual Report*, 2012–13; state-wise details of IEM filed 2012–13; *Fact Sheet on Foreign Direct Investment* (Department of Industrial Policy and Promotion, Ministry of Commerce, Government of India).

TABLE 4.2   Indian States in Terms of Resources for Business and Labour
Market Flexibility

Rank	Industrial Sector's Contribution to NSDP	Private Sector Employment	Labour Market Flexibility
1	Gujarat	Gujarat	Gujarat
2	Maharashtra	Maharashtra	Andhra Pradesh
3	Andhra Pradesh	Andhra Pradesh	Maharashtra
4	West Bengal	West Bengal	West Bengal

Source: Author's classification based on the discussions.

the expectation of business influence being contingent on material resources at their disposal does not seem to hold in the context of labour reforms across the states. There is a clear anomaly in the extent of business resources and corresponding influence over policy understood through labour market reform.

The lack of correspondence between the material resources of business and the degree of labour flexibility suggests the operation of some other causal variable that accounts for the lower level of labour market flexibility in Maharashtra relative to Andhra Pradesh. Existing studies on subnational variations highlight considerable difference in policy design and implementation, due to regional political and institutional dynamics (Bajpai and Sachs 1999; Sinha 2005).

Business Organization and Labour Flexibility

An important factor that may account for the varying ability of businesses to influence policies is the mechanism to access and influence policymakers. It is well recognized that in the absence of proper organization, mere possession of resources may not be adequate to influence policymakers. In a democracy, such policymakers include elected representatives as well as the bureaucracy and political parties. Thus, the extent of interest aggregation by business organizations and business–politics linkages is crucial to the success of a business's influence. The importance of political dynamics in determining the relative influence of a business at the subnational level in India has been recognized in literature (Sinha 2005).

Like any other interest groups, the capacity of a business to effectively influence policy and its outcome depends on the resources of the organization; ability to assimilate interests, that is, extent of centralization; access to policymakers; freedom from government control; and the ability to compete with other contending interests.

The states in our case study are marked by multiplicity of business organizations often based on region, industry, and even rivalry across businesses in that state. Even though all the states have multiple business organizations, Andhra Pradesh and Gujarat are marked by relative centralization of business organizations in comparison to Maharashtra and West Bengal. For example, the Gujarat Chamber of Commerce and Industry (GCCI) is the apex organization in Gujarat with membership of different regional associations and firms. The GCCI offers an extensive range of diversified services to its members such as providing industry information, liaising between business firms and government, sending of budget-related memoranda to various state authorities, and enabling business promotion (GCCI 2010).

West Bengal, in comparison, does not have any overarching business federation, and the state is characterized by a multiplicity of business associations, notably the Bengal Chamber of Commerce, the Bengal National Chamber of Commerce, the Oriental Chamber of Commerce, and the Indian Chamber of Commerce. These chambers of commerce represent the various industry associations and take up policy matters directly with the government. Maharashtra also has a high degree of business organization decentralization. The business associations in the state reflect a diversity of regional interests, in the form of associations such as the Deccan Chamber of Commerce, the Mahratta Chamber of Commerce; community chambers like the Memon Chamber of Commerce, the Dalit Chamber of Commerce; along with statewide business associations like the Bombay Chamber of Commerce and Industry, the Indian Merchants Chamber, and the Maharashtra Chamber of Commerce.

It can be argued that the extent of fragmentation (centralization) could have some influence in determining business influence across the states. However, as Sáez and Mahmood (2016) point out, the extent of centralization of a business is not an exogenous variable and essentially reflects factors like historical–institutional developments, extent of business coordination, and nature of business classes. As such, the extent of organization of business, as a variable in determining business influence, can be marginal at best. What is important, however, is the difference in the relative efficiency of business organizations across the states. Cali and Sen (2009) in the study of state business relations in subnational states of India corroborate a high and increasing state–business relation (SBR) for Gujarat and Andhra Pradesh. The SBR in Maharashtra is comparatively lower than these states, while it is lowest in West Bengal. The evaluation of subnational SBR broadly correlates with the subnational variation in business influence over labour market reforms.

An important question in this context concerns the conditions that augment greater coherence among business. Such a question assumes relevance in the light of the fact that mere possession of resources by business does not translate into influence and points to the role of wider political processes, especially coherence in interest aggregation and business–party linkage.

Partisan Linkage of Business and Labour Flexibility

As the previous discussion suggests, labour policy and outcomes are not merely determined by structural factors like size of private sector or employer coordination. The wider political process and business–government linkage has an important role in defining the impact of business interests on policy. The conventional explanation regarding the subnational variation in business incentives also emphasizes on the nature of government and regional political economy (Sinha 2005). The role of partisan linkage is important, particularly in India due to the historical weakness of interest groups and legacy of state presence in economic policymaking.

The relation between business and government policy, especially labour policy, is not straightforward. As mentioned previously, just as greater business contribution should lead to greater influence of a business over policy, the policies of the government influence the investment decision of business. The partisan orientation of government in terms of a left-to-right spectrum has significant consequences for macroeconomic policies and economic outcomes like employment levels, monetary growth rates, income distributions, growth strategies, and growth rates (Quinn and Shapiro 1991). The partisan-orientation hypothesis claims that governments by parties with a pro-business orientation share close collaboration with a business and favour economic growth and inflation over redistribution and employment. In contrast, the Left governments favour employment and redistribution over growth.

The business–government relations across countries can be understood by examining the institutions through which they interact both formal and informal, such as parties, executive, bureaucrats, and business associations (Hillman 1995). The resources in the hands of businesses for influencing the government and parties vary from investment for states to financial assistance to political parties, personal gratification of political elites, and connection to bureaucracy. The most direct political intervention of business in policy occurs when business is part of the policymaking process. Naturally, if there is greater representation of business in the government, policies are expected to be more responsive to the needs of business.

As the findings of Chapter 3 suggest, linkage between political parties and business groups is significant in determining a business's influence over labour policy. Business, as per Chapter 3, is conceptualized through the wider category of caste, and the configuration of a partisan support base showed that parties with greater support from business castes and relatively homogeneous dominant support base (leadership) undertake greater labour market reform.

Developing on the partisan politics linkage, I assume that relative variation in labour market reform can be associated with the variation in business representation in partisan government. In this section, the data on the profession of MPs across the states between 1980 and 2009 is analysed to evaluate the extent of business representation. The data is collected from *Who's Who*, published by the Lok Sabha Secretariat that provides the professional background of the members along with a short biography.

Analysing the various self-reported professions of the members, this section classifies the occupations into a four major categories, consisting on the following professions: businesses, consisting of industrialists and business persons; agriculturists comprising people who claimed farming or animal husbandry as their profession; professionals, consisting of doctors, lawyers, teachers, and others; and political workers comprising MPs who claimed to be full-time party workers or activists. Four more subcategories, namely—business–agriculturists, business–professionals, professional–agriculturists, and business–agriculturist–professionals, are created to accommodate the members who had more than one declared profession. The eightfold classification of profession is exhaustive and exclusive. However, as the categorization is based on self-declaration of politicians, it will be sensible to consider the data as indicative and not exact.

The relative presence or absence of business persons within the elected MPs across the states matches the caste-wise evaluation in Chapter 3. Gujarat is characterized by a strong presence of businesses as business persons constitute around 40 per cent of all MPs in the state. Table 4.3 corroborates the domination of the regional bourgeoisie (business and professional classes) in the politics of the state. The expected party-wise variation in the representation of regional bourgeoisie is also confirmed by the data as around 80 per cent of all the BJP candidates and around 60 per cent of the Congress belong to the business and profession categories.

The low influence of business in the politics of West Bengal, as revealed by the absence of business castes, is also reflected in terms of the proportion of business persons in elected MPs (Table 4.4). The overall proportion of business persons in total elected representatives is a meagre 4.4 per cent. This marginalization of business interests in the state can be understood in the context of dominance of left ideology in politics and bhadralok community in the socio-cultural life of the state.

At a superficial level, correspondence can be drawn between the extent of presence of business interests in party leadership and extent of labour market reform in the Gujarat and West Bengal. The association

TABLE 4.3   Profession and Party of Elected MPs in Gujarat, 1980–2008

Profession	Congress	BJP	Others	Total
Business	7	3	0	10
Agriculture	28	16	1	45
Profession	12	42	1	55
Political Worker	5	0	0	5
Business and Agriculture	17	5	0	22
Agriculture and Profession	2	4	0	6
Business and Profession	20	18	0	38
Business, Agriculture, and Profession	0	1	0	1
Total	91	89	2	182

Source: Author's classification from *Who's Who* (various issues).

TABLE 4.4   Profession and Party of Elected MPs in West Bengal, 1980–2008

Profession	Congress	Communist	BJP	AITC	AIFB	RSP	Total
Business	3	0	0	2	0	0	5
Agriculture	1	12	0	0	0	4	17
Profession	24	80	1	16	9	17	147
Political Worker	10	89	2	4	9	4	118
Business and Agriculture	0	8	0	0	0	0	8
Total	38	189	3	22	18	25	295

Source: Author's classification from *Who's Who* (various issues).

between business presence among policy framers and extent of labour flexibility is, however, not so direct in the case of Andhra Pradesh and Maharashtra. The business–politics dynamics in the two states highlights that mere presence of business persons in policymaking is inadequate for a business's influence, and the broader composition of partisan policymakers (dominant support base of parties) mediates between business's interest and policy outcomes.

Table 4.5 on the profession of MPs in the state of Andhra Pradesh reveals that around 35 per cent of all the elected MPs have some form

TABLE 4.5   Profession and Party of Elected MPs in Andhra Pradesh, 1980–2008

Profession	Congress	TDP	Communist	BJP	Others	Total
Business	14	7	0	5	0	26
Agriculture	48	35	0	2	5	90
Profession	22	23	3	2	4	54
Political Worker	15	5	6	0	6	32
Business and Agriculture	20	8	0	3	2	33
Agriculture and Profession	7	9	0	0	1	17
Business and Profession	22	10	2	1	1	36
Business, Agriculture, and Profession	5	0	0	0	0	5
Total	153	97	11	13	19	293

Source: Author's classification from *Who's Who* (various issues).

of business interest. This share of business representation appears to be significantly high when compared to the resources at disposal of businesses. As the data shows, out of total 293 elected members between the period 1980 and 2009, 100 members had some sort of business interest distributed across the two major parties. Evidently, the ability of a business to affect policymaking in the state, despite lower share of resources, is due to its representation in politics.

Interestingly, the representation of business in Maharashtra is greater than in Andhra Pradesh (Table 4.6). Overall, around 40 per cent of all elected members have some form of association with business. This representation increases particularly after economic liberalization in the 1990s. In partisan terms, the proportional representation of business interests is greater in the BJP–Shiv Sena alliance compared to the Congress–NCP alliance.

Clearly, the relation between representation of business persons among the policy framers and labour reforms is not direct. In the case of Andhra Pradesh, the reasonably high representation of business in politics translates into greater policy influence due to the relatively homogenous nature of the main political parties. The lower levels of labour market reform in Maharashtra testifies to the fact that business influence over policies is conditioned by the nature of the dominant support base of governments.

TABLE 4.6   Profession and Party of Elected MPs in Maharashtra, 1980–2008

Profession	Congress	BJP	NCP	Shiv Sena	Others	Total
Business	16	2	1	13	0	32
Agriculture	78	17	10	9	2	116
Profession	35	9	0	4	10	58
Political Worker	15	3	0	2	2	23
Business and Agriculture	13	6	1	11	2	33
Agriculture and Profession	4	1	0	0	0	5
Business and Profession	30	16	3	13	0	62
Business, Agriculture, and Profession	2	0	0	0	1	3
Total	193	54	15	52	17	332

Source: Authors classification from *Who's Who* (various issues).

Business Interests and Subnational Labour Reform

The analysis of labour market flexibility through business interest provides support for the partisan-orientation hypothesis. The extent of labour market reforms across the subnational states cannot be explained through material–organizational resources of business (private sector of the economy). Disaggregated analysis reveals that in terms of economic structure, the power of the business sector should have been greater in Maharashtra and Gujarat compared to West Bengal or Andhra Pradesh. However, as the case study reveals, businesses are more successful in influencing labour market policies in Andhra Pradesh and Gujarat due to the greater representation of business interests within political parties. The relation, however, is not simple and direct, that is, it is not that greater business representation is translated into greater business-friendly policies. As pointed out in Chapter 3, the configuration of support base for reform depends on two factors: (a) the presence of business caste/class within parties and (b) the relative homogeneity or heterogeneity of the dominant support base of parties.

The relevance of contending social groups in determining business influence is reflected in the differences in business attitude across the states. An important distinction that can be cited concerns business orientation towards labour flexibility and trade unions. Almost all the respondents in the chambers of commerce of West Bengal and Maharashtra approached questions of labour flexibility with emphasis on socio-economic security, often recognizing the adverse effect of liberalization of labour. Chatterjee, a member of the Employers Federation of India, eastern region, argued 'reforms are a social process that should aim at reducing social tensions'.[1] In contrast, the approach of business towards flexibility in Gujarat resembled the classic neo-liberal paradigm where faith appears to be on operation of market and its beneficial impact. Parekh, a senior consultant with CII in Gujarat, argued 'business logic has never been made subservient to politics in Gujarat and that is why Gujarat has fared so well after liberalisation'.[2]

[1] Personal communication with P.K. Chatterji, Bengal Chamber of Commerce and Industry, Business Representative to State Labour Advisory Board, 15 October 2009, Kolkata, India.

[2] Personal communication with S. Parekh, CII, Committee on Industries in Gujarat, 26 March 2010, Ahmedabad, India.

Most business leaders in Gujarat emphasized on the benefits of growth reflected through enlightened interaction between business and labour that resulted in very low confrontation.

The argument of partisan orientation in explaining subnational variation can be theoretically substantiated in India, as interest groups historically developed along pluralist lines and were often divided along nature of capital, regional concentration, and even caste. The post-Independence legacy of dirigisme meant that the influence of interest groups dependent on their capacity to influence parties in government and electoral outcomes (Sáez and Mahmood 2016). As such, the relevance of business within electoral support base for parties emerged as critical to determining its influence.

The conclusion stands in contrast to the conventional notion of variegated business influence across subnational states due to cultural differences. An extension of the cultural variation argument is the debate about nature of business class, specifically in terms of social origin. It is argued with some degree of veracity that regionally loyal bourgeoisie with ties to the political elites has been one of the conditions of economic development. Even in this case study, the emergence of agriculture-turned-industrial class in Gujarat and Andhra Pradesh with ties to political parties appears to facilitate industrial growth and pro-market reforms. In contrast, West Bengal, in particular, is affected because of non-emergence of an integrated and regionally orientated capitalist class (Banerjee 1998). The argument is stylistic and fails to explain the development of Maharashtra, which, like West Bengal, has been characterized by the dominance of non-Marathi capital. The difference between the two states remains in the extent of integration of business in politics.

Trade Unions

The analysis of political economy of labour market reforms remains incomplete without reference to trade unions. Everyday explanation of reform variation emphasizes on the strength of trade unions to describe the extent of labour market flexibility. I have argued and shown that trade unions do not offer a strong rationalization for reform variation and partisan support base provides a more robust explanation. The marginal space to the agency of labour or trade unions is due to two interrelated factors, namely the gradual relegation of trade unions in policymaking, especially politics of labour reform in India, and the dependence of trade union on government patronage for effective intervention, which in turn depends on partisan support base. The pivotal role of partisan government, in regulating the power of interest groups, is also relevant for trade unions. Consequently, under conditions of globalization trade unions are unable to prevent reforms when the government is pro reform or reform-oriented.

This section is devoted to an analysis of trade union movement and reforms to supplement and reinforce the arguments of the book regarding partisan orientation.

Trade Unions, Globalization, and Reforms

As a voluntary association of employees in industrial enterprises, trade unions pursue objectives embodying workers' interests. The literature on trade union shows a general consensus that trade unions have largely resisted labour market reforms under conditions of globalization that weaken their position. Unions, by the very logic of their existence, seek to protect and increase wages, work conditions, and social benefits for its constituents (Chatterjee 1980). Naturally, reforms that negatively affect established privileges of labour, such as work conditions and wages, elicit opposition from trade unions. Horton, Kanbur, and Mazumdar (1991), in their study of reforms in Latin America, found that strong trade unions impeded not only labour, but overall economic reforms. Garrett (1998b) and Downes, Gomez, and Gunderson (2004) have argued that trade unions use their collective status and significant voting power to prevent or extract compensation for reforms that have implications for wage, employment, and job security. Apart from direct collective mobilization, trade unions often make use of institutional framework, such as access to decision-making and legal prerogatives, to prevent labour market flexibility.

The empirical evidence of union response to labour reform, however, has been mixed. In some instances, firm-level unions have supported wage gains at the cost of employment, while in cases of corporatist arrangements labour unions had to accept austerity for broader macroeconomic gains (Anderson 2001). Whatever be the cause of acquiescence, in most countries, economic reforms have been accompanied by significant reorganization of the labour market marked by losses of real wages, rise in precarious employment, and decreasing implementation of labour rights (Tardanico and Menjívar 1997). Unions have been largely unsuccessful to impede reforms in the face of altered politico-economic context, especially competitive pressure for attracting investments, technological transformations, and shift towards market growth strategies (Gillan and Pokrant 2009; Miller 2005; Shyam Sundar 2005).

Since labour is a factor of production, the effect of globalization on labour is subject to specific structural–institutional context. Wage and employment are conditioned by not only through bargaining, but factors such as composition of domestic economy (restructuring process involves job loss with outsourcing, industrial demand shift, along with job creation with investment). The varieties of capitalism literature attributes differences in labour market, between the liberal market economies and the coordinated market economies, to institutional comparative advantage and coordination among businesses (Hall and Soskice 2001). Similarly, scholars like Rogowski (1987a) and Rodrik (2007) have repeatedly emphasized the role of regulations and institutions in determining socio-economic outcomes. Political factors such as strength of interest groups and the composition and preference of social groups have also featured as determinants of the labour market outcomes (Frieden and Rogowski 1996; Garrett 1998b). Therefore, the capacity of trade unions to influence the outcome of labour market and policy is related to the complex interplay of economic, institutional, and political factors in which both labour and capital are embedded.

In India, observers have pointed out that corroborating the global experience, liberalization has preceded emaciation of the organized sector and declining fortunes of trade unions (Banerjee 2005; Nagaraj 2007; Roychowdhury 2003). Two broad indicators of labour market flexibility, namely wage share and share of contractual workforce, reveal steady liberalization of the labour market and suggests that trade unions have been unable to protect existing privileges (Mahmood 2016). The increase in the rate of economic growth with inflow of investments after economic liberalization has not been accompanied by corresponding employment generation. According to Sharma (2006), there has been a steady slowdown in the rate of employment generation with liberalization, and employment generation declined from 2 per cent between 1961 and 1980 to around 1 per cent in between 1990 and 2000. Much of the new employment is in the informal sector and employment in organized sector has witnessed an absolute decline.

While scholars like Patnaik (2003) and Guha-Khasnobis and Kanbur (2006) attribute such a development (jobless growth) to the peculiar nature of neo-liberal capitalism, mainstream economists and policy-makers identify institutional constraints in encouraging job creation in formal sector. Besley and Burgess (2004) identify the institutional constraints, especially rigid labour regulations as the cause for existence of dual labour market and unemployment in India. Trade unions have often featured as a crucial interest group in preventing liberalization of the economy and legislative reforms (Papola 1994). Theoretically, the subnational variation in labour market flexibility may be linked to the strength of trade union movement in the states. The discussions in this section, however, reveal the non-correspondence between trade union movement and labour reforms in the selected states.

Trade Unionism and Labour Flexibility

Trade unions essentially function to overcome the weakness of individual labour in capitalist wage system through collective action. The unions gain power from their capacity to withdraw labour and prevent alternative allocation of labour by acting monopolistic. Hence, membership is the primary source of strength of a trade union. Union mobilization and action such as strikes provide important and complementary information about the strength of unions (Flanagan 1999). As trade unions are interest-aggregating organizations, an important determinant of a union's strength is the extent of fragmentation. Competition among trade unions for the representation of the same group of workers weakens the unions internally and intra-union coordination externally (Murillo 2001).

In India, the analysis of trade unions based on organizational strength is challenging due to the absence of reliable and comparable data (Bhattacherjee 1999). The abundance of unions in the liberal–pluralist framework with a flippant attitude to record keeping (the trade unions as well as the government) has meant that most scholars rely on data on industrial disputes, specifically strike and lockout data to evaluate trade unionism. The data on workdays lost due to strike and lockout provide some measure of relative strength of business and labour (Datt 2003). The choice of such a measurement is not only due to the availability of data, but also the recognition that strikes initiated by workers and lockouts declared by employers represent their respective capacity to extract economic costs.

Comparing strikes and lockouts in the subnational states to examine the strength of labour (vis-à-vis capital) reveals that militancy reflected through strikes have declined secularly across the states. In all states except West Bengal, workdays lost due to strikes and lockouts are comparable. Figures 4.3 to 4.6 show the share of workdays lost due to strikes and lockouts across the states with a standardized axis to allow comparisons.

In Andhra Pradesh, workdays lost due to strikes have declined since the mid-1980s and lockouts outweigh strikes after liberalization (Figure 4.3). Overall industrial disputes reveal a declining trend in the state. A similar trend can be noted in the case of Maharashtra where strikes declined severely around the same time (the end of the Bombay Textile Mills strike) and lockouts gained prominence (Figure 4.4).

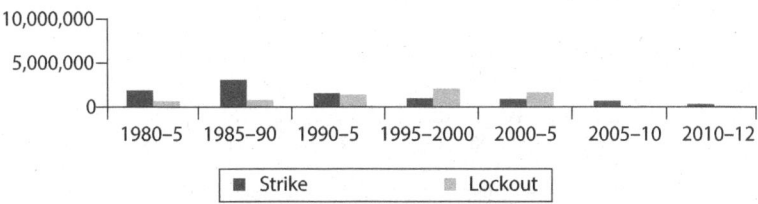

FIGURE 4.3 Aggregate Share of Workdays Lost Due to Strikes and Lockouts in Andhra Pradesh, 1980–2012
Source: Indian Labour Yearbook (various issues).

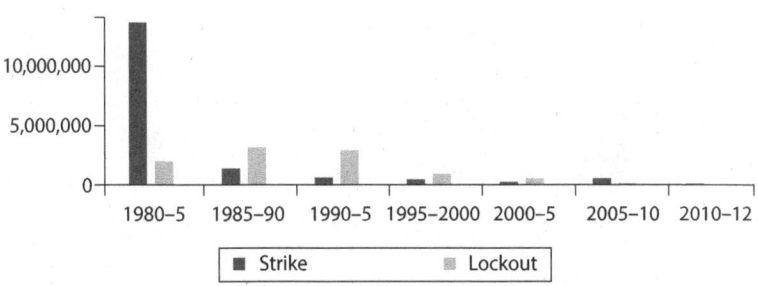

FIGURE 4.4 Aggregate Share of Workdays Lost Due to Strikes and Lockouts in Maharashtra, 1980–2012
Source: Indian Labour Yearbook (various issues).

In contrast to Maharashtra and Andhra Pradesh, the workdays lost due to strikes and lockout appear historically very low and equivalent in Gujarat (Figure 4.5). The state confirms to the image of peaceful industrial relations with minimum workdays loss and no significant difference between lockouts and strikes. The period since the mid-2000s is marked by no notable strikes or lockouts in the state.

The most interesting outcome is, however, in West Bengal, conventionally characterized as pro-labour state. Compared to other states, the workdays loss due to strike is higher in West Bengal (Figure 4.6). However, the share of workdays loss due to lockouts far outweighs strikes in West Bengal (except for a brief period in the 1980s).

The comparative estimation of union strength based on strikes and lockouts suggests that employers have gained ascendance since liberalization, indicating declining powers of trade unions (Datt 2003).

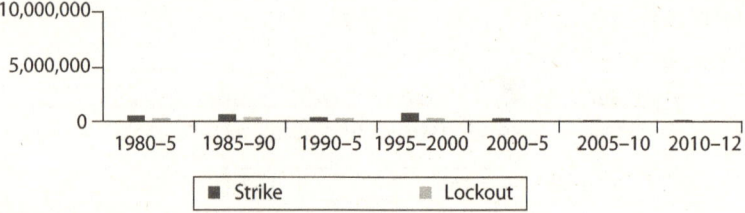

FIGURE 4.5   Aggregate Share of Workdays Lost Due to Strikes and Lockouts in Gujarat, 1980–2012
Source: Indian Labour Yearbook (various issues).

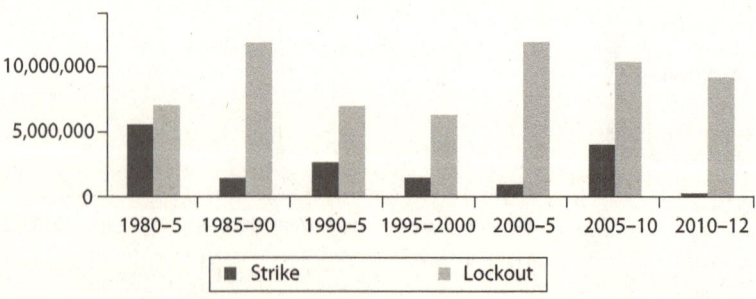

FIGURE 4.6   Aggregate Share of Workdays Lost Due to Strikes and Lockouts in West Bengal, 1980–2012
Source: Indian Labour Statistics (various issues).

Thus, the argument of strong trade unions counteracting the interests of business in the labour market does not appear convincing. In terms of union mobilization (strike), West Bengal is the highest but so is employer mobilization (lockout). Trade union mobilization in the state can be hierarchically arranged in the following order: West Bengal, Andhra Pradesh, Maharashtra, and Gujarat.

This comparative arrangement of trade unions is also reflected in trade union density measures. Trade union density is the measure of the number of trade unions normalized by the number of industrial units in the state. Trade union density is an alternate measure to strikes and lockouts, which have their inherent limitations. Strikes and lockouts are not only the reflection of relative power of capital and labour, but also the overall economic situation. Lockouts can be the outcome of employer assertion as well as deteriorating viability of industry. Similarly, a strike can be the assertion of organized labour or a purely political gesture. Trade union density, with limitations, can provide the comparative incidence of trade unions in the industrial sector and the likelihood of collective action.

Figure 4.7 shows the high presence of trade unions in the industrial sector of West Bengal, although the period since the late 1990s reveals a declining trend. Among the other states, union density is comparatively higher in Andhra Pradesh followed by Maharashtra, and both show an increasing trend since the 1990s. Gujarat has the lowest levels of union density, indicating a weak trade union presence. Although the measure of union density is at best indicative due to the limitations in data on number of trade unions it corroborates the classification of union strength in the states.

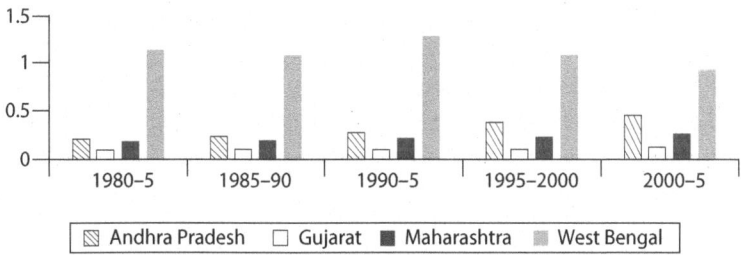

FIGURE 4.7   Average Density of Trade Unions across the States, 1980–2005
Source: Authors calculation based on *Indian Labour Yearbook* (various issues).
Note: Trade Union Density = number of registered trade unions in the state/ number of firms under Factories Act.

The strength of trade unions, like any other interest group, cannot be properly evaluated simply through workdays lost or union presence. Unions derive their strength from their ability to act as the monopoly supplier of labour in the firm.[3] As such, mobilization during collective action can provide some indication of union power. Considered over a long period of time, such a measure can accommodate state-specific variables such as nature of industrial relations and condition of industries. Consequently, we consider the average strike participation of workers across the states over the period as a measure of relative strength of unions (Figure 4.8).

Figure 4.8 reveals some interesting dimensions of trade unionism across the states. Overall, there has been a steady decline of worker participation in strikes across the states (except in Maharashtra and West Bengal for the period 2005–10). Gujarat clearly has the lowest worker participation in industrial action, which also corroborates the low rates of unionization in the state. Interestingly, during the period 1980–90, Andhra Pradesh has the highest worker participation in industrial action (40–50 per cent), which, however, declined remarkably after liberalization. West Bengal has a relatively high (20–30 per cent) worker

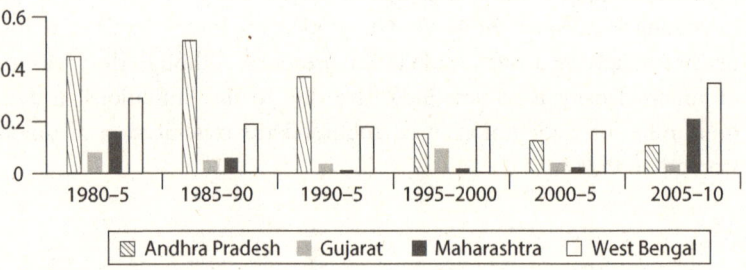

FIGURE 4.8   State-wise Average Worker Participation in Strikes, 1980–2010
Source: Author's calculations based on *Indian Labour Yearbook* (various issues).
Note: Average strike participation = Total workers participating in strikes/Average daily employment in industries.

---

[3] The trade union's strength depends on the power to prevent employers from employing outside workers during strikes and ensuring workers close ranks during strikes. In case trade unions cannot perform these tasks, their power is undermined significantly.

participation across the period with some increasing trends in the recent period. This increasing trend is also noted in Maharashtra and recent strike participation rates mirror the rates of the early 1980s when the state witnessed widespread mill strikes.

Combining the measures of strikes–lockouts, union density, and strike participation rates across the states suggests that unions are strongest in West Bengal and weakest in Gujarat. The condition of unions in Maharashtra and Andhra Pradesh can be labelled as intermediate between the two extremes. The presence of trade unions and strikes is greater in Andhra Pradesh compared to Maharashtra. The comparative evaluation of trade unions, however, does not correspond to the aggregate labour market situation. The effectiveness of labour in impeding flexibility appears lower in Andhra Pradesh compared to Maharashtra despite higher mobilization.

Institutional Dynamics and Trade Unionism

A possible argument for the disproportionate strength of trade unions in Maharashtra compared to Andhra Pradesh may be due to the economic–institutional context. Evaluation of trade unionism across the world shows that economic conditions and relevant institutional framework such as participation in decision-making, ownership structure of firms, and legal rights significantly determine union strength (Paczynska 2006).

Trade union power is intrinsically connected to the prevalent economic condition and unions are found to be more assertive during periods of boom (Kume 1998). Such an understanding does not consider trade unions as exogenous but rather endogenous to the economy, conditioned by the arrangement of production (Kume 1998; Miyamura 2011). The impact of economic structure on a trade union's power can be narrowed down to the industry structure in terms of ownership of firms, nature of industry, and product market. Given the carefully selected cases, factors like nature of industry are highly similar across the paired set of states, rendering their impact, if any, largely similar. The only distinguishing feature of the states considered is the share of public sector enterprises in the economy.

There is empirical evidence that trade unions are more powerful in the public sector compared to the private sector. Public sector enterprises are generally considered model employers with extensive legal and procedural rights for the workforce along with a distinct social responsibility. Heller and Tait (1984) point out in developing economies the impact of trade union largely operates through the public sector and government decision on wages are likely to affect 15–40 per cent of the employed workers in the urban labour market having a pervasive 'leverage effect' on domestic unit wage cost. Forteza and Rama (2006) have argued that the size of the public sector has relation to the strength of unions due to electoral considerations of the government. It can be presumed that greater proportion of employment in the public sector not only implies greater capacity of governments to influence economic outcomes like wage and production, but also increases the power of labour to influence outcomes.

In terms of overall employment, private employment is lowest in the state of Andhra Pradesh (around 30 per cent as a proportion of total employment), and highest in Gujarat, reaching nearly 60 per cent of the total employment in that state for the period 2000–10. In the factory sector (manufacturing industries), the share of private employment is highest in Gujarat reaching around 90 per cent, while West Bengal has the lowest employment at around 68 per cent in the post-2000 period. Clearly, public sector employment as a cause of trade union strength does not correspond to the situation in the states, especially in the case of Andhra Pradesh and Maharashtra.

Another potential factor affecting the strength of trade unions that is subsumed under the nature of industry is the nature of bargaining. The literature on collective bargaining suggests that firm-level bargaining and corporatist unions generate weak pressure, compared to sector- or industry-level bargaining (Anderson 2001). As such, differences in the levels of union bargaining may lead to variations in a trade union's strength across the subnational states. The state with historical–institutional preponderance of industry-level bargaining may be characterized by stronger and more aggressive trade unions.

At an aggregate level, the data on collective bargaining across the states does not exist. As such, we take recourse to secondary literature, specifically the micro case studies to categorize the dominant modes of bargaining in the states. An important literature Bhattacherjee (1999) provides an interesting insight into the nature of collective bargaining in India. Analysing trade unionism in the states of West Bengal and

Maharashtra, he shows that firm-level bargaining is more prevalent in high-skilled industries marked by independent trade unions. In contrast, industry-level bargaining characterizes traditional and declining industries dominated by political trade unions. The underlying reason is the diverging incentives in the wage–employment trade-off for trade unions. In industrially dynamic regions, trade unions opt for wage increase, while in stagnant regions unions prefer employment over wage. In the former, there is a strong incentive for unions to seek company-based 'rents' rather than political rents that are more attractive in less industrially dynamic regions (Miyamura 2011). Company-based unions are confined within firms without explicit political agenda and perceive themselves as a professional organization.

The data on industrial growth reveals that economies of Gujarat, Maharashtra, and Andhra Pradesh are comparatively more dynamic than West Bengal. Micro-level study of trade unionism in the states corroborates greater prevalence of company-based trade unions in Gujarat, Maharashtra, and Andhra Pradesh (Davala 1992). As such, the impact of level of bargaining should be relevant for West Bengal but marginal for the other states. In fact, the presence of company-based unions should be greater in Maharashtra compared to Andhra Pradesh, simply due to the size and nature of its industrial economy. Further, the influence on trade union bargaining is marginal given the limited presence of trade unions.

The incongruence between institutional framework and a trade union's strength also extends to the regulatory framework. As discussed in the section titled 'Legal Amendments' in Chapter 2, legislative amendments in West Bengal substantiate the conventional classification of West Bengal as a regulated labour market with most number of pro-labour amendments and not a single pro-employer amendment. Andhra Pradesh is next in terms of pro-labour amendments, but unlike West Bengal, it has some pro-employer amendments, which occur after economic liberalization. Gujarat has the least number of amendments in labour laws, but the direction of such amendment has been explicitly pro employer. In Maharashtra, the extent of amendments reveals some sort of balance between pro-labour and pro-employer amendments.[4]

[4] See Table 2.11 in Chapter 2.

The preceding discussion on the organizational, structural, and institutional dimensions of the trade union movement across the states underlines the non-correspondence between trade unionism and labour market flexibility. As the discussion suggests, trade union movement can be hierarchically arranged in terms of relative strength with West Bengal as the strongest, followed by Andhra Pradesh, Maharashtra, and lastly Gujarat as the weakest. The condition of the labour flexibility in the states, however, does not tally with such an arrangement of states. Particularly, Andhra Pradesh with higher share of public sector and legal protection for labour is marked by greater flexibility compared to Maharashtra.

Political Dynamics and Unionism

The limitation of the organizational, structural, and institutional dimensions of unionism to account for labour condition in the states indicates the marginalization of trade unions in the politics of reform. As the discussion in the previous chapters reveals, the extent of labour market flexibility can be explained thorough partisan support base and the presence of business in the partisan base. Intuitively, greater presence of business in partisan base should imply less representation to labour and trade unions.

This section considers the relation between labour and partisan governments to explain the variation in extent of labour reforms. Such an analysis substantiates the argument of partisan politics with reference to business representation.

The literature on trade union highlights the role of political competition and loyalties to government in affecting a trade union's strength and response. Based on comparative study of Latin America, Murillo (2001) has argued that the political relation between government and trade union facilitates cooperation, whereas political competition for trade union control provides incentives for militancy. The relation is particularly relevant for India due to the historical–institutional legacy of state intervention in industrial relations institutionalized through an elaborate system of control, creation of large public sector enterprises, and decision-making prerogative of the state. The state sought to control industrial disputes through development of pluralist–corporatist industrial relations and complex legal system (Bhattacherjee 1999).

Such developments ensured that the labour movement relied more on political negotiations and patronage than mobilization and bipartite bargaining. As Rudolph and Rudolph (1987) have argued, industrial relation in India was characterized by state domination and 'involuted pluralism' where the trade union's movement proliferated massively along territorial, horizontal, and vertical partisan lines, but was marked by decline or loss of vigour. Even though a decline in the state intervention in industrial relations can be noted under conditions of globalization, historical institutional developments ensure continued relevance of wider politics in industrial relations. Thus political–ideological context of trade unionism across the states offers a better explanation of a trade union's role in labour reforms.

The power of trade unions remains significantly regulated by their linkages to the government and more specifically to the political party in government. Contemporary literature on party–union relation highlights the growing distance between unions and government after liberalization (Bhattacherjee 1999; Uba 2008). As governments across the states increasingly adopted neo-liberal policies, the linkage between party and affiliated trade unions has come under strain. Based on a study of labour protests across subnational states of India, Uba (2008) has argued that all parties that were long identified with a labour-friendly, left-of-centre, predominantly statist position, initiated market reforms at their respective levels indicating certain convergence on the issue of labour rationalization regardless of their ideological orientation. This changing orientation of political parties, especially when in government, has been an important variable in determining the relative importance of trade unionism and labour policy.

To interrogate the relation between the government and trade unions, this section looks at two variables, specifically the presence of trade unionist within leadership of political parties and the disputes in public sector firms. Theoretically, greater representation of trade unionist within parties would not only increase the access of labour to political decision-makers, but also provide greater support for a trade union movement. Industrial dispute in public sector, on the other hand, would indicate the gap between government and labour. Following the methodology outlined in the analysis of partisan support base, the section looks at the proportion of trade unionists elected as MP from the selected states during the period 1980–2009 (Figure 4.9).

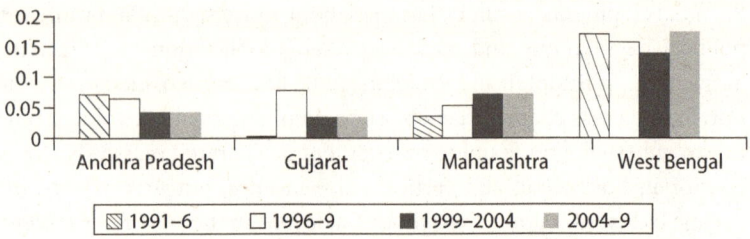

FIGURE 4.9   State-wise Share of Trade Unionists Elected to the Parliament,
1981–2008
Source: Author's calculation based on *Who's Who* (the Lok Sabha Secretariat).

A cursory glance of the share of elected trade union representatives across the states reveals some association with the general trend of flexibility. The least flexible is West Bengal, marked by significant presence of trade unionists, and the most flexible is Gujarat, which has marginal presence of unionists. Maharashtra represents increasing representation of trade unionists, whereas in Andhra Pradesh, trade union representation has declined since liberalization. As such, it may be argued that the strength of a trade union in impeding flexibility has some correspondence to the presence of trade unions in the dominant support base.

The linkage between trade unions and the government can also be analysed through data on public sector disputes. In public sector, the government is the direct employer and greater disputes would indicate a rift between government and trade unions. Public sector reorganization and deregulation have been important issues of contention between reformist governments and trade unions. Scholars like Venkataratnam (1993) and Venkataratnam and Verma (1997) have pointed out that prior to liberalization, industrial conflicts occurred mainly in the private sector but since the 1990s, industrial disputes in public sectors have increased significantly due to reform orientation of governments. Intuitively, the variation in reform orientation of governments (measured by public sector disputes) should have some correspondence to subnational labour market flexibility. In the context of selected cases, especially Andhra Pradesh and Maharashtra, public sector industrial dispute should be greater in the former compared to the latter.

Figure 4.10 provides important indications about the dynamics between partisan governments and trade union across the subnational

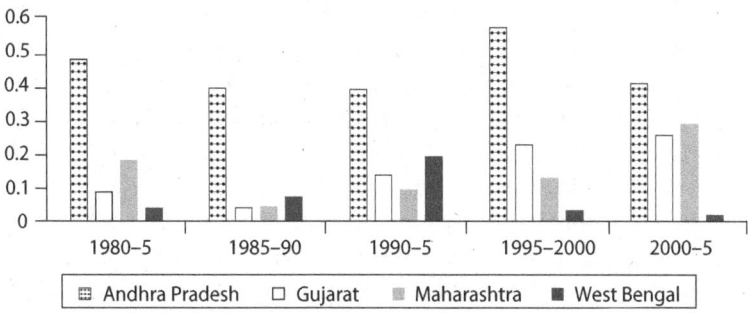

FIGURE **4.10**   State-wise Proportion of Workdays Lost in Public Sector
Disputes, 1980–2005
Source: Indian Labour Yearbook (various issues).

states. The extent of public sector workdays lost reveals an increasing
trend across the states, reflecting the growing tension between trade
unions and government. The most remarkable outcome is the high
level of dispute in public sector in Andhra Pradesh accounting for
three-quarters of total workdays lost since the 1980s. This indicates a
deep schism between trade unions and government, leading to direct
conflict and it rationalizes the high levels of flexibility despite significant
levels of unionization in the state. The literature on subnational reform
supports the leading position of Andhra Pradesh in public sector reform
which has been vigorously but unsuccessfully opposed by organized
labour (Mooij 2005).

Confirming expectation, the extent of public sector dispute is significantly lower in Maharashtra compared to Andhra Pradesh. The
number of workdays lost in public sector reveals an upward trend since
economic liberalization in the state. Public sector dispute is lowest in
West Bengal among the states which can be attributed to the ideological and political congruence between Left government and the trade
unions. Interestingly, the dispute in public sector of Gujarat also exhibits an upward trend since liberalization, despite the inherent weakness
of trade union movements in the state. The analysis of linkage between
the government and the trade unions suggests that trade unions have
greater leverage in influencing policies in the state of West Bengal and
least in Andhra Pradesh. In Maharashtra, increasing government–trade
union difference can be argued to limit the influence of trade unions
although to a much lesser extent than Andhra Pradesh.

Overall, the analysis of trade union movement reveals that, in terms of organizational strength and mobilization, labour is strongest in West Bengal and weakest in Gujarat. The extent of unionism is higher in Andhra Pradesh compared to Maharashtra. However, a stronger trade union movement in Andhra Pradesh has to confront a more reformist government which accounts for greater labour flexibility. The declining presence of labour in the partisan support base is unable to counter the reformist orientation of the government. In Maharashtra, the reform orientation of government is not only perceptibly lower (public sector dispute) but trade unions have greater presence in wider politics. As such, trade unions in Maharashtra are more effective, in comparison to Andhra Pradesh, in influencing labour market policies and outcome.

Interest Groups, Partisan Government, and Reform

The preceding discussion on the role of business and trade unions in affecting labour market reforms adequately demonstrates that relation to the government significantly shapes the power of interest groups. The relevance and ability of interest groups to influence policy are conditioned by their interaction with the partisan government. This brings us back to the argument in Chapter 3 about the nature of support base and representation of economic interests within parties as critical to shaping labour market policies and outcomes. In a sense, the ability of interest groups to affect policy and outcome is significantly predisposed by their political manifestation within governing parties. Thus, partisan government provides a more credible explanation for reform variation contrary to the interest groups explanations for variation in reforms.

5

Party System

Partisanship, Interest Groups, and Politics

The discussion to this point presents the variations in labour flexibility across the states as an outcome of partisan governments, specifically the socio-economic support bases of parties (caste/class composition). The nature of support base determines not only the developmental orientation of governments, but also shapes interest group–government interrelation. Parties with representation of business caste/class and a relatively homogenous support base undertake greater labour reforms when in government compared to parties with a heterogeneous support base or marginal business representation. This is due to the logic of intra-party compromises and party–interest group interrelation. When the support base of the party is wide and heterogeneous, the party has to accommodate contending and contradictory pressures from the diverse support base. Such a support base also provides greater opportunity to interest groups for accessing policymakers.

Maharashtra is an example where business interests have to be negotiated with contradictory pressures emanating from a wide and heterogeneous support base of regimes. Contrary to such a situation are Gujarat and Andhra Pradesh, where the domination of business caste/class in politics (political parties) and the relatively homogenous support base ensures fulfilment of business interests in the form of greater labour market reforms. In West Bengal, the absence of business in politics and the homogeneous support base of a radicalized middle class and the poor has meant non-incorporation of business interests in politics.

The argument of domination of a support base and partisan government, however, requires several contextual appraisals. Political parties, social groups, interest groups, and even individuals function in an environment inhabited by other contending forces. As such, their interests and responses are influenced by the wider context of politics. In democracies, this wider political context is provided by the party system. Naturally, an argument of partisan government and political dynamics requires some discussion on the prevalent party system.

The choice of policy alternatives, for governments, is conditioned or constrained by the political system, more specifically the party system. The number and the nature of parties in a polity determine the political opportunities for furtherance of interest groups agenda, representation of socio-economic groups, type of political discourse, and other factors. As Sartori (2005) points out, the party system reflects the dominant social cleavages and political discourse in a society. In the context of policy choice, the party system acts as an intermediate variable influencing the behaviour of interest groups and political parties. There is evidence that partisanship, that is, support for a particular party is conditioned by the political alternatives available both in terms of electoral as well as ideological choice (Budge, Crewe, and Farlie 1976). The importance of a party system is further augmented in the politico-economic analysis due to the supposedly negative relation between fragmentation in the party system and policy reform (Tsebelis 2002).

As the detailed case study reveals, the party system has a bearing on labour market reforms, as an endogenous variable, by shaping partisan support bases, and influencing partisan–ideological competition and the instrumental interest of parties. The operation of the party system in certain situations facilitate the formation of homogenous and heterogeneous support bases that have consequences for the reform orientation of governments. The findings also challenge the conventional relation of the party system and reform that highlight fragmentation in party system as an impediment to reform. In the context of the selected states, political fragmentation and labour market reforms proceed simultaneously, suggesting a more nuanced interrelation between party fragmentation and reform.

Party System and Public Policy

Any policy reform is the outcome of a government's response to issues and situations, articulation of interest groups, and ideological and instrumental interests of parties. The party system provides the political context for all policy decisions. As Chhibber (2001) argues, parties operate within a dynamic environment and choices are significantly shaped by the available political and policy alternatives in an institutional and historical setting. The choice of policy by a government is the outcome of the interaction between ideological and instrumental objectives of the party, in a context characterized by the existence of oppositional parties. Chhibber (1995: 77) points out that short-term electoral incentives of political parties are important considerations in policy choice. As such, the nature and operation of the party system need to be incorporated in any analysis of policy reform. An inherent limitation of many rational actor analyses, including that of party behaviour, stems from the static view of actors, whereas the reality is dynamic (Chhibber 1995). The interaction between intrinsic utility of agents and a complex changing environment need to be considered in analysis to arrive at inferences (Chai 2001: 14–15).

The party system refers to the system of interactions resulting from inter-party competition (Sartori 2005). Intuitively, inter-party competition includes primarily two dimensions, namely the number of parties and the nature of parties, that characterize a party system. Consequently, the classification of party system has been along two dimensions, namely, number of parties and ideological distinction. The evaluation of number of parties has generally proceeded along enumeration of parties in electoral competition. However, enumeration of parties in a party system must go beyond simple description of number of parties, as many registered political parties, although officially in existence, have little influence on electoral outcomes, public opinion, or policy due to their limited or marginal support. A simple enumeration of parties can often be misleading, especially in a multiparty system with a low cost of party registration, as parties without popular support (consequently impact) may be included in the analysis. To remedy the issue, parties have been increasingly measured on the basis of percentage of votes received and proportion of seats in the legislature, which is labelled as effective number of parties.[1] To account for the ideological distance, parties are generally placed along a left–right continuum according to the ideological position.

The literature on party system and policymaking highlights a number of characteristics that influence policy choice. There is a body of literature that emphasizes on the institutional features of the party system, such as electoral rules and nature of the political system (unitary or federal), which determine social and economic policies (Rogowski 1987b). This study, however, does not focus on institutional dimensions of the party system as they are similar in the context of subnational states. Rather, it focuses on the other dimensions of the party system, specifically the party institutionalization, the scope of party operation (national or regional), party competition, and extent of fragmentation, as variables with implications for policy choice.

Party institutionalization refers to the stability of the party system with regard to the presence of stable and coherent parties. An institutionalized party system is marked by the presence of programmatic political parties with coherent policy orientation. In such a system, parties perform aggregative and mobilization functions and have high levels of legitimacy. In contrast, weakly institutionalized party systems are marked by non-programmatic or personality-based parties with short-term populist policy proposals. According to Mainwaring (1998), the level of institutionalization is a critical dimension for understanding party systems. The extent of institutionalization is determined by internal party organization, stability of inter-party competition, strength of party roots in society or support base, and legitimacy of parties and elections.

In an institutionalized party system, policy orientation of competing parties is relatively stable and consistent due to the ideological and

---

[1] Effective number of parties recalculates the number of parties based on their vote percentage and share of seats in the legislature (Laakso and Taagepera 1979). The number of parties equals the effective number of parties only when all parties have equal strength. In any other case, the effective number of parties is lower than the actual number of parties.

instrumental stability of parties. On the other hand, in a weakly institutionalized system, policy stability is relatively weak due to weaknesses of political parties. Consequently, under weak party institutionalization, voters and interest groups have curtailed expectation from parties, with lower policy stability and consistency.

The scope of party operation, which is understood as the extent of party presence, has important implications for policymaking, as regional parties are likely to have a limited political agenda focusing on the specific region, while national parties would have a wider agenda. A party system dominated by national parties will be characterized by a greater emphasis on the national agenda both among voters and parties. However, if regional political parties dominate, local and subnational issues are likely to dominate the political discourse.

The extent of ideological polarization and number of competing parties are the most consequential determinants of policy choice. The literature on the relation between the party system and socio-economic reforms suggests that fragmentation in the party system prevents alteration in socio-economic policies or reforms by creating a large number of decision-makers and making consensus elusive (Tsebelis 2002). Emphasizing on the extent of party competition, it is argued that as a party system becomes fragmented, economic reforms become challenging as an increasing number of decision-makers creates policy stalemate (Haggard and Kaufman 1995; Roubini and Sachs 1989).

Like numerical fragmentation, the ideological polarity is an important determinant of policy reform, as policy changes are most likely under conditions of low levels of ideological polarization among the principal parties. Based on the study of post-communist societies, Horowitz and Browne (2008) have shown that strong far-Left parties and identity-based far-Right parties have inhibiting effects on policy reform. The extent of ideological polarity between parties acts as an important determinant of policymaking in democracies, and governments are able to effectively implement policies on which there exist low levels of difference.

The impact of party system on policy reform is not a one-way road and just as party system exerts influence on policymaking, adoption of policies or policy reforms have consequences for party system and politics. Although this book confines itself to one dimension, that is, the impact of politics on policy (labour reforms), it is important to remember the dynamic two-way relationship between politics and reforms. In this context, it is imperative to mention Nayyar (1998) who highlights three broad effects of reform on politics in India. He argues that implementation of economic reforms has led to restructuring or creation of several political institutions. These new institutional structures transform the nature of citizen–government interaction, enabling them to negotiate, bargain, and control. Such developments have emaciated political parties and interest groups that dominated the role of interest aggregation and articulation.

Second, economic reforms have created a new political culture. At one level, economic reform has led to the generation of a climate of competition aided by the exposure to the international market. At another level, the process has led to the resurgence of regional or local cultural issues as national identities gave way to regional or local identities.

Finally, economic reform has influenced the process of political mobilization. In an earlier era of populism, the promise of economic incentives was widely used to arouse the masses during the election. In the age of 'limited' state[2] and fiscal austerity, political parties use sentimental issues of caste, religion, or language in electoral campaigns compared to populist economic issues.

The discussion suggests that party system has important implications for policy reform that needs to be incorporated in policy or reform analysis. The nature of political competition can provide an opportunity for generating demands as well as constraining social demands depending on specific ideological and political dynamics.

Party System in Indian States

The politico-electoral system adopted in India after Independence was based on the Westminster model of single member plurality electoral system in a constitutionally arranged federal framework. Discussions on party system in India invariably begin with the INC, which was the predominant political association during the independence movement and the foremost political party after Independence. In the period between 1952 and 1967, the Congress won over two-thirds majorities

---

[2] A 'limited' or constricted state refers to a state under conditions of globalization as the state cedes functions to the market.

in Parliament and the state legislative elections based on a plurality of votes (44–48 per cent) against a fragmented opposition. The only exception was subnational states of Nagaland, Kerala, and Jammu and Kashmir (Hasan 2002; Yadav and Palshikar 2006).

The dominance of the Congress party during this period led Kothari (1964) to term the Indian party system as the Congress system, characterized by a weak multiparty opposition and a strong dominant party. The preeminent position and the catchall nature of the Congress was possible due to the legacy of the independence movement (Congress being the main party that led the freedom struggle), heterogeneities in the Indian society at the local level in terms of caste, class, region, language that prevented polarization (no group was large enough to dominate over others and all social groups sought association with the Congress party), the organizational and leadership skills, and an elaborate patronage network to build vote banks across communities (Frankel 2005; Manor 2002).

The party system in the states also reflected a similar trajectory with the Congress's dominance and fragmented multiparty opposition. However, an important divergence, despite a uniform Congress dominance, was the nature of the opposition in the states. In Andhra Pradesh, until 1972, the communist party was the principal opposition, winning 51 seats and 19.5 per cent votes in the 1962 elections. There was also some presence of the Socialist Party and economically rightist Swatantra Party. In West Bengal, similar to Andhra Pradesh, the Communist Party emerged as the main opposition during this period with the Forward Block and the Janata Party as minor oppositions.

In Gujarat, the economically rightist Swatantra Party emerged as the main opposition in the 1962 and 1967 elections with 24.4 per cent and 38.2 per cent votes, respectively. In this discussion, Maharashtra presents the most interesting case, as the principal opposition party altered every election. For example, in 1957 the Janata Party emerged as the principal opposition with 36 seats but in 1962 elections the Peasant and Workers Party emerged as the main opposition with 15 seats. Thus, Maharashtra was characterized by a more fragmented opposition compared to other states (Election Commission of India [ECI] various issues).

The Congress's hegemony was broken in 1967 when opposition parties dislodged it in eight of the 16 subnational states. This period witnessed the rise of bipolarization of the state party system where single but different opposition parties tended to dominate non-Congress votes. In West Bengal, the first non-Congress government was formed when the Bangla Congress, a breakaway section of the Congress, and the Left parties formed the United Front. In 1977, the Left Front, a coalition of Left parties, came to office in West Bengal as the Congress was relegated to the third position. Since 1977, the Left Front, constituted by the CPI(M), the CPI, the Forward Block, and the Revolutionary Socialist Party (RSP) formed seven consecutive governments with nearly 50 per cent vote share. In 2011, the Left Front lost the election to an alliance of the AITC and the Congress party.

In Andhra Pradesh, there was a gradual polarization of opposition parties and, in the 1978 elections, the Janata Party emerged as the principal opposition with 28.9 per cent of the votes possibly due to the merger of the Swatantra Party, the Jana Sangh, the socialists, and others. Interestingly, the prominence of the Left in the state underwent a secular decline from a high of 51 seats in 1962 to 14 seats in 1978 (CPI and CPI(M)). The party system underwent a transformation in the state when the newly formed TDP swept the elections and came to power in, the state in 1983.

In Gujarat, the first non-Congress government was formed in 1975 through a coalition of the Congress (O),[3] the Bharatiya Jana Sangh, the Samyukta Socialist Party, and the Swatantra Party (ECI various issues). However, Congress returned to office in Gujarat and Maharashtra in the elections of 1980 and 1985, with massive majorities.

Analysing the fragmentation of party system and the rise of oppositional parties, observers like Hasan (2002) have ascribed splits in the Congress, increasing inability of the Congress to mediate the cleavages of a heterogeneous society, and a marked tendency towards centralization as responsible for the fragmentation. Sridharan (2002), however, associates increasing regionalization of party politics to structural

[3] Congress (O) stood for Congress (Organization). This was a contending group after the split of the Indian National Congress in 1969 after Indira Gandhi, the then prime minister of India, was expelled from the Congress party for violating the party discipline. The party split with Indira Gandhi setting up a rival organization, which came to be known as Congress (R). The Indian National Congress (Organization) was also referred to as the Syndicate (Chandra, Mukherjee, and Mukherjee 2000: 236).

factors, namely the systemic properties of the first-past-the-post electoral system operating in a federal polity. He argues that the federal polity increases the political attractiveness for a party to be in power at the state level and as such opposition emerged at the subnational level when national and state elections were separated. Such an argument, although attractive, cannot eclipse the political dynamics of growing disenchantment of the people with failures of the Congress government, which sympathetic commentator Manor (2002) calls 'failure in governance' as the principle cause of such fragmentation. The exceptional post-Emergency election of 1977 witnessed the first non-Congress government when a temporarily united opposition under the banner of the Janata Party formed the government. By the end of the 1980s, the decline of the Congress system had been complete in essence as well as appearance, and the Indian party system represented multiple bipolarities with two-party competition at the state level with various parties, which aggregated to constitute the party system at the centre (Yadav 2006).

The period since the mid-1980s witnessed several independent but simultaneous trajectories in the party system: First, the period was marked by increased electoral competition and participation. According to Yadav (1996: 102–3), this period marked the assertion of Dalit identity politics. Second, there was a shift of level of politics from all India to the states. Such a development was complemented by the rise in the number of parties based on regional, ethnic, and ascriptive appeals. The rise of regional parties and the shift of level of politics were mutually reinforcing developments as the prevalence of regional parties prevented the growth of national parties (Sáez 2002).

The period since the 1980s, has been marked by a dual political system with continued bipolarization of party system at the subnational level and multiparty system and coalition politics at the centre (De Souza 2006; Sridharan 2002). The bipolar political competition at the state level represents specific regional political dynamics. In Andhra Pradesh, the emergence of the TDP ensured a stable two-party competition between the Congress and the regional TDP. Like Andhra Pradesh, Gujarat has moved towards two-party competitions but between the national parties, that is, BJP and Congress.

The political competition in Maharashtra and West Bengal took the shape of bipolar competition, not between two parties but rather two stable coalitions largely homogenous in terms of agenda and outlook.

In Maharashtra, the 1990s witnessed the rise of the Shiv Sena as an electorally significant political force and the BJP–Shiv Sena coalition came to power in 1995 with a vote share of 29.2 per cent. In the 1999 elections, the state saw the rise of the NCP after a split in the Congress, and the Congress–NCP alliance formed the government. The Congress–NCP alliance continued in office with the BJP–Shiv Sena alliance as the principal opposition until 2014. In West Bengal, the Congress party also underwent a split, leading to the formation the AITC, which emerged as the principal opposition to the Left Front, relegating the Congress to the third position. The AITC, under a maverick leader, Mamata Banerjee, dislodged the Left Front government in 2011 after 34 years of uninterrupted rule.

The party system in the states represents either a two-party competition or bipolar competition. The fragmentation and transformation in the party system were also contributed by profound socio-economic changes that marked Indian polity since the mid-1980s. According to Heath and Yadav (1999), politics in the post-liberalization period has been characterized by four distinctive features: First, there is a participatory upsurge among the hitherto marginalized sections of society. Second, there is an influx of lower-order beliefs, vocabularies, and homespun ideologies in the discursive practice of democracy. Third, the contest for manufacturing electoral majorities has resulted in a redefinition of caste identities at a macro plane. Fourth, the states have emerged as the relevant unit for party and social identity choice.

Party System and Labour Reforms

The complex multilayered relation between the party system and policy becomes relevant from the earlier discussion. The task of decoding the relation is, however, simplified by the research design of comparison of 'most alike' subnational states. As the subnational states share institutional similarities, this section focuses on party system characteristics that vary across the states. Features of the party system like electoral rules, nature of the political system, extent of institutionalization, and scope of operation are not considered in the analysis due to their similarity across the selected cases. As mentioned previously, all the selected states are characterized by a stable two-party or bipolar competition, and parties have some programmatic coherence despite the variations in origin. The analysis of partisan support base in Chapter 4 adequately displays the institutionalized party system based on a stable support base and programmes.

The scope of party operation in the states reveals that in all the states, national parties are present either in government or as the principal opposition. The determination of national and regional party follows the categorization of the ECI, which classifies parties as regional or national (the INC, the BJP, the CPI(M), the Bahujan Samaj Party [BSP], the CPI, and the NCP) on the basis of percentage of seats in the Lok Sabha and vote shares.

In Andhra Pradesh, the main political parties are the regional TDP and the INC. In West Bengal, the competition is also between regional and national parties, albeit in the form of coalitions. The Left Front, dominated by the CPI(M) and the AITC,[4] constitutes the contending party in the state. In Maharashtra and Gujarat, the party system is somewhat similar to national parties, that is, Congress and BJP, as the major political actors. In Maharashtra, however, the two national parties are in coalition with regional parties, namely NCP (a breakaway faction of the Congress) and Shiv Sena (a right-wing regional political outfit).

Theoretically, the role of the scope of party as a variable that influences reforms should be quite limited. The dominant view on the party system in India contends that since the 1990s, states have emerged as the relevant unit for party organization. Even national parties in India have regional character and the diverse nature of social mobilization has led to the creation of diverse regional political parties across regions (Sridharan 2002; Yadav 1996). As such, the impact of the scope of parties on policy reform can be theoretically argued to be marginal.

Significant variation in the party system across the subnational states, however, can be noted in the extent of party competition and party fragmentation. To conceptualize the extent of fragmentation and competition in party system, I borrow the concept of the effective number of parties from Laakso and Taagepera (1979). The effective number of parties measures parties by the number of seats in the state assembly and votes received in a given election. The quantification is based on the least

---

[4] The AITC is a regional party, presently in power in the state. It is a breakaway faction of the Congress, which was the principal opposition to the Left Front till 2001.

arbitrary method of treating vote share or seat share of parties by their own weight and adding such weighted measures to arrive at a composite number. In short, the effective number of parties gives us a quantification of political parties that have significance for government formation or electoral competition. The data on effective number of parties is derived from Sáez and Sinha (2010) who discuss the impact of political cycles on public sector expenditure in the subnational states of India.

To analyse the ideological distinction in the party system, I consider the share of Left party vote in the state assembly elections. It is difficult to capture ideological polarity in the party system across India due to the absence of a clear left/right ideological position of most political parties. As discussed in the previous section, divergence in economic policy, especially labour policy, is essentially non-existent among the non-Left parties. The political parties with an explicit position on labour reform are the communist parties. As such, I consider Left party presence in selected states as a proxy for presence of ideological divergence. The underlying assumption is that greater Left support potentially indicates greater opposition to labour reform.

Ideological Competition and Labour Flexibility

To scholars and observers, the role of the ideological dimension of party system in the reform process is marginal except maybe in West Bengal where Left parties are dominant. Such an evaluation is because programmatic difference, especially on economic reforms, is negligible among the non-Left parties. As articulated in Chapter 3, ideological orientation of parties does not explain either the extent of labour reforms in the states or the variation in parties across states (such as the Congress in Gujarat and Andhra Pradesh). Even if the ideological explanation appears weak at the level of individual parties, there is the potential for ideological discord in the party system to influence reforms. At a macro level, government decisions have to take into account the response of opposition parties who have the ability to pressurize the government, shape public opinion, and undertake political mobilization. Thus, at a macro level, ideological dissonance in the party system has the potential to shape reforms. There is evidence to show that presence of Left parties in the party system significantly hampers the extent of reforms (Haggard and Kaufman 1995). The discussion on trade unions also shows that the presence of

Left parties has favourable consequences for the workers through greater accommodation of trade unions and articulation of workers issues.

As such, greater presence of Left parties in the party system (when not major parties) should increase the extent of class discourse and union mobilization, leading to impediments to reforms. The presence of the Left party, measured through share of votes in election, can provide a clear proxy for the extent of ideological polarity in the party system.

Figure 5.1 shows the low levels of ideological polarity (on economic reforms) in the selected states except for West Bengal where Left parties were dominant. Excluding the specific case of West Bengal, the vote shares of Left parties did not cross the threshold of 10 per cent of votes in any of the states to have any significant impact. Further, in a comparative evaluation, the presence of Left parties is relatively greater in Andhra Pradesh followed by Maharashtra and Gujarat where Left parties have minuscule electoral support. Incidentally, Left parties had historic presence in Andhra Pradesh and Maharashtra, particularly among labour, which has emaciated over time. Thus, in the context of relative ideological polarity (measured by presence of Left parties in the party system), one is confronted with the problem of higher labour reform in Andhra Pradesh despite relatively higher electoral support for Left parties compared to Maharashtra.

Clearly, ideological polarity in the party system as a determinant of reform variation does not appear to be convincing. The findings corroborate the argument of broader impact of Left parties in terms of organization of the working class as the extent of unionization correlates to proportional presence of the Left. It is plausible to argue that the existence of Left parties leads to significant organization of labour. However, such organization of labour does not appear to impede flexibility when faced with a reformist government.

Fragmentation and Labour Market Reforms

Another aspect of party system with implications for reforms is the extent of fragmentation of the party system. Theoretically, as a party system becomes fragmented in a democracy, economic reforms become challenging, as an increasing number of decision-makers creates what Tsebelis (2002: 17–18) calls a 'policy stalemate'. Increasing fragmentation in the party system is likely to lead to weak governments, inhibiting

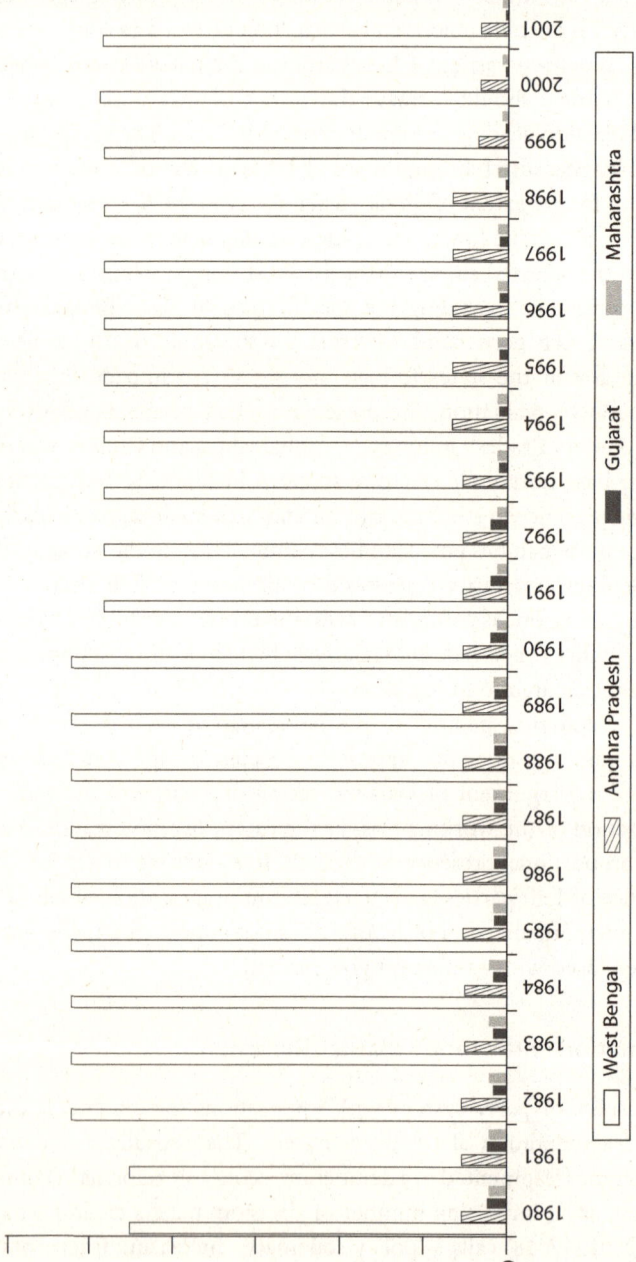

FIGURE 5.1   State-wise Percentage of Votes Obtained by Left Parties in State Elections, 1980–2001

Source: Malhotra and Bhattacharya (2003).

Note: Left parties are communist parties and allied parties with left-leaning ideology.

strong or unpopular decisions often associated with reforms. Alesina and Drazen (1991) argue that ceteris paribus, reforms are adopted slowly in countries with more political fragmentation due to increasing difficulty in making compromises between small groups and instability of governments. The implications of fragmentation and reform have also been noted by Haggard and Webb (1993) and Roubini and Sachs (1989).

Apparently, the states with lower labour flexibility, that is, West Bengal and Maharashtra, are characterized by coalition governments, while states with higher flexibility have largely been single-party governments. The negative relation between party fragmentation and policy reform appears to hold in the case of labour market reforms when we consider the effective number of parties in the states. Apparently, states with greater number of parties are characterised by lower labour flexibility. Higher party fragmentation in West Bengal and Maharashtra corroborates the lower levels labour market flexibility observed in the states. It appears that higher levels of party-system fragmentation and coalition government may be factors in the subnational variations in labour reforms.

However, a careful evaluation of the state-specific political condition suggests that such a conclusion may be premature. In terms of partisan competition, especially government formation, both West Bengal and Maharashtra are also characterized by bipolar competition. In both the states, parties of similar ideological orientation coalesce into two stable opposing poles, as the NCP–Congress share broad ideological congruity. Similarly, in West Bengal the Left Front is a coalition of Left parties, while the opposition (the coalition of Congress and the breakaway AITC) broadly shares same core values. Fragmentation, as Tsebelis (2002) points out, is not merely a greater number of decision-makers, but crucially the policy distance between decision-makers. In the context of stable political alliances in West Bengal and Maharashtra between like-minded parties, the states are not effectively characterized by greater fragmentation.

The explanations through the party system emphasizing on greater reforms in states with two-party competitions compared to states with multiparty coalition governments also appear untenable. This is because of the stability of alliances and lack of intra-coalition divergence on reform issues. The coalition governments in Maharashtra and West Bengal are

formed of parties with similarity in ideological position and partisan support. For all effective purposes, the alliance governments in Maharashtra
and West Bengal act like a single party with minor intra-party differences.

Interestingly, if we study labour market reforms across the states,
we find that political fragmentation has actually accompanied
reforms. Contrary to conventional expectation, increased political
fragmentation has paralleled labour market reforms across the states.
Importantly, this does not imply that states with greater fragmentation have greater labour flexibility. Rather, it suggests that party fragmentation and labour reforms increase simultaneously which can be
attributed to intermediate variables.

The data on political fragmentation across the states measured by
the number of effective parties shows that effective number of parties
have a positive correlation with labour market flexibility. We can identify periods of changing party competition in terms of the number of
parties with periods of increased labour flexibility.

Figure 5.2 presents the extent of party system fragmentation in the
states through the effective number of parties. Evidently, fragmentation has been higher in Maharashtra over the period, with around five

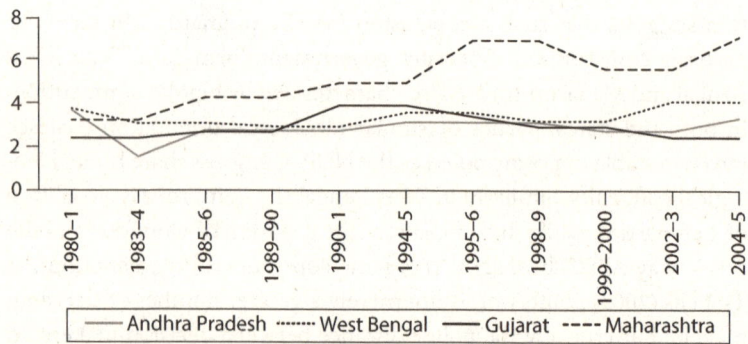

FIGURE 5.2   State-wise Numbers of Effective Parties in Terms of Votes
Polled, 1980–2005
Source: POLEX data from Sáez (2008).
Note: The data presented is of select years, hence the years given on the x-axis do
not have a consistent gap between them.

[5] Since effective number of parties is an arithmetic calculation, the numerical
value can be in decimals. While interpreting the result, only the whole number is
considered for analysis.

parties in the party system since the mid-1990s. Specifically, in terms of votes, Maharashtra witnessed a steady growth in the number of effective parties from 3.27 in 1980 which reached its peak around 1995–6 to 7 parties. Similarly, Gujarat experienced a period of increasing number of parties between 1980 and 1995, when the effective number of parties increased from 1.46 to 3.46.[5] Then on, the number of parties appears to decrease and since 1995 the party system is characterized by a stable two-party competition. In West Bengal, there is an increase in the number of effective parties since 1985. Since the late 1990s, the party system in the state is characterized by the presence of 4 effective parties. In Andhra Pradesh, the number of parties remains somewhat stable across the period since 1983, after the emergence of the TDP in the state.

Interestingly, increased fragmentation across the states corresponds with increasing flexibility in the labour market. For example, in terms wage share one can identify a sharp decline in Gujarat and Maharashtra between 1985 and 1995, which corresponds to the period of increase in the number of parties. Similarly, in West Bengal, the increase in the number of parties since the 1990s corresponds with a marked increase in labour flexibility. Comparable trends could be identified in case of Andhra Pradesh although the extent of fragmentation is relatively smaller.

A simple correlation graph of party system fragmentation and wage share (an indicator of labour flexibility) for the subnational states illustrates the point (Figure 5.3). Although correlation does not necessarily mean causation, the graphical representation clearly indicates the negative correlation between fragmentation (y-axis) and wage share (x-axis) across the states. The direction of the relation contradicts the conventional wisdom, as increasing fragmentation should inhibit reforms.

Fragmentation and Labour Reforms

The positive correspondence between labour reforms and party system fragmentation is somewhat expected, as the period of economic liberalization has also been a period of increasing democratization. The period since the early 1990s witnessed increased democratic participation and electoral competition largely through mobilization based on religious, caste, and regional appeals (Yadav 1996). The natural question

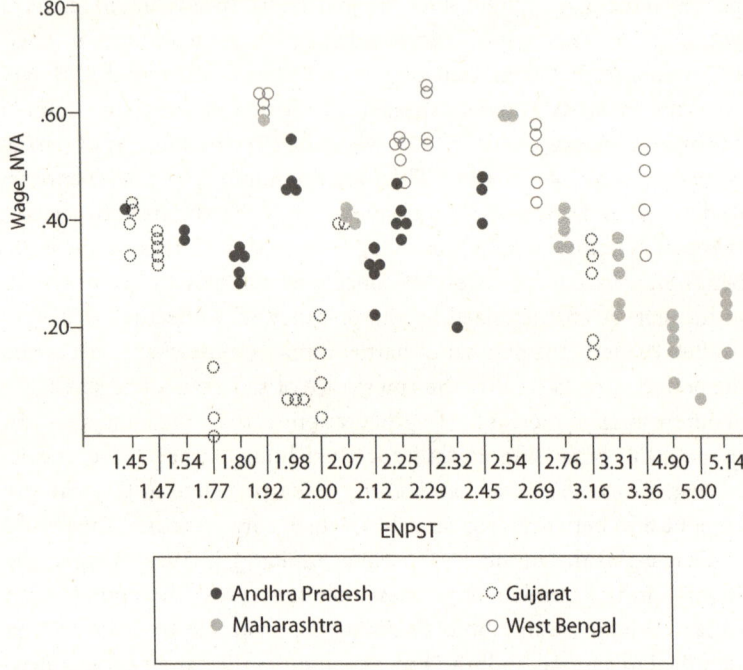

FIGURE 5.3   State-wise Correlation between Party Fragmentation and Wage
Share, 1980–2005

Source: Effective number of parties derived from POLEX data (Sáez 2008) and
wage share data from *ASI* (various issues).

in this context is whether increasing fragmentation and labour reforms
are contemporaneous or correlated developments.

The detailed case study of subnational labour market reforms
reveals that fragmentation in the party system is correlated to labour
flexibility. To put simply, increasing competition at the partisan level has
actually facilitated labour market reforms. This counter-argument to
conventional wisdom builds on the wider political experiences of the
states. The relation is multilayered and can be interrogated at multiple
levels, specifically transformations in (a) political discourse, (b) socio-
economic configurations, (c) instrumental imperative of parties, and
(d) labour interest groups. These factors are mutually interconnected,
and it is only for analytical clarity that they are discussed separately.

Transformations in Political Discourse

The incidence of increasing labour market flexibility in the face of increasing number of parties can be accounted through the transformations in wider polity. There is a large body of literature on party system in India that highlights the emergence of identity-based politics since the 1990s. A prominent example of such a contention is the elite–mass dichotomy argument of Varshney (1999). He makes a distinct between elite politics that occurs largely within institutional confines of parliament, bureaucracy and cabinet, and mass politics that take place in the streets. Mass politics are usually issues with emotive appeal, arouse passion and take forms of agitations and movements. Depending on issues that make demand on the energies of electorate and politicians such as ethnic strife, corruption, and crime, economic reforms may sometimes not become central to politics. In the context of India, reforms under a minority government were achievable, as reform issues were crowded out of mass politics by emotive issues of Hindutva and caste reservations that aroused greater passion and anxiety among people and political parties.

The politics of India underwent a shift in the late 1980s and early 1990s. The election results of 1989 witnessed an electoral wave against the Congress party with increased opposition unity like in the 1977 elections. However, the distinct development during this period was the increased importance of regional parties in national politics, and shifting social basis of politics. According to Yadav (1999: 2394), the period carried signs of a shifting social basis of Muslims in UP and Dalits and OBCs in Bihar that upset the social equations for political parties. The decisive stimulus for change occurred through three independent yet correlated developments, namely *mandal*, mandir, and market, during the period 1989–91. The period witnessed the implementation of the Mandal Commission's recommendations for OBC reservations, which made caste as an issue of political contention. The BJP's *rathyatra* for Ram Mandir catapulted religion as the dominant fissure and culminated in the demolition of Babri Masjid in 1992 with nationwide communal riots. Finally, the forex crisis of 1990 paved the way for economic policy shift and implementation of an IMF-sponsored structural adjustment programme. All these developments created the conditions for shifts in existing political alignments and a transition in the electoral system with religion and caste reservation becoming the dominant political fissure driving politics. Such a transformation in the politics, on the one hand, increased scope of participation by previously marginalized groups through emergent political parties but, on the other hand, also led to muting of issues like class and labour.

The relation between identity politics and reforms has also been addressed in the wider literature. Barber (1996) has argued that in the realm of culture, globalization not only leads to certain homogenization with creation of global culture of consumption, but also reinforces regional identities through reactive cultural assertion. According to Scholte (2005: 168), the assertion of ethnic identity under conditions of globalization is reinforced through various channels. Globalization provides space to ethnic groups by reducing the operative space for the nation states. The withdrawal of the state vacates space for ethnic and ascriptive groups to fulfil local needs of constituents.

In India, liberalization of the economy has corresponded with changes in the wider political milieu as issues of identity and ethno-nationalism have increasingly dominated the political space. Such a development, however, is not exceptional. Due to historical–institutional factors, politics in India has had strong undercurrents of identity and ascriptive issues. As Chhibber (2001) argues, in the absence of strong associational heritage, electoral competition over state has led to the politicization of social cleavages in India. Democratization in India has proceeded along ethnic and caste lines and such a democratic upsurge has undermined non-ascriptive differences such as class and gender.

For labour and trade unions, this development has two important consequences: First, the old patronage structure where organized labour was accommodated through public sector and patronage has increasingly been replaced by new patronage politics based on communal, ethnic, and regional issues. Second, the discourse and agenda of politics has also witnessed a progressive marginalization of labour. Thus, increasing number of political parties did not necessarily provide labour or other social groups opposed to liberalization any increased scope to affect policy choices. Rather, democratization in this context led to the emergence of new issues of political discourse based on caste, religion, and region at the expense of issues like welfare state, liberalization, and labour.

The political developments in the selected subnational states corroborate such an understanding. Ahmedabad in Gujarat and Mumbai in Maharashtra were both characterized by huge textile industries that provided employment in the formal sector and constituted the bedrock of organized labour movement in the two cities. The end of 1980s witnessed industrial restructuring as the textile mills gradually closed down and most workers had to shift to the informal sector (Breman 2002). Interestingly, the closure of mills in Gujarat was rather peaceful compared to Maharashtra, which witnessed massive labour unrest. According to Breman (2002) in Ahmedabad, many of the displaced workers were accommodated politically through the discourse of religion and communal identity. Sinha (2007: 50) while commenting on the politics of mill closure has argued that many workers joined the ultra-rightist religious organization Vishwa Hindu Parishad (VHP), its youth wing the Bajrang Dal, or other organizations dedicated to the militant promotion of Hindutva. Thus, opposition to closure was transformed into communal opposition through the emergent discourse of religion and caste. Gujarat provides an instance when identity issues marginalized issues of labour and facilitated adoption of flexible labour market policies.

Transformation in Socio-economic Configurations

The impact of political fragmentation on wider politics is not confined only to political ideology and discourse. Fragmentation has more tangible consequences in terms of alignment of social groups and political cleavages. As discussed in the previous chapters, socio-economic support base of parties has important consequences for the reform orientation of government. Naturally, political fragmentation and realignment of social groups have consequences for policy reform.

The historical account shows that the period between the 1970s and the 1980s marked a profound transformation in the political economy of India. The green revolution and renewed investment in public sector during this period led to economic growth and the creation of a regional capitalist-agrarian class, which later transformed into the industrial class (Damodaran 2008; Sinha 2005). These classes, that is, the agriculture-turned-industrial capitalists along with the professional middle classes sought to augment their position by seeking political and material patronage from regional governments and political parties. As the case study reveals, Andhra Pradesh and Gujarat were characterized by such developments whereby the regional agrarian-turned-industrial class maintained close interconnection with political parties which influenced the reform orientation of parties.

The professional middle classes created through the public sector expansion and welfare activities of the state also witnessed significant transformations and political reorientation. As the intellectual constituent of Indian society (Bardhan [1984] considered the professional middle class as one of the proprietary classes with control over education), the middle class also has an important role in influencing the extent of reforms. Corbridge and Harriss (2000) have pointed out that structural changes in the Indian economy led to the emergence of a new middle class that benefited from globalization. This transformation in the professional classes and growing distance between the concerns of the middle class and that of organized labour marked the break in the historic alliance between white-collar and blue-collar workers (Anderson 2001).

This realignment of socio-economic groups has been facilitated by the reconfiguration of the party system through fragmentation and regionalization. As discussed in the previous section, the fragmentation of party system in Andhra Pradesh marked by the emergence of TDP, or the emergence of BJP in Gujarat, facilitated the political reorganization of socio-economic interests. The literature on party system at the subnational level also points out shifting caste alliance of backward castes and Kammas towards TDP in Andhra Pradesh (Suri 2004a), use of religious idioms and identity in popular mobilization in Gujarat (Shah 2002), and instability of the social bases of parties, leading to a new structure of caste competition in Maharashtra (Palshikar 2004).

Importantly, the impact of fragmentation on reorganization of socio-economic interests is not automatic, but affected by the nature of political actors, particularly parties and pre-existing cleavages. In other words, the emergence and persistence of particular political cleavage is a product of both environmental conditions and elite choices. In our study, the impact of fragmentation on the support base of parties does not appear to be in any definite direction in terms of making it more homogenous or heterogeneous across the states. Perhaps, that is why fragmentation in the party system in West Bengal and Maharashtra does not seem to lead to clear socio-economic cleavage-based political alignment unlike Andhra Pradesh and Gujarat.

Transformation in Instrumental Imperative of Parties

Compared to reorganization of social bases of party support, which is a gradual and historical process, the immediate impact of fragmentation is on instrumental interest of parties. The literature on party system points out perceived differences in party objectives due to the party system. In his examination of public expenditure across subnational states of India, Chhibber (1995) has found that fragmented multiparty systems are marked by intense electoral competition and smaller party support base. This, he argues, leads parties to focus on their voting blocs for electoral prospects. Thus, increasing fragmentation of the party system can potentially lead to the emergence of sectional interests in terms of agenda and social group.

As cultural and ethnic identities reaffirm their presence through revival of primordial identities, scholars have identified the growth of political parties based on narrow and specific interests (Sridharan 2002). In India, the process (cleavage-based politics) has been variegated due to variations in social heterogeneity. In the context of this research, TDP in Andhra Pradesh and Shiv Sena in Maharashtra are examples of parties that have been able to arouse local and regional identities and reap electoral dividends. Even the national political parties have not been devoid of such regionalization. Although not visible at the macro level, national parties like Congress and BJP have generated their own subnational and region-specific agendas.

In a party system marked by the mobilization according to identity issues, political parties tend to be dominated by specific groups and increasingly, relate to support base through the segmented identities of caste, religion, and region due to instrumental imperative of nurturing a stable support base. Clearly, political competition largely based on issues of identity has significantly different outcomes than one based on issues of class, in terms of the political agenda and policy orientation.

In sum, as the party system becomes fragmented and increasingly regionalized, instrumental imperative of parties tend to highlight certain identities at the expense of others. Under conditions of regionalization and withdrawal of the state due to liberalization, political parties have to relate to the people through narrow ascriptive identities like caste or region. Thus, increasing fragmentation of the party system leads to the emergence of narrow sectional interests that marginalize broader interests.

Transformation in Labour Interest Groups

Fragmentation in the party system has had adverse consequences for interest groups, especially trade unions. The historical–institutional developments in India have encouraged inter-connection between parties and interest groups. Such a relation is most apparent in the case of labour movement, which has been closely identified with political parties. As such, ideological and political rivalries that characterize the general politics significantly determine the characteristics and behaviour of the labour movement in India (Bhattacharjee 1996). Naturally, fragmentation of the party system is continued in the division of organized labour movement, leading to emaciation of worker strength.

Increasing fragmentation of labour movement contributes to what Rudolph and Rudolph (1987) term as involuted pluralism, where increase in the number of trade unions is associated with decline in strength. Although data on extent of trade union fragmentation does not exist, based on qualitative interview of trade unionists across the four subnational states we can argue that trade unionism has been affected by both political fragmentations as well as growing disenchantment with political trade unionism.

Further, the political importance of trade unions has been undermined by the shifts in process of political mobilization from welfare populism to ascriptive issues, as the promises of economic incentives have been driven out by the logic of market economy. Traditionally, organized groups such as trade unions, which had been stable source of political mobilization, have increasingly been marginalized by emergent caste, linguistic, and regional associations. Interviews of left trade unionists and political activists reveal that caste identity more often than not overrides class identity of workers during elections. The situation is aptly summed by one left trade unionist who pointed out that workers unite under the red flag to wage struggle against capital but return home as Brahmans, Harijans, and Dalits, and not as workers.

Party System, Partisan Government, and Interest Groups

The preceding discussion on the party system provides the context background to the core argument of the book regarding subnational variations in reform. Partisan government analysed through support base is the crucial variable determining reform. The nature of party system also has an important influence on the conduct of political parties and interest groups.

The particular subnational case study presents a situation where increasing democratization, that is, mobilization and representation, facilitates reforms contrary to the conventional arguments. In the subnational states, experience of labour reforms reveals that periods of increasing competition and fragmentation in the party system expedited labour flexibility. Such an outcome challenges the conventional argument and highlights the limitations of purely structuralist understanding of the relation between party fragmentation and reforms. The features of party system share a complex interdependence, and the consequence of fragmentation on policy is contingent upon wider politics such as ideological distance, impact on partisan linkage of social groups, and interest groups.

As the case study reveals, fragmentation in party system increases labour market flexibility as the emergent political groups and prevailing political agenda highlight identity issues at the expense of class and labour. The occurrence of governments with a homogenous support base consisting of business castes is due to the peculiar intersection between caste and class and the pre-existing caste configurations in the states. Intuitively, the creation of such support bases has been due to the reconfiguration of party system and dominance of ascriptive mobilization. As the patronage power of the state declines and identity issues dominate political mobilization, the parties have to reorient through regionalized identity to create stable linkage to social groups. As Nayyar (1998) points out, the fragmentation in the party system has led to the emergence of several regional parties and even the national parties have tended to view their regional units as the focal points in inter-party competition. This regionalization is also reflected in the socio-economic support base of parties. In the earlier era of consensual politics, parties tried to appeal to cross-sections of society, irrespective of caste, religion, community, or class. In the absence of economic resources and need-based agenda, parties try to associate with voters through ascriptive linkages. As such, there has been a qualitative change in the way in which parties relate themselves to the people, leading to a significant reconfiguration of the socio-economic support base and electoral inconsequence of traditional interest groups, especially trade unions.

A reader might get the impression that political mobilizations in India are all about caste and ascriptive identity. That is certainly not true or the complete truth, to be precise. I do not imply the complete absence of rhetoric of class, gender, or other forms of non-ascriptive mobilization and recognize the potential for commixing of class and caste concerns. However, one must recognize that the process of increasing democratization in India has largely relied on the rhetoric of ethnicity, both for mobilization as well as policy orientation. As DeSouza and Sridharan (2006) have argued, democratic upsurge although representative (providing representation to marginalized groups) has not been translated effectively into the formal politics, as the emergence of new political actors has little scope for transformative politics.

The impact of party system is not as an exogenous variable in the labour market. Rather, it is endogenous and influences the behaviour and functions of key political actors. The party system influences labour market reforms through its impact on wider political discourse, instrumental objective of parties, and reconfiguration of socio-economic cleavages. Interestingly, political fragmentation and economic liberalization in India are mutually reinforcing developments.

Conclusion

Political Economy of Reforms

This book highlights the significance of political variables in determining labour market reforms. The case study of four subnational states shows that despite similar institutional and structural constraints, the outcome of labour market across Gujarat–Maharashtra and Andhra Pradesh–West Bengal diverges due to political–economic dynamics. The relevance of political variables in determining labour reforms underlines the importance of politics in shaping policy transformations. The subnational variations also demonstrate the intra-national dynamics of the reform process. Reforms under conditions of globalization have a political logic; one that operates not only at the central level, but also in subsequent levels, even if forces of globalization are attributed causal importance in policy transformations.

The specific analysis of labour market variation highlights the role of regional political–economic dynamics, specifically the nature of support base of governments and the extent of business representation. Evidently, it is the political salience of economic interests that plays a critical role in shaping socio-economic policies. Policy reform is the outcome of negotiation and bargaining between relevant interests mediated through political processes. The role of caste/class interest in the adjustment process remains significant and public policies under globalization continue to be nuanced if not shaped by distributive conflicts between major socio-economic groups. Naturally, at the level of governance, it seems that who governs matters for how globalization unfolds in a society.

The opportunities and constraints for political negotiations and bargaining are conditioned by the prevailing political system, reflected through the party system. The party system influences reforms by providing or constraining policy alternative and electoral choices for social groups and interests in society. The configuration of socio-economic groups, prevalent political agenda, or relative importance of interest groups is determined within a wider political environment that influences how individuals or groups locate themselves in the economic structure and consequently their attitude to reforms.

In sum, the book identifies two sets of explanatory variables, namely partisan orientation and political competition, which have an impact in determining the extent of reforms. Such a research outcome builds on the literature that emphasizes on political variables to explain policy heterogeneity across societies (Esping-Andersen 1996; Garrett 1998c; Korpi 2003). The subnational case study also provides insights regarding the location of policymaking in a multilevel polity. The findings reiterate recent literature on federalism, which argues that regional states have emerged as important actors mediating the process of structural adjustment (Sáez 2002; Sinha 2005).

Politics of Labour Market Reform

The central issue which this book is concerned with is the variation in labour reform across the four selected subnational states of India, namely Gujarat, Maharashtra, Andhra Pradesh, and West Bengal, despite similar economic and institutional framework. The variation is not confined to labour policy (regulation) only, but also extends to labour market outcome (wage share and the proportion of contractual labour). The index of labour market reform based on the concept of labour flexibility reveals the magnitude and variations in reform across the states. Broadly, the labour markets of Andhra Pradesh and Gujarat have higher levels of flexibility compared to that of Maharashtra and West Bengal. This variation across the states cannot be accounted through economic factors or institutional framework. As an indicator of the degree of global integration, FDI also does not corroborate the extent of reforms. The non-correspondence between economic openness and labour market reforms is also corroborated by Marjit, Kar, and Maiti (2007) in their study on trade and poverty. They have calculated the trade openness of subnational states based on industry-wise annual value added for each state vis-à-vis the shares of the products in total exports and imports (Table C1). The data reveals that Maharashtra has been the foremost state in terms of economic liberalization, while the trade component in Gujarat industry is relative low. Thus, labour market reform cannot be reduced to forces of economic liberalization.

The source of the variation in labour flexibility as revealed in the course of the book is due to political factors, namely partisan orientation of governments and party system dynamics. States with governments backed by a homogenous dominant support base with business representation undertake greater labour reforms. In contrast, when governments rely on a heterogeneous support base or have a marginal representation of business, labour market flexibility is lower. When the dominant support base is wide, governments have to formulate broader socio-economic policies and maintain a wider network of political patronage. Evidently, labour policy and outcome under conditions of globalization are shaped as much by political consideration as under economic obligation.

A regime with relatively heterogeneous socio-economic support base is exemplified by the Congress party in Maharashtra that tends to reform gradually. In contrast, the predominant socio-economic base of BJP and TDP, originating in urban middle class and business class/caste sections, provides both the parties with a relatively homogenous dominant support base. When such parties are in government, like those in Andhra Pradesh and Gujarat, greater reforms in the labour market can be noted. The opposite situation prevails when parties with a homogenous support base without business representation are in government. In West Bengal, the initial pro-labour policy in spite of industrial stagnation was driven by the support base of labour, a radicalized bhadralok community, and agrarian sections.

TABLE C1 Index of Subnational Trade Openness in India

	1980–5	1985–90	1990–5	1995–2000	2000–3
Andhra Pradesh	7.50	5.30	8.80	21.20	49.67
West Bengal	8.00	5.20	5.40	3.80	10.50
Gujarat	7.90	8.00	8.70	8.20	7.17
Maharashtra	11.20	10.70	10.50	10.10	34.67

Source: Marjit, Kar, and Maiti (2007).

The creation of such homogenous or heterogeneous socio-economic support bases for governments across the states is due to certain socio-political dynamics. The existence of caste cleavages specific to regions and the general correlation of caste and class in society provides the social context of the support base. The peculiar configurations of caste and its correlation with class have meant that generally upper castes are concentrated in the high classes and vice versa. The caste–class correlation is particularly strong in the context of landowning and industrial sections of society. The historic weakness of civic associations in India has meant that social cleavages and ascriptive identities such as caste, region, religion, and ethnicity are the aggregating categories in politics (Chhibber 2001). As political mobilization is significantly guided by these ascriptive values and identities, certain political conditions lead to the formation of homogeneous or heterogeneous support bases. It is the peculiar intersection of caste and class and the political mobilization based on identity that contributes to the creation of a distinct socio-economic support base for parties. The case study reveals that even national parties like the Congress party exhibit state-level differences due to local socio-political dynamics. Reforms under the Congress regime in Andhra Pradesh and Maharashtra seem to vary due to regional specificities, particularly the composition of social castes and classes.

The composition of the dominant support base is not static, as the political configuration of pre-existing caste cleavage is structured by political competition. The party system operates as an endogenous variable, influencing political discourse, the instrumental imperative of parties, and political alignment of socio-economic cleavages. The nature of ideological polarity in the party system determines the political discourse and, as the case study suggests, the predominance of ascriptive issues and identity-based political parties marginalizes issues of class and labour. As such, the nature of political competition operating in a particular socio-economic situation can provide the opportunity for generating demands as well as constraining social demands depending on ideological and political dynamics. As the case study reveals, contrary to established ideas, an increasing number of parties facilitates labour market flexibility. Notably, the ascendance of an ethnic identity is by no means inevitable but rather the product of actions taken by elites within the group and favourable conditions which arise from the broader political and economic environments (Brass 1984; Manor 2002).

As the discussion in the book reveals, the TDP in Andhra Pradesh utilized an ascriptive identity for political mobilization in the name of *telugugauravam* or Telugu pride. Similarly, the BJP regime in Gujarat has sought to redefine identity-based mobilization and incorporate the economically marginalized groups through the construction of an extensive Hindu identity. The role of the Congress party in conceptualizing voters through caste identity can also be identified in their framing of welfare policies that were a precursor to identity politics. The study of particular mechanisms adopted by parties that contribute to identity politics constitutes an important and urgent area of research.

Coming back to the issue at hand, it is reasonable to argue that political dynamics has a greater role is shaping reforms than perhaps one attributed in contemporary reform literature. It can be argued that policy reform towards neo-liberal consensus is the outcome of the interaction between structural (economic) features and political dynamics, particularly partisan orientation and the nature of party competition. Despite the uniformity of structural pressures on subnational states for increasing labour market flexibility, the unfolding of reforms, that is, the pace and orientation of reform, is significantly affected by political dynamics.

The findings of this book suggest that domestic political factors significantly influence how globalization unfolds in a particular society. Contextualizing the argument in broader terms even though global transformations in the economy and polity (liberalization and internationalization) exert significant pressures on domestic economies to adopt certain policies, such pressures are negotiated by domestic constituents, and specific policy outcome is always conditioned by the prevalent political economy. There is always a relative autonomy of politics that is reasonably free from structural and institutional constraints.

The argument stands in contrast to both the globalist argument of structural determination that marginalizes the role of political factors as well as sceptic assertion about the myth of globalization. The research contributes to the literature on reforms, particularly the strain of political economy of reforms literature by highlighting the role of political dynamics, specifically the partisan orientation of governments and political competition in determining reform outcome. The findings augment literature such as Rudra (2008), who reasons that negative impact of greater trade flows and capital mobility on welfare spending in less developed economies is due to the weakness of democratic institutions and collective action problem of labour.

Given the subnational comparative framework and specific focus of this book, it is not possible to empirically comment on the potential of the political factor to alter or reject forces of globalization completely.

Accounting for Variations in Labour Market Flexibility

The perceived variation in the extent of labour market flexibility across the selected states is the outcome of historical–institutional developments and regional political economy. The relative strength of different politico-economy agents and the political setting determines the nature and extent of labour reforms in the states.

The two principal contending actors in the labour market, business and labour, seek to influence labour market policies and outcomes to their benefit. Trade unions want to limit labour flexibility and consider neo-liberal reforms as an attack on the rights and privileges of trade unions. Businesses, specifically private businesses, on the other hand, seek greater labour flexibility to adjust factors of production in an environment of increased global competition. Intuitively, the relative strength of trade unions and businesses (greater trade unionism and share of private sector) provides the immediate context for politics of labour reform.

As the state-level case study shows, the strength of trade unions or business groups does not correspond to the extent of labour market flexibility. Although there appears to be some correspondence between the union strength and labour reform in the cases of West Bengal (strong trade union and low labour reform) and Gujarat (weak trade union and high labour reform), the situation is not so in the cases of Andhra Pradesh and Maharashtra. In Andhra Pradesh, a visible trade union movement is unable to prevent reforms, while in Maharashtra, labour market flexibility is low despite a weak and emaciated trade union movement. This non-correspondence between the powers of interest groups and public policy is also evident in the case of business influence. Measured through all relevant indicators, business strength is greater in Maharashtra, which is characterized by lower labour reforms. Clearly the relative strength of labour and business interest groups cannot explain the situation of labour market reforms in the subnational states.

A detailed analysis of politics in the selected states reveals that the influence of interest groups is dependent on the orientation of government and the interest group linkage to the party in power. The influence of trade unions and businesses over labour markets is determined by wider political dynamics. Analysis of the different dimensions of trade union strength shows that the capacity of unions to influence the labour market is significantly constrained by its relation to the government. In terms of unionization, labour is strongest in West Bengal and weakest in Gujarat, which broadly corroborates with the situation of labour market, but not in Maharashtra and Andhra Pradesh. In fact, the orientation of the government provides a more credible interpretation of the relation between trade unionism and labour flexibility.

Likewise, the source of divergence in business influence emanates from the nature of party in power, more specifically the nature of business–party interaction. A business's capacity to influence policy is fundamentally associated with the presence of the business's representation in the support base of parties in government. States where business classes and castes constitute an important support base for government are characterized by greater reforms. The assertion of business interests within parties is, however, constrained by the composition of a wider support base for parties.

The prominence of the government becomes comprehensible in the light of the historical–institutional development of state-dominated industrial relations and weakness of civic associations, including interest groups. The continued relevance of the state in reform brings into focus the partisan orientation of the government. As the book shows, partisan orientation is a major factor in determining reform across the subnational states. Empirical evidence reveals that the variation in flexibility across parties, especially Congress and BJP (who have a similar position on economic reforms), is due to the region-specific dominant support base. Reform is greater in states where governments are backed by a relatively homogeneous dominant support base with significant presence of business classes/castes. In states like Gujarat and Andhra Pradesh, business castes constitute a significant part of relatively homogeneous socio-economic support base of the main parties (BJP in

Gujarat and TDP and Congress in Andhra Pradesh), which appears to undertake greater reforms and is less amenable to trade union influence. In contrast, governments backed by a support base with marginal or no business presence, as in West Bengal, appear to undertake least reform.

The differences in the pace and orientation of the government to reforms is attributed to few interconnected factors: First, political representation of business interests is correlated to the pace of reforms even under conditions of globalization. Second, a homogenous support base allows parties to formulate coherent and focused policies with relatively fewer contradictory distributive and redistributive pressures. Finally, parties with a narrow and homogenous support base are more likely to resist interest group pressures not amenable to their support base. If the support base is wide and heterogeneous, governments often find it difficult to pursue reforms due to the distributive and redistributive pressures emanating from the support base. Such homogeneous dominant support base with socio-economically alike caste-class groups is made possible due to the peculiar interrelation between caste and class in India. Caste as a hereditary, hierarchical social stratification has a correlation to class, which is understood as groups with relatively similar economic endowments that define similarities in their opportunities and constraints.

The specificity of the dominant support base of parties across the states has been noted in contemporary literature on party politics. For example, Heath and Yadav (1999) show that in Gujarat the electoral support of BJP has been concentrated more among the upper castes and middle and upper classes, and is weakest among Muslims and underprivileged. In contrast, the Congress party relied on the underprivileged, minorities, lower classes, and sections of upper castes for electoral support. The case study shows that despite wide electoral support, the dominant support base of Congress has significant representation of regional bourgeoisie. In Maharashtra, they found that the Congress voters were generally less well off than the BJP–Shiv Sena voters although the difference was much less than in case of the direct Congress–BJP contest. Clearly, the Congress party in Maharashtra is characterized by a relatively wider socio-economic support base than BJP, which is more homogeneous.

The creation of specific (homogenous or heterogeneous) socio-economic support bases for parties is an outcome of region-specific caste cleavages and prevailing party system. The wider political system, that is, nature and extent of political competition, determines the array of choices for voters and policymakers and condition the interaction between political actors such as parties and interest groups. As the study reveals, the party system acts as an endogenous variable in case of labour reforms. Political fragmentation facilitates labour market reforms through distinct yet interrelated factors: First, the emergent political groups and prevailing political agenda highlight identity issues at the expense of class and labour. Second, the creation of a homogenous support base consisting of business castes is often facilitated by the reconfiguration of the party system and ascriptive mobilization. Third, fragmentation influences instrumental interest of parties. As the party system becomes fragmented and increasingly regionalized, parties tend to highlight the narrow ascriptive identities like caste or region to relate to the people. The appeal for ascriptive identities for political mobilization assumes prominence as the power of state patronage (material benefits) becomes constrained under conditions of globalization. Finally, the historical interconnection between parties and interest groups, especially labour movement, has meant that fragmentation in the party system is reflected in organized labour movement leading to emaciation of worker strength.

Bringing Back the Political

The findings of this book have implications for the wider debate on the relation between politics and economic policy under conditions of globalization. This research outcome answers some pertinent questions and raises a few others in the process.

In generic terms, the research findings suggest that economic reforms are mediated and influenced by political dynamics, particularly political parties and party system, at least in the transitional economies. The orientation of a political party is determined by the composition of the support base. The extent of competition and fragmentation in the party system provides the macro-political context in which parties and interest groups operate. It is important to mention that institutional and structural conditions like electoral system, nature of political cleavages, and historical–institutional developments also wield significant influence that has not been considered in this study.

It also affirms the relevance of political economy by showing that even though external pressures for reform may be significant, the outcome is always contingent on domestic political dynamics. The findings corroborate that policy change towards neo-liberal consensus is shaped by the nature of party competition and presence of specific interests within the support base of parties. As such, it is the political relevance of the social groups that structure political choices of governments. Distributive conflicts between major social groups reflected through the political process remain an important determinant of socio-economic policies. Simply put, globalization is not a class-neutral process and has particular consequences for different socio-economic groups in society. The emphasis on partisan politics based on the support base of regimes suggests the continued relevance of class-related socio-economic interests in the process.

The findings mirror the importance of socio-economic groups in reforms emphasized in contemporary literature, especially welfare state literature and opposition to reforms literature. Corbridge and Harriss (2000) in their study of India have argued that economic reforms in India were the revolt of an upper-class minority against a pro-poor state. Their argument highlights the emergence of the new middle class, which was a beneficiary of globalization, and other backward castes, who challenged the domination of rich peasants and became the centre of social mobilization. In welfare state literature, the transformation in the professional classes and growing distance between the concerns of the middle class and that of organized labour have been characterized as the break in the historic alliance between white-collar and blue-collar workers (Anderson 2001).

The outcome also contradicts the spatial theories of parties such as median voter theory. According to the median voter choice argument, most voters are massed in the median region and as such parties adopt largely median policies to appeal to the largest constituency of voters. Even though the dissertation cannot comment on the broader spectrum of public policies, in terms of labour policy such an argument does not appear to hold. Rather, differences in labour market policy and outcome are a function of nature of the specific support base of the political party in power. The variation in labour reform is influenced by the specific partisan support bases.

Globalization, Public Policy, and Reform

In conclusion, the arguments of this book emphasize on the importance of politics fit into a wider body of theoretical work on globalization and public policy. It substantiates the literature on the political economy of reforms that seeks to explain scope and contents of policy alterations through political variables. The outcome derived from labour reform can be interpolated to a larger argument of the political economy of globalization.

The general shift in economic policy paradigm, growing internationalization of production and consumption, and mobility of capital create structural pressures on states to adopt neo-liberal policies to maintain international competitiveness. As Rudra (2008: 414) points out, globalization discourages governments from raising revenue through taxes due to footloose (mobile) capital, and instead encourages reduction in welfare spending as well as taxes to improve export competitiveness and attract international investment. However, this behaviour of the state is contingent on the strength of labour, as the strength of the labour induces governments to increase welfare spending. The global transformations are accompanied by changes in domestic economic arrangements such as the transition from an industrial to a service economy, shifting patterns of demand, and de-industrialization. The liberalization of the economy usually corresponding globalization, thus, increases the role for market forces in the determination of economic outcomes and weakens the role of politics to influence policy, specifically economic policy. These developments have called into question the limits of political control over economic processes.

Given the limited scope and objectives of this book, it is not possible to comment decisively on the extent of political control over the market at a macro level. The case study of variation in labour market reform, however, suggests that even when economic pressures necessitate adjustment, the choice of policies and reforms remains intrinsically a political choice. It points to the potential space for domestic constituents to influence economic reforms that emerge in the interrelation between economic considerations vis-à-vis political imperatives. At a theoretical level, it indicates a greater role for political factors in the determination of policies than conventionally regarded in globalization literature. As the case study reveals, labour market flexibility has not only varied across states, but was initiated at different times. For example, increasing flexibility in the labour market can be noticed in Gujarat much prior to the reforms of 1991, while in West Bengal, it is evident nearly one and a half decade later only after liberalization. This variation appears to be explained not by global structural transformation, but by partisan orientation and political configuration. Thus, contrary to arguments of increasing irrelevance of traditional political actors such as parties, this book argues for continued relevance of political actors under condition of globalization.

Clearly, even if certain trends towards policy convergence can be noted across economies the extent, pace and intensity of change vary due to politico-economic reasons. Globally, policy paradigms are filtered differently through distinct traditions of welfare capitalism, power resources, institutional lock-in effects, and configurations of national political systems. Consequently, it cannot be argued that increasing economic linkages or globalization has been the sole source of labour market flexibility.

The recognition of politico-economic factors in the determination of reforms suggests that globalization processes are more complex than dichotomy of divergence and convergence. The exact outcome of globalization in a national economy is profoundly shaped by political agents and institutional agency (Christopherson 2002). The argument can be located somewhere between the literature that expounds the supremacy of global economic transformations (Strange 1996) and literature that doubts the effect of globalization on national state capacity (Garrett 1998a). The book provides a sophisticated model of political economy of labour policy that reinstates the importance of political variables in determining reforms that are neglected in the dominant structural interpretation.

Appendix: Labour Law Amendments at the Subnational Level

Table A1 presents data derived from P.L. Malik (2009). The computation and coding of labour law amendments is based on Contract Labour (Regulation and Abolition) Act, 1970; Factories Act, 1948; and Industrial Disputes Act, 1947.

Although Employees' Provident Fund and Miscellaneous Provisions Act, 1952; Employees' State Insurance Act, 1948; and Trade Union Act, 1926 were also considered, there were no subnational amendments found.

The classification results are similar to that of Besley and Burgess (2004) except for a few cases where the classification should be pro state rather than pro employer or pro labour. A typical example would be the West Bengal 1989 amendment of the Industrial Disputes Act, which empowers the government to stop or retain the enforceability of award in order to prohibit disputes. While Besley is not incorrect to classify it in the particular context of West Bengal as a pro-labour amendment, the most appropriate classification should be pro state, as the amendment empowers the state.

Moreover, the subnational amendment is much wider in scope, which is particularly relevant, as contractual worker and trade unionism have emerged as important indicators of the labour market under conditions of globalization. The most significant labour law amendments in recent past have been regarding the employment of contractual labour.

TABLE A1 Index of Labour Amendments at the Subnational Level

State	Year	Amendment and Codes	Overall Code	Besley and Burgess
Andhra Pradesh	2003	Expanding the scope of Contract Act although prohibiting contract labour in core activity	Pro Employer	
	2003	Abolition of State Advisory Board in determining Contract Labour, abolition of rule-making power for State Labour Board	Pro Employer	
	1968	Expands definition of Essential Services to prohibit strikes and lockouts in hospitals and dispensaries	Pro Employer	Pro Employer
	1949	State schedule to expand the industries under IDA; creation of tribunal	Pro State	Pro Employer
	2008	Definition as per the central act	Neutral	
	1987	Individual Dispute can be directly addressed to court	Pro Labour	Pro Labour
	1987	Government has special power to contain disputes	Pro Employer	Pro Employer
	1987	Payment of wages and due prior to closure	Pro Labour	Pro Labour
	1987	Workers in muster roll of a reopened unit receive precedence	Pro Labour	Pro Labour
	1987	Where a workman is reinstated by award, reinstatement considered from day of award	Pro Labour	Pro Labour
	1987	Voluntary agreement at par with conciliation	Neutral	
	1987	Power to recover dues extended to chief judicial magistrates	Pro Labour	Pro Labour
	1982	Facilitates settlement of industrial disputes in labour courts	Pro Labour	Pro Labour

State	Year	Provision		
	1987	Penalty for not complying with govt. Order for prohibiting disputes	Pro Employer	Pro Employer
	1987	Individual worker can move the court	Pro Labour	Pro Labour
	1987	Lengthens the notice period for change of work conditions	Pro Labour	Pro Labour
Maharashtra	2006	Expansion of definition of contract labour	Pro Employer	
	2003	Contract labour in SEZ cannot be scrutinized under central act	Pro Employer	
	2006	Expands the definition of Factory	Pro Labour	
	1981	Expands the scope of layoff: Compensation due to layoff	Pro Labour	Pro Labour
	2006	Enhanced the ambit of worker by increasing the salary to 6,500	Pro Labour	
	1974	Procedural: Labour court is empowered to act as an industrial Tribunal	Neutral	Neutral
	2006	Expanding the list of exceptions when notice of termination is not required	Pro Employer	
	1972	Qualifies the term worker and recognizes union	Pro Labour	
	1972	Recognized union can sign agreements on behalf of all workers	Unclear if it is Pro Labour or Pro State	
	1972	New unions can terminate old settlements within 2 months	Pro Labour	
	1981	100% wage in case of layoff due to contravention of Electricity Act	Pro Labour	Pro Labour

(Cont'd)

TABLE A1 (Cont'd)

State	Year	Amendment and Codes	Overall Code	Besley and Burgess
	1981	Government can update Chapter VB to extend rules in layoff, retrenchment, and closure	Pro Labour	Pro Labour
	1982	Application for closure must be made 90 days prior and no communication within 60 days ensures automatic permission	Pro Employer	
	1972	Only recognized trade unions can represent workers in case of industrial disputes	Pro State, Anti Labour	
	1981	Expansion of scope of IDA to firms employing more than 100 workers	Pro Labour	Pro Labour
West Bengal	1983	Right to appeal decision of industrial tribunal	Pro Labour	Pro Labour
	1958	Qualification of presiding officer of industrial tribunal	Neutral	Neutral
	1959	Tenure of presiding officer	Neutral	Neutral
	2007	Procedural: Specifying conciliation officers	Neutral	
	1974	Amending the definition of lay off two limit 2 hours. Prohibits lay off in the same day.	Pro Labour	Pro Labour
	1974	Defining public utility to prohibit strikes and lockouts	Pro Employer	
	1980	Definition of retrenchment expanded and ill health removed from clause	Pro Labour	Pro Labour
	1980	Expands definition of worker to include sales workers	Pro Labour	Pro Labour
	1989	Termination of individual worker to be deemed industrial dispute	Pro Labour	Pro Labour
	1989	Enhancing definition of dispute to include refusal of employment	Pro Labour	Pro Labour

Year	Provision	Neutral	
1980	Formation of works committee in IDA	Pro Labour	Pro Labour
1987	Notice period for change of work condition increased	Pro Employer	Pro Labour
1980	Increasing the time frame for conciliation	Pro labour	Pro Labour
1989	Voluntary arbitration	Pro Labour	Pro Employer
1980	Empowered labour courts to issue decree	Pro Labour	Pro Labour
1989	Facilitates judicial settlement of labour dispute. Regular hearing in court	Pro Labour	Pro Labour
1980	Government may stop or retain the enforceability of award	Pro State	Pro Labour
1980	Expunged the continuous 45 layoff qualification for retrenchment. Limit on layoff removed	Pro Labour	Pro Labour
1980	Laid off worker to report once a week if laid off more than 7 days	Pro Labour	Pro Labour
1989	Payment of wages and due prior to closure	Pro Labour	Pro Labour
1980	Workers in muster roll of a reopened unit receive precedence	Pro Labour	Pro Labour
1980	Where a worker is reinstated by award, reinstatement considered from day of award	Pro Labour	Pro Labour
1980	Expanding the scope of chapter VB from 300 to 50 workers	Pro Labour	Pro Labour
1989	Computation of compensation specified and Government may issue direction as required	Pro Labour	Pro Labour
1989	Closure must ensure due payment of wages	Pro Labour	Pro Labour
2007	Penalty for breach of award increased	Pro Labour	Pro Labour
1980	Power to recover dues extended to chief judicial magistrate	Pro Labour	Pro Labour

(Cont'd)

TABLE A1 (Cont'd)

State	Year	Amendment and Codes	Overall Code	Besley and Burgess
	1989	Section 38 procedural change	Neutral	Neutral
	1980	Period of 60 days increased to 90 days in case of permission for layoff	Pro Labour	Pro Labour
	1990	Qualification of labour judge	Neutral	Neutral
	1986	Greater power of labour courts in industrial disputes	Pro Labour	Pro Labour
	1989	Right of individual to approach labour court after conciliation	Pro Labour	Pro Labour
Gujarat	1962	Qualification of presiding officer of Industrial tribunal	Neutral	Neutral
	1977	Qualification of labour court judge and presiding office of tribunal	Neutral	Neutral
	1984	Procedural: Defining closure	Neutral	
	2004	Termination is put outside the scope of IDA	Pro Employer	
	2004	Procedural: Defining layoff	Neutral	
	2004	Constricting the definition of retrenchment to exclude SEZs	Pro Employer	
	2004	Defining termination as in principal act	Neutral	
	1972	Work committee and joint management	Neutral	
	1977	Procedural labour court Neutral		
	2004	Unfair labour practices applicable in SEZs	Pro Labour	Pro Worker
	1972	Fine for non-application of joint management council	Pro Labour	Pro Worker

Bibliography

Abraham, John Joseph. 2014. 'The Political Economy of Hindu Nationalism in India: 1998–2004', PhD thesis on politics and international relations, University of London.

Aghion, Philippe, Robin Burgess, Stephen J. Redding, and Fabrizio Zilibotti. 2008. 'The Unequal Effects of Liberalization: Evidence from Dismantling the License Raj in India', *American Economic Review*, 98(4): 1397–412.

Ahsan, Ahmad. 2006. 'Labor Regulations In India: Impact and Policy Reform Options', Presentation to Human Development Network, New Delhi and Washington, DC.

Ahsan, Ahmad, Carmen Pages, and Tirthankar Roy. 2008. 'Legislation, Enforcement and Adjudication in Indian Labour Markets', in Dipak Mazumdar and Sandip Sarkar (eds), *Globalization, Labour Markets and Inequality in India*, pp. 247–82. Oxon: Routledge.

Ahuja, Sandeep, Jaime Allentuck, Jimin Chung, Charles Corrigan, Ian Hathaway, Christopher Martin, Micki O'Neil et al. 2006. *Economic Reform in India: Task Force Report*. Chicago: Harris School of Public Policy, University of Chicago.

Aizenman, J., M.D. Chinn, and H. Ito. 2010. 'The Emerging Global Financial Architecture: Tracing and Evaluating New Patterns of the Trilemma Configuration', *Journal of International Money and Finance*, 29(4): 615–41.

Alcaraz, Carlo. 2009. 'Informal and Formal Labour Flexibility in Mexico', *Desarrollo Y Sociedad*, Primer Semestre De: 115–43.

Alesina, A., and A. Drazen. 1991. 'Why Are Stabilizations Delayed?', *American Economic Review*, 81(5): 1170–89.

Alesina, Alberto, and Enrico Spolaore. 1997. 'On the Number and Size of Nations', *Quarterly Journal of Economics*, 112(4): 1027–56.

Alivelu, G., K. Srinivasulu, and M. Gopinath Reddy. 2009. 'State Business Relations and Performance of Manufacturing Sector in Andhra Pradesh:

A Case Study', Discussion Paper Series No. 31, Research Programme Consortium on Improving Institutions for Pro-Poor Growth, University of Manchester.

Alvarez, Michael A., Geoffrey Garrett, and Peter Lange. 1991. 'Government Partisanship, Labor Organiszation and Macroeconomic Performance', *American Political Science Review*, 85(2): 539–56.

Aman, Alfred C. 2004. *The Democracy Deficit: Taming Globalization Through Law Reform*. New York and London: New York University Press.

Anderson, Karen M. 2001. 'The Politics of Retrenchment in a Social Democratic Welfare State: Reform of Swedish Pension and Unemployment Insurance', *Comparative Political Studies*, 34(9): 1063–91.

Arulanantham, D.P. 2004. 'The Paradox of the BJP's Stance towards External Economic Liberalisation: Why a Hindu Nationalist Party Furthered Globalisation in India', Asia Programme Working Paper. London: Chatham House.

Bajpai, Nirupam, and Jeffrey Sachs. 1999. 'The Progress of Policy Reform and Variations in Performance at the Sub-National Level in India', Development Discussion Paper No. 730. Cambridge, Massachusetts: Harvard Institute for International Development.

Banerjee, Debdas. 1998. 'Indian Industrial Growth and Corporate Sector Behaviour in West Bengal, 1947–97', *Economic and Political Weekly*, 33(47/48): 3067–74.

Banerjee, Debdas. 2005. *Globalisation, Industrial Restructuring and Labour Standards: Where India Meets the Global*. New Delhi: Sage.

Barber, Benjamin R. 1996. *Jihad vs. McWorld*. New York: Ballantine Books.

Bardhan, Pranab. 1984. *The Political Economy of Development in India*. Oxford: Blackwell.

Basu, Kaushik. 2003. 'A Theoretical Evaluation of India's Labour Laws: What Role Should Government Play?', in Pulin Nayak, Ranjan Ray, and Kaushik Basu (eds), *Markets and Government*, p. 288. New Delhi: Oxford University Press.

———. 2004. *India's Emerging Economy: Performance and Prospects in the 1990s and Beyond*. Cambridge, Massachusetts: MIT Press.

Bawn, Kathleen, Martin Cohen, David Karol, Seth Masket, Hans Noel, and John Zaller. 2012. 'A Theory of Political Parties: Groups, Policy Demands and Nominations in American Politics', *Perspectives on Politics*, 10(3): 571–97.

Bello, W., S. Cunningham, and B. Rav. 1994. *Dark Victory: The United States, Structural Adjustment, and Global Poverty*. London: Pluto.

Besley, Timothy, and Robin Burgess. 2004. 'Can Labor Regulation Hinder Economic Performance? Evidence from India', *Quarterly Journal of Economics*, 119(1): 91–134.

Béteille, Andre. 1965. *Caste, Class, and Power: Changing Patterns of Stratification in a Tanjore Village*. Berkeley: University of California Press.

Bhagwati, Jagadish. 2004. *In Defense of Globalisation*. New York: Oxford University Press.

Bharatiya Janata Party. 2010. 'Freedom Charter'. Available at http://www.bjp.org/index.php?option=com_content&view=article&id=409: freedom-charter& catid=50: election-manifestos&Itemid=446, last accessed on 5 February 2017.

Bhattacharjea, Aditya. 2006. 'Labour Market Regulation and Industrial Peformance In India: A Critical Review of the Empirical Evidence', *Indian Journal of Labour Economics*, 49(2): 211–32.

Bhattacharjee, Debasish. 1996. 'Economic Liberalisation, Democracy and Industrial Relations: India in a Comparative Perspective', *The Indian Journal of Labour Economics*, 39(4): 1011–21.

Bhattacharya, B.B., and S. Sakthivel. 2007. 'Regional Growth and Disparity in India: Comparison of Pre- and Post-reform Decades', in Baldev Raj Nayar (ed.), *Globalization and Politics in India*, pp. 458–76. New Delhi and Oxford: Oxford University Press.

Bhattacherjee, Debashish. 1999. 'Organized Labour and Economic Liberalization India: Past, Present and Future', *Discussion Paper Series* No. DP/105/1999, Labour and Society Programme. Geneva: International Labour Organization.

Bonoli, G., and T. Shinkawa. 2005. *Ageing and Pension Reform Around the World: Evidence from Eleven Countries*. Cheltenham, UK and Northampton, Massachussets: Edward Elgar.

Borensztein, E., J. Zettelmeyer, and T. Philippon. 2001. 'Monetary Independence in Emerging Markets: Does the Exchange Rate Regime Make a Difference?', *IMF Working Paper* No. 01/1, Washington, DC: International Monetary Fund.

Brass, Paul R. 1984. *Caste, Faction, and Party in Indian Politics*, 2 vols. Delhi: Chanakya Publications.

———. 1991. *Ethnicity and Nationalism: Theory and Comparison*. Thousand Oaks, California: Sage.

Breman, Jan. 2002. 'An Informalised Labour System: End of Labour Market Dualism', *Economic and Political Weekly*, 36(52): 4804–21.

Budge, I., I. Crewe, and D. Farlie. 1976. *Party Identification and Beyond: Representations of Voting and Party Competition*. London: Wiley.

Burgess, Katrina. 2004. *Parties and Unions in the New Global Economy*, Pitt Latin American Series. Pittsburgh: University of Pittsburgh Press.

Calì, Massimiliano, and Kunal Sen. 2009. 'Do Effective State Business Relations Matter for Economic Growth? Evidence from Indian States', *World Development*, 39(9): 1542–57.

Castells, Manuel, and Roberto Laserna. 1989. 'The New Dependency: Technological Change and Socioeconomic Restructuring in Latin America', *Sociological Forum*, 4(4): 535–60.

Central Statistical Office (CSO). Various Issues. 'Statistical Abstract'. New Delhi: Central Statistical Office, Deparment of Statistics.

———. Various Issues. *Annual Survey of Industries*. Kolkata: Central Statistics Office.

Chai, Sun-Ki. 2001. *Choosing an Identity: A General Model of Preference and Belief Formation*. Ann Arbor, Michigan: University of Michigan Press.

Chakrabarty, Bidyut. 1998. '1998 Elections in West Bengal: Dwindling of the Left Front?', *Economic and Political Weekly*, 33(50): 3214–20.

Chandra, Bipan, Mridula Mukherjee, and Aditya Mukherjee. 2000. *India after Independence: 1947–2000*. New Delhi: Penguin Books.

Chandra, Kanchan. 2004. *Why Ethnic Parties Succeed: Patronage and Ethnic Headcounts in India*. Cambridge: Cambridge University Press.

Chandrasekhar, C.P., and Jayati Ghosh. 2000. *The Market that Failed*. New Delhi: LeftWord Books.

Chatterjee, Rakahari. 1980. *Unions, Politics and the State in India: A Study of Indian Labour Politics*. New Delhi: South Asian Publishers.

———. 2001. *Politics India: The State–Society Interface*. New Delhi: South Asian Publishers.

Chaudhuri, Kalyan. 1987. 'Left Front's Ten Years in Power', *Economic and Political Weekly*, 22(30): 1230–1.

Chhibber, Pradeep K. 1995. 'Political Parties, Electoral Competition, Government Expenditures and Economic Reforms in India', *Journal of Development Studies*, 32(1): 74–96.

———. 1997. 'Who Voted for the Bharatiya Janata Party?', *British Journal of Political Science*, 27(4): 631–9.

———. 2001. *Democracy without Associations: Transformation of Party System and Social Cleavages in India*. Ann Arbor, Michigan: University of Michigan.

Christopherson, Susan. 2002. 'Why Do National Labor Market Practices Continue to Diverge in the Global Economy? The "Missing Link" of Investment Rules', *Economic Geography*, 78(1): 1–20.

Communist Party of India (Marxist). 2005. 'Political Resolution Adopted at the 18th Congress', Communist Party of India (Marxist), New Delhi.

Cook, María Lorena. 2002. 'Labor Reform and Dual Transitions in Brazil and the Southern Cone', *Latin American Politics and Society*, 44(1): 1–34.

———. 2007. *The Politics of Labor Reform in Latin America : Between Flexibility and Rights*. University Park, Pennsylvania: Penn State University Press.

Coppens, D., and B. de Meester. 2005. 'Public Policy and WTO Law: Regulating Globalization', *International Law Forum*, 7(2): 138–43.

Corbridge, Stuart, and John Harriss. 2000. *Reinventing India: Liberalization, Hindu Nationalism and Popular Democracy*. Cambridge: Polity Press.

Cortázar, R., N. Lustig, and R.H. Sabot. 1998. 'Economic Policy and Labor Market Dynamics', in C. Graham, R. Sabot, and N. Birdsall (eds), *Beyond*

Tradeoffs: Market Reforms and Equitable Growth in Latin America. Washington, DC: Brookings Institution Press/Inter-American Development Bank.

Crouch, Colin. 1990. 'Trade Unions in the Exposed Sector: Their Influence on Neo-Corporatist Behaviour', in Renato Brunetta and Carlo Dell'Aringa (eds), *Labour Relations and Economic Performance*, pp. 68–91. New York: New York University Press.

Dahl, Robert A. 2005. *Who Governs? Democracy and Power in an American City.* New Haven, Connecticut: Yale University Press.

Daly, Herman E. 1999. 'Globalization versus Internationalization: Some Implications', *Ecological Economics*, 31(1): 31–7.

Damodaran, Harish. 2008. *India's New Capitalists: Caste, Business, and Industry in a Modern Nation.* Basingstoke, Hampshire: Palgrave Macmillan.

Das, Ritanjan, and Zaad Mahmood. 2015. 'Contradictions, Negotiations and Reform: The Story of Left Policy Transition in West Bengal', *Journal of South Asian Development*, 10(2): 199–229.

Das, S. 2001. 'New Left Has to Please All', *Economic and Political Weekly*, 36(24): 2116–18.

Dasgupta, Sreemanta. 1998. 'West Bengal and Industry: A Regional Perspective', *Economic and Political Weekly*, 33(47/48): 3049–60.

Datt, Ruddar. 2003. *Lockouts in India.* New Delhi: Manohar.

Datta Chaudhuri, Mrinal. 1996. 'Labour Markets as Social Institutions in India', IRIS-India Working Paper, Center for Institutional Reform and the Informal Sector (IRIS), University of Maryland, College Park, Maryland.

Davala, S. 1992. *Employment and Unionisation in Indian Industry.* New Delhi: Friedrich-Ebert-Stiftung.

Davidson, Carl, and Steven J. Matusz. 2000. 'Globalization and Labour Market Adjustment: How Fast and at What Cost?', *Oxford Review of Economic Policy*, 16(3): 42–56.

Davies, Ronald B., and Krishna Chaitanya Vadlamannati. 2013. 'A Race to the Bottom in Labor Standards? An Empirical Investigation', *Journal of Development Economics* 103(July): 1–14.

DeSouza, Peter Ronald, and E. Sridharan. 2006. *India's Political Partics: Readings in Indian Government and Politics.* New Delhi: Sage.

Deshpande, Lalit, Alakh N. Sharma, A. Karan, and S. Sarkar. 2004. *Liberalisation and Labour Market Flexibility in India.* New Delhi: Institute for Human Development.

Devitt, Camilla. 2009. 'The Migrant Worker Factor in Labour Market Policy Reform', ECPR Joint Sessions of Workshops, Lisbon, 14–19 April.

Dicken, P. 2011. *Global Shift: Mapping the Changing Contours of the World Economy*, Sixth edition. London: Sage.

Dougherty, Sean M. 2009. 'Labour Regulation and Employment Dynamics at the State Level in India', *Review of Market Integration*, 1(3): 295–337.

Downes, Andrew, Raphael Gomez, and Morley Gunderson. 2004. 'The Two-way Interaction between Globalization and Labour Market', *Oxford Development Studies*, 32(1): 135–52.

Drezner, Daniel. 2001. 'Globalization and Policy Convergence', *International Studies Review*, 3(1): 53–78.

Dunning, John H. 1997. *Governments, Globalization, and International Business*. Oxford: Oxford University Press.

Election Commission of India. Various Issues. *Statistical Report on General Election to Legislative Election of Maharashtra*. New Delhi: Government of India.

Esping-Andersen, Gosta (ed.). 1996. *Welfare States in Transition: National Adaptations in Global Economies*. London: Sage.

Fallon, Paul, and Robert Lucas. 1993. 'Job Security Regulations and the Dynamic Demand for Industrial Labor in India and Zimbabwe', *Journal of Development*, 40: 214–75.

Flanagan, Robert J. 1999. 'Macroeconomic Performance and Collective Bargaining: An International Perspective', *Journal of Economic Literature*, 37(3): 1150–75.

Flanders, A. 1970. *Management and Unions*. London: Faber.

Forteza, Alvaro, and Martin Rama. 2006. 'Labor Market Rigidity and the Success of Economic Reforms across More than 100 Countries', *Journal of Policy Reform*, 9(1): 75–105.

Frankel, Francine R. 2005. *India's Political Economy 1947–2004: The Gradual Revolution*. New Delhi: Oxford University Press.

Frieden, J.A., and R. Rogowski. 1996. 'The Impact of the International Economy on National Policies: An Analytical Overview', in H.V. Milner and R.O. Keohane (eds), *Internationalization and Domestic Politics*, pp. 25–47. Cambridge: Cambridge University Press.

Friedman, Thomas L. 1999. *The Lexus and the Olive Tree*. New York: Farrar Straus Giroux.

———. 2007. *The World is Flat: The Globalized World in the Twenty-first Century*. Updated and expanded edition. London: Penguin.

Furlong, Scott. 1997. 'Interest Group Influence on Rule Making', *Administration and Society*, 29(3): 325–47.

Galli, Rossana, and David Kucera. 2003. 'Informal Employment in Latin America: Movements over Business Cycles and the Effects of Worker Rights', Discussion Paper No. DP/145/2003, Decent Work Research Programme, International Institute for Labour Studies, International Labour Organization, Geneva.

———. 2004. 'Labor Standards and Informal Employment in Latin America', *World Development*, 32(5): 809–28.

Garrett, Geoffrey. 1998a. 'Global Markets and National Politics: Collision Course or Virtuous Cycle?' *International Organization*, 52(4): 787–824.

———. 1998b. *Partisan Politics in the Global Economy*. Cambridge, UK and New York: Cambridge University Press.

———. 2000. 'The Causes of Globalization', *Comparative Political Studies*, 33(6–7): 941–91.

Gillan, Michael, and Bob Pokrant. 2009. 'The Social Impact of Trade and Production Networks on Labour and Local Communities in Asia', in Michael Gillan and Bob Pokrant (eds), *Trade, Labour and Transformation of Community in Asia*, pp. 3–23. New York: Palgrave Macmillan.

Godbole, Madhav. 2004. 'Good Governance: A Distant Dream', *Economic and Political Weekly*, 39(11): 1103–7.

Guha-Khasnobis, Basudeb and S.M. Ravi Kanbur (eds). 2006. *Informal Labour Markets and Development*, Studies in Development Economics and Policy. Basingstoke, UK: Palgrave Macmillan.

Gujarat Chamber of Commerce and Industry (GCCI). 2010. 'Vision & Mission'. Available at http://www.gujaratchamber.org/about-us/profile.aspx, last accessed on 4 April 2016.

Haggard, S., and S.B. Webb. 1993. 'What Do We Know about the Political Economy of Economic Policy Reform?' *The World Bank Research Observer*, 8(2): 143–68.

Haggard, Stephan, and Robert Kaufman. 1995. *The Political Economy of Democratic Transitions*. Princeton: Princeton University Press.

Hall, Peter A., and David Soskice (eds). 2001. *Varieties of Capitalism: The Institutional Foundations of Comparative Advantage*. Oxford: Oxford University Press.

Hankla, Charles R. 2006. 'Party Strength and International Trade: A Cross-National Analysis', *Comparative Political Studies*, 39(9): 1133–56.

Harris-White, Barbara. 2003. *India Working: Essays on Society and Economy*. Cambridge: Cambridge University Press.

Hasan, Rana, Devashish Mitra, and Beyza Ural Marchand. 2006. 'Trade Liberalization, Labor market Institutions and Poverty Reduction: Evidence from Indian States', *India Policy Forum*, 3(1): 71–122.

Hasan, R., and Karl Robert L. Jandoc. 2012. 'Labor Regulations and the Firm Size Distribution in Indian Manufacturing', *Program on Indian Economic Policies Working Papers*. New York: Columbia University Academic Commons.

Hasan, Zoya. 2002. *Parties and Party Politics in India*. Themes in Politics Series. New Delhi and New York: Oxford University Press.

Hazan, Reuven, and Gideon Rahat. 2006. 'Candidate Selection: Methods and Consequences', in Richard Katz and William Crotty (eds), *Handbook of Party Politics*, pp. 109–21. London: Sage.

Heath, Anthony, and Yogendra Yadav. 1999. 'The United Colours of Congress: Social Profile of Congress Voters, 1996 and 1998', *Economic and Political Weekly*, 34(35): 21–7.

Held, David, and Anthony G. McGrew. 2000. *The Global Transformations Reader: An Introduction to the Globalization Debate*. Cambridge: Polity.

———. 2007. *Globalization Theory: Approaches and Controversies*, Global Transformations. Cambridge: Polity.

Held, David, Anthony G. McGrew, David Goldblatt, and Jonathan Perraton. 1999. *Global Transformations: Politics, Economics and Culture*. Oxford: Polity.

Heller, Peter S., and Alan A. Tait. 1984. 'Government Employment and Pay: Some International Comparisons', *Occasional Papers* No. 24. Washington, DC: International Monetary Fund.

Hensman, Rohini. 2001. 'The Impact of Globalisation on Employment in India and Responses from the Formal and Informal Sectors', *CLARA Working Paper No. 15*. Amsterdam: International Institute of Asian Studies and International Institute of Social History.

Hillman, Amy, and Gerald Keim. 1995. 'International Variation in the Business-Government Interface: Institutional and Organizational Considerations', *The Academy of Management Review*, 20(1): 193–214.

Hirst, P., and G. Thompson. 1996. 'Globalization: A Necessary Myth?', in P. Hirst and G. Thompson (eds), *Globalization in Question*, pp. 1–17. Cambridge: Polity.

Horowitz, S., and E.C. Browne. 2008. 'Party Systems and Economic Policy Change in Postcommunist Democracies: Ideological Consensus and Institutional Competition', *Comparative Politics*, 41(1): 21–40.

Horowitz, Shale Asher, and Uk Heo. 2001. *The Political Economy of International Financial Crisis: Interest Groups, Ideologies, and Institutions*. Lanham, Maryland and Oxford: Rowman & Littlefield.

Horton, Susan, Ravi Kanbur, and Dipak Mazumdar. 1991. 'Labor Markets in an Era of Adjustment: An Overview', WPS 694, *Policy, Research, and External Affairs Working Papers*, World Bank, Washington, DC.

Horton, Susan, Ravi Kanbur, and Dipak Mazumdar. 1994. *Labor Markets in an Era of Adjustment*. 2 vols. Vol. 1. Washington, DC: World Bank.

Huber, Evelyne, and John D. Stephens. 2001a. 'Welfare State and Production Regimes in the Era of Retrenchments', in Paul Pierson (ed.), *The New Politics of the Welfare State*, pp. 107–45. New York: Oxford University Press.

———. 2001b. *Development and Crisis of the Welfare State: Parties and Policies in Global Markets*. Chicago: University of Chicago Press.

Indian National Congress (INC). 2004. 'Economic Growth: The Congress Agenda', in *Congress Sandesh*.

Inglehart, Ronald. 1997. *Modernization and Postmodernization: Cultural, Economic, and Political Change in 43 Societies*. Princeton, New Jersey: Princeton University Press.

International Labour Organization. 1996. *World Employment 1996–97: National Polices in a Global Context*. Geneva: International Labour Office.

Jayal, Niraja Gopal, and Pratap Bhanu Mehta. 2010. *The Oxford Companion to Politics in India*. New Delhi: Oxford University Press.

Jenkins, Rob. 1999. *Democratic Politics and Economic Reform in India, Contemporary South Asia*. New York: Cambridge University Press.

Jha, Praveen, and Sakti Goldar. 2008. 'Labour Market Regulation and Economic Performance: A Critical Review of Arguments and Some Plausible Lessons for India', *Economic and Labour Market Paper* 1. Geneva: International Labour Organization.

Jones, Philip, and John Hudson. 1998. 'The Role of Political Parties: An Analysis Based on Transaction Costs', *Public Choice*, 94(1): 175–89.

Kapila, Raj, and Uma Kapila. 2002. *A Decade of Economic Reforms in India*. Delhi: Academic Foundation.

Karan, Anup K., and Sakthivel Selvaraj. 2008. 'Trends in Wages and Earnings in India: Increasing Wage Differentials in a Segmented Labour Market', *ILO Asia-Pacific Working Paper Series*. New Delhi: International Labour Organization.

Katzenstein, Peter J. 1976. 'International Relations and Domestic Structures: Foreign Economic Policies of Industrial States', *International Organization*, 30(1): 1–45.

Kellner, Douglas. 2002. 'Theorizing Globalization', *Sociological Theory*, 20(3): 285–305.

Keohane, Robert O., and Joseph S. Nye. 2002. 'Realism and Complex Interdependence', in Frank J. Lecher and John Boli (eds), *The Globalization Reader*, pp. 77–83. Malden, USA: Blackwell.

King, Gary, Robert O. Keohane, and Sidney Verba. 1994. *Designing Social Inquiry: Scientific Inference in Qualitative Research*. Princeton, New Jersey: Princeton University Press.

Knill, Christoph. 2005. 'Introduction: Cross-national Policy Convergence—Concepts, Approaches and Explanatory Factors', *Journal of European Public Policy*, 12(5): 764–74.

Kochanek, Stanley A. 1995. 'The Transformation of Interest Politics in India', *Pacific Affairs*, 68(4): 529–50.

Kohli, Atul. 2001. *The Success of India's Democracy, Contemporary South Asia*. Cambridge, UK and New York: Cambridge University Press.

Kohli, Atul, and Pranab Bardhan. 1988. *India's Democracy: An Analysis of Changing State–Society Relations*. Princeton, New Jersey: Princeton University Press.

Kong, Tat Yan. 2006. 'Labour and Globalization: Locating the Northeast Asian Newly Industrializing Countries', *Review of International Political Economy*, 13(1): 103–28.

Korpi, Walter, and Joakim Palme. 2003. 'New Politics and Class Politics in the Context of Austerity and Globalization: Welfare State Regress in 18 Countries, 1975–95', *The American Political Science Review*, 97(3): 425–46.

Kothari, Rajni. 1964. 'The Congress System in India', *Asian Survey*, 4(12): 1161–73.

Kume, Ikeo. 1998. *Disparaged Success: Labor Politics in Post-War Japan*. Ithaca, New York: Cornell University Press.

Laakso, M., and R. Taagepera. 1979. '"Effective" Number of Parties: A Measure with Application to West Europe', *Comparative Political Studies*, 12(1): 3–27.

Labour Bureau. Various Issues. *Statistics on Factories*. Chandigarh/Shimla: Labour Bureau.

Lamy, Pascal. 2006. 'Humanising Globalisation', Speech delivered in Santiago, Chile, 30 January, World Trade Organization.

Levitsky, Stephen, and Lucan Way. 1998. 'Between a Shock and a Hard Place: The Dynamics of Labor-Backed Adjustment in Poland and Argentina', *Comparative Politics*, 30(2): 171–92.

Lewis, Arthur W. 1954. 'Economic Development with Unlimited Supplies of Labour', *The Manchester School*, 22(2): 139–91.

Lillie, Nathan, and Ian Greer. 2007. 'Industrial Relations, Migration and Neoliberal Politics: The Case of the European Construction Sector', *Politics and Society*, 35(4): 551–81.

Lindblom, Charles Edward. 1977. *Politics and Markets: The World's Political Economic Systems*. New York: Basic Books.

Lingguang, B. 2001. 'Economic Globalization, WTO and Tax Reform in China', *Intertax*, 29(10): 341–7.

Lipset, S.M., and S. Rokkan. 1967. *Party Systems and Voter Alignments: Cross-national Perspectives*. New York: Collier Macmillan.

Lucas, John. 1997. 'The Politics of Business Associations in the Developing World', *The Journal of Developing Areas*, 32(1): 71–96.

Mahadevia, Darshini. 2005. 'From Stealth to Aggression: Economic Reforms and Communal Politics in Gujarat', in Jos Mooij (ed.), *The Politics of Economic Reforms in India*, pp. 291–321. New Delhi: Sage.

Mahmood, Zaad. 2016. 'Trade Unions, Politics and Reform in India', *Indian Journal of Industrial Relations*, 51(3): 531–49.

Mainwaring, S. 1998. 'Party Systems in the Third Wave'. *Journal of Democracy*, 9(3): 67–81.

Malhotra, K., and H. Bhattacharya. 2003. 'Statistical Supplement', *Journal of Indian School of Political Economy*, 15(1 & 2): 289–605.

Malik, P.L. 2009. *Handbook of Labour and Industrial Laws*. Lucknow: Eastern Book Company.

Mankiw, Gregory. 2010. *Macroeconomics*. 7th ed. New York: Worth Publisher.

Manning, Bayless. 1977. 'The Congress, the Executive and Intermestic Affairs: Three Proposals', *Foreign Affairs*, 55(2): 306–24.

Manor, James. 2002. 'Parties and Party System', in Zoya Hasan (ed.), *Parties and Party System in India*, pp. 431–74. New Delhi: Oxford University Press.

Marjit, Sugata, Saibal Kar, and Dibyendu Maiti. 2007. 'Regional Trade Openness Index and Income Disparity', *Economic and Political Weekly*, 42(9): 757–69.

Márquez, G. 1998. 'Ties that Bind: Employment Protection and Labour Market Outcomes in Latin America', working paper. Washington, DC: Inter-American Development Bank.

Martin, C.J., and D. Swank. 2004. 'Does the Organization of Capital Matter? Employers and Active Labor Market Policy at the National and Firm Levels', *The American Political Science Review*, 98(4): 593–611.

Mathur, A.N. 1994. 'Labour Market Flexibility: Holy Grail or Banquo's Ghost?', *Indian Journal of Labour Economics*, 37(4): 481–7.

Mazumdar, Dipak, and Sandip Sarkar. 2008. *Globalization, Labor Markets and Inequality in India, Routledge Studies in the Growth Economies of Asia*. London and New York: Routledge and International Development Research Centre.

Mehta, Pratap Bhanu. 2004. 'A Crisis of the State Structure', *The Hindu*, 20 May.

Meyer, John W., John Boli, George M. Thomas, Francisco O. Ramirez. 1997. 'World Society and the Nation-State', *American Journal of Sociology*, 103(1): 144–81.

Miller, Max H. (ed.). 2005. *Worlds of Capitalism: Institutions, Governance and Economic Change in the Era of Globalization*, Routledge Studies in Governance and Change in the Global Era. London and New York: Routledge.

Minami, R., F. Makino, and K.S. Kim (eds). 2014. *Lewisian Turning Point in the Chinese Economy: Comparison with East Asian Countries*. Basingstoke, UK: Palgrave Macmillan.

Ministry of Labour. Various Issues. *Indian Labour Yearbook*. Shimla / Chandigarh: Ministry of Labour.

Misra, Kavita. 2006. 'Politico-Moral Transactions in Indian Aids Service: Confidentiality, Rights and New Modalities of Governance', *Anthropological Quarterly*, 79(1): 33–74.

Mitra, Arup. 2008. 'The Indian Labour Market: An Overview', *ILO Asia-Pacific Working Paper Series*. New Delhi: International Labour Organization.

Miyamura, Satoshi. 2011. 'Diversity of Labour Market Institutions in Indian Industry: A Comparison of Mumbai and Kolkata', *The Indian Journal of Labour Economics*, 54(1): 113–30.

Mooij, Jos E. 2005. *The Politics of Economic Reforms in India*. New Delhi: Sage.

Morehouse, S. 1973. 'The State Political Party and the Policy-Making Process', *The American Political Science Review*, 67(1): 55–72.

Mosley, Layna and Saika Uno. 2007. 'Racing to the Bottom or Climbing to the Top? Economic Globalization and Collective Labour Rights', *Comparative Political Studies*, 40(8): 923–48. doi: 10.1177/0010414006293442.

Mueller, Hannes. 2007. 'Political Support and Candidate Choice', *JEPS Working Paper* 07-002. London: London School of Economics.

Mukherjee, Rahul. 1999. 'Caste in Itself, Caste and Class, or Caste in Class', *Economic and Political Weekly*, 34(27): 1759–61.

———. 2007. 'Economic Transition in a Plural Polity', in Rahul Mukherjee (ed.), *India's Economic Transition: The Politics of Reform*, pp. 117–45. New Delhi: Oxford University Press.

Murillo, Maria Victoria. 2001. *Labour Unions, Partisan Coalitions, and Market Reform in Latin America*. Cambridge: Cambridge University Press.

———. 2005. 'Partisanship Amidst Convergence: The Politics of Labor Reform in Latin America', *Comparative Politics*, 37(4): 441–58.

———. 2009. *Political Competition, Partisanship, and Policy Making in Latin American Public Utilities*, Cambridge Studies in Comparative Politics. New York and Cambridge, UK: Cambridge University Press.

Nagaraj, R. 2004. 'Fall in Organised Manufacturing Employment: A Brief Note', *Economic and Political Weekly*, 39(40): 3387–90.

———. 2007. 'Labour Market in India: Current Concern and Policy Responses', Seminar on Labour Markets in Brazil, China, and India, 28 March, Paris.

Naim, Moises. 2000. 'Fads and Fashion in Economic Reforms: Washington Consensus or Washington Confusion?' *Third World Quarterly*, 21(3): 505–28.

Nayar, Baldev Raj. 2000. 'The Limits of Economic Nationalism in India: Economic Reforms under the BJP-Led Government, 1998–1999', *Asian Survey*, 40(5): 792–815.

———. 2007. *Globalization and Politics in India*, Themes in Politics. New Delhi and New York: Oxford University Press.

Nayyar, Deepak. 1998. 'Economic Development and Political Democracy: The Interaction of Economics and Politics in Independent India', *Economic and Political Weekly*, 33(49): 3121–31.

Nelson, Joan M. (ed.). 1990. *Economic Crisis and Policy Choice: The Politics of Adjustment in the Third World*. Princeton, New Jersey: Princeton University Press.

Nelson, Joan M., Jacob Meerman, and Embong Abdul Rahman (eds). 2008. *Globalization & National Autonomy: The Experience of Malaysia*. Singapore Bangi, Malaysia: Institute of Southeast Asian Studies and Institute of Malaysian & International Studies.

O'Rourke, Kevin H. 2003. 'Heckscher-Ohlin Theory and Individual Attitudes Towards Globalization', *NBER Working Paper 9872*. Cambridge, Massachusetts: National Bureau of Economic Research.

O'Rourke, Kevin H., and Alan M. Taylor. 2006. *Democracy and Protectionism.* Cambridge, Massachusetts: National Bureau of Economic Research.

Obstfeld, M., J.C. Shambaugh, and A.M. Taylor. 2005. 'The Trilemma in History: Tradeoffs Among Exchange Rates, Monetary Policies, and Capital Mobility', *Review of Economics and Statistics*, 87(3): 423–38.

Omae, Kenichi. 1995. *The End of the Nation State: The Rise of Regional Economies.* New York: Free Press.

———. 1999. *The Borderless World: Power and Strategy in the Interlinked Economy.* Revised edition. New York: HarperBusiness.

Omvedt, Gail. 1983. 'Textile Strike Turns Political', *Economic and Political Weekly*, 18(35): 1509–11.

Paczynska, Agnieszka. 2006. 'Globalization, Structural Adjustment, and Pressure to Conform: Contesting Labor Law Reform in Egypt', *New Political Science*, 28(1): 45–64.

Palshikar, Suhas. 2004. 'Shiv Sena: A Tiger with Many Faces?', *Economic and Political Weekly*, 39(14/15): 1497–507.

Palshikar, Suhas, and Rajeshwari Deshpande. 1999. 'Electoral Competition and Structures of Domination in Maharashtra', *Economic and Political Weekly*, 34(34/35): 2409–22.

Pant, B.P. 2010. 'Secretary, Labour and Skill Development, Federation of Indian Chamber of Commerce and Industry'. PhD Dissertation, SOAS, University of London.

Papola, T.S. 1994. 'Structural Adjustment, Labour Market Flexibility and Employment', Conference of Indian Society of Labour Economics, 21–23 January, Ahmedabad.

Papola, T.S. and P.P. Sahu. 2012. 'Growth and Structure of Employment in India: Long-Term and Post-reform Performance and the Emerging Challenge', Study prepared as a part of a research programme, 'Secondary Growth and Structure of Employment in India: Long-Term and Post-Reform Performance and the Emerging Challenge', sponsored by Indian Council of Social Science Research. Available at http://isidev.nic.in/pdf/ICSSR_TSP_PPS.pdf, last accessed in March 2017.

Patnaik, Prabhat. 2003. *The Retreat to Unfreedom: Essays on the Emerging World Order.* New Delhi: Tulika Press.

Petrocik, J.R., and T.A. Brown. 1999. 'Party System Structure and Electoral Realignment', in B.A. Yeşilada (ed.), *Comparative Political Parties and Party Elites: Essays in Honor of Samuel J. Eldersveld*, pp. 11–54. Ann Arbor, Michigan: University of Michigan Press.

Pierson, Paul. 1994. *Dismantling the Welfare State? Reagan, Thatcher and the Politics of Retrenchment.* Cambridge: Cambridge University Press.

———. 2001. *The New Politics of the Welfare State.* New York: Oxford University Press.

Piore, Micheal, and Charles Sabel. 1984. *The Second Industrial Divide: Basic, Possibilities for Prosperity.* New York: Basic Books.

Planning Commission. 2013. Press Note on Poverty Estimates, 2011–12. New Delhi: Press Information Bureau, Government of India.

Polanyi, Karl. 2001. *The Great Transformation: The Political and Economic Origins of Our Time,* Second edition. Boston: Beacon Press.

Przeworski, Adam. 1991. *Democracy and the Market: Political and Economic Reforms in Eastern Europe and Latin America.* Cambridge: Cambridge University Press.

Przeworski, Adam, and Fernando Limongi. 1993. 'Political Regimes and Economic Growth', *Journal of Economic Perspectives,* 7(3): 51–69.

Quinn, Dennis P., and Robert Y. Shapiro. 1991. 'Business Political Power: The Case of Taxation', *American Political Science Review,* 85(3): 851–74.

Radice, Hugo. 2000. 'Globalization and National Capitalisms: Theorizing Convergence and Differentiation', *Review of International Political Economy,* 7(4): 719–42.

Rama, Martin. 1995. 'Do Labor Market Policies and Institutions Matter? The Adjustment Experience in Latin America and the Caribbean', *Labour: Review of Labour Economics and Industrial Relations,* 9(Special): 243–68.

Ramaswamy, E.A. 1988. *Worker Consciousness and Trade Union Response.* New Delhi: Oxford University Press.

Ramaswamy, K.V. (ed.). 2015. *Labour, Employment and Economic Growth in India.* New Delhi: Cambridge University Press.

Raychaudhuri, Ajitava, and Gautam Kumar Basu. 2007. 'The Decline and Recent Resurgence of the Manufacturing Sector of West Bengal: Implications for Pro-Poor Growth from an Institutional Point of View', *IPPG Discussion Papers* No. 10. Manchester: IPPG, University of Manchester.

Reddi, Agarala Easwara, and D. Sundar Ram (eds). 1994. *State Politics in India: Reflections on Andhra Pradesh.* New Delhi: M.D. Publications.

Reserve Bank of India. Various issues. 'Components of Net State Domestic Product at Factor Cost by Industry of Origin', *Database on Indian Economy.* New Delhi: Reserve Bank of India.

Rodrik, Dani. 1997. *Has Globalization Gone Too Far?* Washington, DC: Institute for International Economics.

———. 2007. *One Economics, Many Recipes: Globalization, Institutions, and Economic Growth.* Princeton, New Jersey and Oxford: Princeton University Press.

Rogowski, Ronald. 1987a. 'Political Cleavages and the Changing Exposure to Trade', *American Political Science Review,* 81(4): 1121–37.

———. 1987b. 'Trade and the Variety of Democratic Institutions', *International Organization,* 41(2): 203–23.

Rosenau, James N. 1997. *Along the Domestic–Foreign Frontier: Exploring Governance in a Turbulent World.* Cambridge, UK and New York: Cambridge University Press.

Roubini, Nouriel, and Jeffrey Sachs. 1989. 'Government Spending and Budget Deficits in the Industrial Economies', *Economic Policy*, 4(8): 99–132.

Roy, Ramashray, and Paul Wallace. 2007. *India's 2004 Elections: Grass-roots and National Perspectives*. New Delhi and Thousand Oaks, California: Sage.

Roychowdhury, Supriya. 2003. 'Public Sector Restructuring and Democracy: The State, Labour and Trade Unions in India', *Journal of Development Studies*, 39(3): 29–50.

Rudolph, L.I. and S.H. Rudolph. 1987. *In Pursuit of Lakshmi: The Political Economy of the Indian State*. Mumbai: Orient Longman.

Rudra, Nita. 2002. 'Globalization and the Decline of the Welfare State in Less-Developed Countries', *International Organization*, 56(2): 411–45.

———. 2008. *Globalization and the Race to the Bottom in Developing Countries: Who Really Gets Hurt?* Cambridge, UK and New York: Cambridge University Press.

Rueda, David. 2007. *Social Democracy Inside Out: Partisanship and Labor Market Policy in Industrialized Democracies*. Oxford: Oxford University Press.

Sachs, Jeffrey D., and Andrew Warner. 1995. 'Economic Reform and the Process of Global Integration', *Brookings Papers on Economic Activity*, 26(1): 1–118.

Sáez, Lawrence. 2002. *Federalism Without a Centre: The Impact of Political and Economic Reform on India's Federal System*. New Delhi and Thousand Oaks, California: Sage.

———. 2008. POLEX: India Dataset, version 2008, edited by Faculty of Law and Social Sciences. London: SOAS, University of London.

Sáez, Lawrence, and Zaad Mahmood. 2016. 'Business and Labor Market Flexibility in India: The Importance of Caste', *Business and Politics*, 18(2): 171–98.

Sáez, Lawrence, and Aseema Sinha. 2010. 'Political Cycles, Political Institutions, and Public Sector Expenditure in India, 1980-2000', *British Journal of Political Science*, 40(1): 91–113.

Sarfati, Hedva, and Catherine Kobrin (eds). 1988. *Labour Market Flexibility: A Comparartive Anthology*. London: Gower.

Sartori, Giovanni. 2005. *Parties and Party System: A Framework for Analysis*. ECPR Classics, Alan Ware (ed.). Oxford: ECPR Press.

Sato, H., and M. Mayumi (eds). 2008. *Globalisation, Employment and Mobility: The South Asian Experience*. New York: Institute of Developing Economies and Palgrave Macmillan.

Schoenmaker, D. 2011. 'The Financial Trilemma', *Economics Letters*, 111(1): 57–9.

Scholte, Jan Aart. 2005. *Globalization: A Critical Introduction*, second edition. Basingstoke: Palgrave Macmillan.

Schonfeld, William R. 1983. 'Review: Political Parties: The Functional Approach and the Structural Alternative', *Comparative Politics*, 15(4): 477–99.

Sen, S., and B. Dasgupta. 2009. *Unfreedom and Waged Work: Labour in India's Manufacturing Industry*. New Delhi: Sage.

Shah, Ghanshyam. 2007. 'Gujarat after Godhra', in P. Wallace and R. Roy (eds), *India's 2004 Elections: Grass-roots and National Perspectives*, pp. 151–79. New Delhi: Sage Publications.

Shah, Ghanshyam and Mario Rutten. 2002. 'Capitalist Development and Jan Breman's Study of Labouring Class in Gujarat', in Ghanshyam Shah, Mario Rutten, and Hein Streefkerk (eds), *Development and Deprivation in Gujarat: In Honour of Jan Breman*, pp. 17–36. New Delhi: Sage.

Sharma, Alakh N. 2006. 'Flexibility, Employment and Labour Market Reforms in India', *Economic and Political Weekly*, 41(21): 2078–85.

Shyam Sundar, K.R. 2005. 'Labour Flexibility Debate in India: A Comprehensive Review and Some Suggestions', *Economic and Political Weekly*, 40(22/23): 2274–85.

———. 2008. *Impact of Labour Regulations on Industrial Development and Employment: A Study of Maharashtra*, Vol. 6 of *Labour Regulation in Indian Industry*, edited by T.S. Papola. New Delhi: Bookwell on behalf of Institute for Studies in Industrial Development.

———. 2010. *Labour Reforms and Decent Work in India: A Study of Labour Inspection in India*. New Delhi: Bookwell.

Sikdar, Soumyen. 2004. *Contemporary Issues in Globalization: An Introduction to Theory and Policy in India*, Oxford India Paperbacks. New Delhi: Oxford University Press.

Sinha, Aseema. 2005. *The Regional Roots of Developmental Politics in India: A Divided Leviathan*. Bloomington: Indiana University Press.

———. 2007. 'India's Unlikely Democracy: Economic Growth and Political Accommodation', *Journal of Democracy*, 18(2): 41–54.

Sklair, Leslie. 1995. *Sociology of the Global System*. London: Prentice Hall.

Slaughter, Matthew J., and Phillip Swagel. 1997. *Economic Issues*, Vol. 11 of *Does Globalization Lower Wages and Export Jobs?*. Washington, DC: International Monetary Fund.

Snyder, Richard. 2001. 'Scaling Down: The Subnational Comparative Method', *Studies in Comparative International Development*, 36(1): 93–110.

Solow, Robert M. 1998. 'What is Labour-market Flexibility? What is it Good For?', Keynes Lecture in Economics, The British Academy, London.

Sridharan, E. 2002. 'The Fragmentation of the Indian Party System, 1952-1999: Seven Competing Explanations', in Zoya Hasan (ed.), *Parties and Party System in India*, 473–502. New Delhi: Oxford University Press.

Srinivasulu, K., and Prakash Sarangi. 1999. 'Political Realignments in Post-NTR Andhra Pradesh', *Economic and Political Weekly*, 34(34/35): 2449–58.

Srivastava, Ravi, and S.K. Sasikumar. 2003. 'An Overview of Migration in India, Its Impacts and Key Issues', Regional Conference on Migration, Development and Pro-Poor Policy Choices in Asia, Dhaka, 22–24 June.

Stiglitz, Joseph E. 2002. *Globalization and Its Discontents*. New York: W.W. Norton.

Strange, Susan. 1996. *The Retreat of the State: The Diffusion of Power in the World Economy*. Cambridge: Cambridge University Press.

Suri, K.C. 2002. 'Democratic Process and Electoral Politics in Andhra Pradesh, India', ODI Working Paper No. 180, Overseas Development Institute, London.

———. 2003. 'Andhra Pradesh: From Populism to Pragmatism: 1983–2003', *Journal of Indian School of Political Economy*, 15(1): 45–78.

———. 2004a. 'Telugu Desam Party: Rise and Prospects for Future', *Economic and Political Weekly*, 39(14–15): 1481–90.

———. 2004b. 'Democracy, Economic Reforms and Election Results in India', *Economic and Political Weekly*, 39(51): 5404–11.

Tardanico, Richard, and Rafael Menjívar. 1997. *Global Restructuring, Employment, and Social Inequality in Urban Latin America*. Coral Gables, Florida: North-South Center Press.

Telugu Desam Party. 2009. 'About Us'. Available at http://www.telugudesam. org/tdpcms/index.php?option=com_content&view=frontpage& Itemid=1, last accessed in March 2016.

Tendulkar, Suresh D. 2004. 'Organised Labour Market in India: Pre and Post Reform', Conference on Anti Poverty and Social Policy in India, 2–4 January, Alwar, Rajasthan.

The Indian Express. 2015. 'New Gujarat Labour Bill Passed, Set to Give Govt More Control Over Industries', 26 February.

The Times of India. 2014. 'Govt Considering Amendment to Labour Laws', 26 November.

Thompson, G.F. 1998. 'Fordism, post-Fordism and the Flexible System of Production' Center for Digital Discourse and Culture, Virginia Tech. Available at http://www.cddc.vt.edu/digitalfordism/fordism_materials/ thompson.htm, last accessed on 13 February 2017.

Tsebelis, George. 2002. *Veto Player: How Political Institutions Work*. Princeton, New Jersey: Princeton University Press.

Tuman, John P. 2000. 'Labor Markets and Economic Reform in Latin America: A Review of Recent Research', *Latin American Research Review*, 35(3): 173–87.

Uba, Katrin. 2008. 'Labour Union Resistance to economic Liberalisation in India', *Asian Survey*, 48(5): 860–84.

Vaid, Divya. 2012. 'The Caste-Class Association: An Empirical Analysis', *Asian Survey*, 52(2): 395–422.

Varshney, Ashutosh. 1999. 'Mass Politics or Elite Politics?: India's Economic Reform in Comparative Perspective', in Jeffrey D. Sachs, Ashutosh Varshney, and Nirupam Bajpai (eds), *India in the Era of Economic Reform*, pp. 222–60. New Delhi: Oxford University Press.

Venkataratnam, C.S. 1993. 'Impact of New Economic Policies on the Role of Trade Unions', *Indian Journal of Industrial Relation*, 29(1): 56–77.

Venkataratnam, C.S., and Anil Verma. 1997. *Challenge of Change: Industrial Relations in Indian Industry*. New Delhi: Allied Publishers.

Vogel, S.K. 2001. 'The Crisis of German and Japanese Capitalism: Stalled on the Road to the Liberal Market Model?' *Comparative Political Studies*, 34(10): 1103–33.

Waters, Malcolm. 2001. *Globalization*, Second edition. London: Routledge.

Weir, Margaret, and Theda Skocpol. 1985. 'State Structures and the Possibilites for "Keynesian" Responses to the Great Depression in Sweden, Britain and the United States', in by B. Evans Peter, Dietrich Rueschemeyer and Theda Skocpol (eds), *Bringing the State Back In*, pp. 107–68. Cambridge: Cambridge University Press.

Williamson, John. 1994. 'In Search of a Manual for Technopols', in John Williamson (ed.), *The Political Economy of Policy Reform*, pp. 9–48. Washington, DC: Peterson Institute.

Wolf, Martin. 1997. 'Why This Hatred of the Market?', *Le Monde diplomatique*, May. Available at http://mondediplo.com/1997/05/globalisation3155, last accessed on 15 March 2017.

Wood, Adrian. 1994. *North-South Trade, Employment, and Inequality: Changing Fortunes in a Skill-driven World*. Oxford: Clarendon Press.

Wood, J.R. 1984. 'Congress Restored? The KHAM Strategy and Congress (I) Recruitment in Gujarat', in J.R. Wood (ed.), *State Politics in Contemporary India: Crisis or Continuity?*, pp. 197–228. Boulder: Westview Press.

World Commission on the Social Dimension of Globalization. 2004. *A Fair Globalization: Creating Opportunities for All*. Geneva: International Labour Organization.

Yackee, Jason, and Susan Yackee. 2006. 'A Bias Towards Business? Assessing Interest Group Influence on the US Bureaucracy', *Journal of Politics*, 68(1): 128–39.

Yadav, Yogendra. 1996. 'Reconfiguration in Indian Politics: State Assembly Elections, 1993–95', *Economic and Political Weekly*, 31(2/3): 95–104.

———. 1999. 'Electoral Politics in the Time of Change: India's Third Electoral System, 1989-99', *Economic and Political Weekly*, 34(34/35): 2393–9.

Yadav, Yogendra, and Suhas Palshikar. 2006. 'Party System and Electoral Politics in Indian States, 1952-2002: From Hegemony to Convergence', in Peter R. deSouza and E. Sridharan (eds), *India's Political Parties*, pp. 73–115. New Delhi: Sage.

Index

About the Author

Zaad Mahmood is a departmental lecturer of South Asian politics and development, Oxford Department of International Development, University of Oxford, UK, and teaches at Presidency University, Kolkata, India. He has also taught at the Seth Anandaram Jaipuria College, Kolkata, served as a guest lecturer at Presidency College, Kolkata, and was a resource person for Netaji Subhas Open University, Kolkata.

Mahmood's focus of research has been political economy of reforms, labour politics, public policy, and electoral politics in South Asia, specifically India. He has written for journals such as *Business and Politics*, *Journal of South Asian Development*, *Indian Journal of Labour Economics*, and *Industrial Law*, besides contributing chapters in books and commentaries.